THE NEW TYCOONS

THE NEW TYCOONS

*Judi Bevan and
John Jay*

SIMON & SCHUSTER

LONDON • SYDNEY • NEW YORK • TOKYO • TORONTO

First published in Great Britain by
Simon & Schuster Ltd in 1989
Copyright © Judi Bevan and John Jay 1989

Simon & Schuster Ltd
West Garden Place
Kendal Street
London W2 2AQ

Simon & Schuster of Australia Pty Ltd
Sydney

British Library Cataloguing-in-Publication Data available
ISBN 0-671-69927-X

Typeset by Selectmove Ltd, London in Palatino 11/13
Printed and bound in Great Britain by
Richard Clay Ltd, Bungay, Suffolk

Contents

To David and Susy

Preface

We began working on this book in the spring of 1987. The original idea came from Judi. She had been watching with some fascination the rapid emergence of a new wave of young entrepreneurs on the British takeover scene. Financed by a euphoric City in the giddy days before the October crash, a group of men and women, a generation or more younger than the great heroes of the 1980s' takeover boom like Lord Hanson and Sir Owen Green, were building substantial businesses virtually from nowhere. Judi strolled into my office one morning in a state of some excitement and floated the possibility of a book on 'the new tycoons'. Within minutes we had assembled a list of people and companies who were dazzling the City of London with daring deals.

We already knew many of them personally, having reported on their progress towards stock market stardom, and a few phone calls indicated that most would be prepared to cooperate in a venture that would lead to far greater exposure of their private lives than that faced by the average public company chairman. We were in business.

Then came Black Monday, the financial melt-down of October 19. As the share prices of the companies plummeted we wondered if we should carry on. Our decision to do so has been vindicated. The stock market gradually recovered and there was a resurgence of corporate activity in 1988 and 1989. All but one of the people we chose to write about came through the crash relatively unscathed and have continued to prosper.

We would like to thank all the individuals who feature in this book. They gave generously of their time. We would also like to thank their financial advisers, stockbroking analysts, friends and competitors, who helped us to piece together the reality behind the public facade. Our thanks also to Ann Dewe, our agent.

Finally we would like to thank Nick Brealey, our editor, who patiently endured our perennial tardiness in delivering copy, and prodded us along when spirits began to flag.

John Jay
July 1989

Chapter I

Introduction

The 1980s have been the decade of the entrepreneur. Young, lean and fit, the modern heads of growing businesses work punishing hours, turning themselves and others into millionaires. Obsessive, visionary and ruthless, they fire the imagination of investors, staff and customers.

Not since the heyday of mid-Victorian capitalism has the individual creator of wealth been so lionised by society. The entrepreneur, the businessman and the corporate executive have become modern-day heroes, in charge of their own destinies. Their adrenalin-packed lifestyles have become the raw material for aspirational advertising.

In the Thatcher era it has become acceptable to be rich, just so long as you work a fourteen-hour day and give time and money to charity. The advent, in 1980, of the Unlisted Securities Market (USM), designed for young companies to raise capital from the City, has created a new breed of entrepreneurial millionaire. By 1989, over 600 companies had been launched on the USM.

The men and women in this book exemplify the new spirit. They are the younger generation: the people in their thirties and forties who have brought their companies through the infant stage – in which so many entrepreneurs get stuck – to maturity. They have spotted new opportunities and have had the talent and determination to achieve their ambitions. Many of them appear 'driven', not just by the thirst for material wealth, but also to create something substantial out of nothing. Some, like Martin Sorrell of WPP, have done this with amazing speed.

Some are friendly rivals: Michael Green of Carlton and Gerald Ratner grew up together in the same wealthy North London circle. They remain great friends, discussing their latest business coups and comparing their share prices over games of snooker and poker with their mentor, Charles Saatchi of Saatchi &

Saatchi. Others have clashed in less friendly circumstances. Ratner himself lost out to George Davies in the 1987 takeover battle for Combined English Stores, only to take his revenge a year later by forcing Davies into a cut-price sale of much of the CES group to reduce Next's high debts. There is also no love lost between John Ashcroft of Coloroll and Nigel Rudd of Williams Holdings. It was Rudd who deprived Ashcroft of the chance of taking over Crown Paints, where he had begun his career, by outbidding him in an auction.

They are the newcomers, the people who have challenged the status quo, and from their ranks will be drawn the leading businesss figures of the 1990s. In the process, they have changed the image of the businessman. Gone is the grey-haired corpulent figure in his fifties sitting at his desk. His replacement is a generation younger, and works from a mobile telephone and a fax machine in his car. Increasingly, 'he' is a woman.

Their achievements are remarkable. From tiny beginnings at the start of the decade have sprung up vibrant young companies like Body Shop International and Sock Shop International. Businesses like Williams Holdings, Amstrad and Carlton Communications have transformed themselves from obscurity into billion-pound combines. Sleepy family firms such as Coloroll, Ratners and Albert Fisher have become market leaders in their fields. At the start of 1985, the combined market value of the eleven companies in this book was well under £1 billion. Four years later they were worth £5 billion.

The appeal of modern entrepreneurs like John Ashcroft of Coloroll, George Davies of Next, and women such as Anita Roddick, the creator of Body Shop, lies in a combination of 'ordinariness' and their ability to make money. They are outside the old Establishment. They come from backgrounds lacking in privilege or tradition. They include women, Jews, northerners and second-generation immigrants. The things they have in common are driving ambition, a passion for competitive sport – at least among the men – and a distaste for abstract intellectualism. Few of the young entrepreneurs to emerge in the 1980s carried their education beyond 'A' level into university, opting either for a professional qualification or to start working. Most married in their early twenties and enjoy stable, traditional family life.

All the entrepreneurs in this book head (or headed) public companies which have used the financial resources of the City of London to grow dramatically. They have exploited the City at a time when it was becoming increasingly international in outlook. This was symbolised by the 'Big Bang' when the stock exchange opened its doors to foreign securities houses. City investors, in return, have reaped handsome profits.

Their talent and ambition rode the wave of the buoyant Thatcher bull market, which ended abruptly in October 1987. They have taken advantage of the enormous strides in technology which have revolutionised management controls and distribution. They have pandered to increasing consumer demand for design and quality.

These companies are now grappling with tougher economic conditions. City investors, so uncritically enthusiastic before the October 1987 crash, drew back sharply from risk-takers, preferring instead to put their money into rock-solid 'blue chip' leading companies. In some instances, they had good reason to do so. Fourteen months after the crash, George Davies was unceremoniously pitched from his position as chairman of Next. Just a few weeks later, Tony Berry was the victim of a boardroom putsch at Blue Arrow and the share price of Saatchi & Saatchi collapsed along with its profits.

But the achievements of the 1980s have indelibly changed the way people in Britain view entrepreneurs. The British businessman abroad is no longer a subject of ridicule as he was in the 1970s. In the United States, Britain has emerged as the biggest buyer of corporate America, snapping up world-famous names like Technicolor and J. Walter Thompson in audacious, giant-killing deals. On the European Continent there is a new regard for British efficiency and enterprise, while even the Japanese admire British marketing and design skills. The successful entrepreneurs employ workforces which are highly motivated, well trained and well paid.

Yet if these paragons of industry should falter and fail their shareholders, they would be out on their ear. Their status depends solely on performance. The fat-cat capitalism of another age has vanished.

The money men of the past, like Jim Slater, were just that. They bought under-managed assets, cut costs and sold off the superfluous. Post-war entrepreneurs in Britain, unlike those in the United States, were at best tolerated, at worst vilified. Following the collapse of the bull market of the late 1960s and early 1970s, business and finance became profoundly unfashionable. Slater, who for a while had been regarded as a saviour of British industry,

3

saw his empire disintegrate in a welter of scandal. Sir James Goldsmith, who retreated overseas from socialist Britain, came to be seen as a pariah.

What differentiates the wealth creators of the 1980s from the financial dealers of the 1960s and early 1970s is that, as well as making fortunes for themselves and their shareholders, they have helped to change the way we live. The steady rise in prosperity during the 1980s inspired a new interest in comfort, design and choice, and provided rich opportunities for those with the talent to spot them.

Tony Millar brings exotic fruit to our supermarkets, Anita Roddick supplies cruelty-fee cosmetics to our bathrooms and John Ashcroft provides ranges of coordinated wallpaper, china, curtains and carpets for our homes. Alan Sugar has revolutionised the lives of thousands by making home computers and word-processors available to the masses, while John and Peter Beckwith develop stylishly designed offices and shopping centres.

The sea change in attitudes became evident around the middle of the decade. After ten years of drab puritanism, making money was suddenly back in vogue. Not only was it acceptable to be rich again, the tax regime was positively conducive to it – Goldsmith's colourful return to the British stock market in 1989 said much about the economic and social revolution of the 1980s.

The Labour governments of the 1960s and 1970s had actively discouraged the role of the individual in wealth creation. In 1966, John Lennon and Paul McCartney joined the supertax bracket and released 'The Taxman' as part of the Beatles' *Revolver* album. They sang, 'Here's one for you and 19 for me. . .I'm the taxman.' Marginal rates peaked at 98p in the pound and a whole industry was spawned dedicated to the avoidance of income tax. It was hardly an incentive for an individual to build a big company.

However, buried in large conglomerates, talented men and women, some scarcely out of school, were learning basic business practices. George Davies was at Littlewoods, developing his reverence for Marks & Spencer, Sophie Mirman was at Marks & Spencer wondering how she could make it onto the board, and the young John Ashcroft was climbing the executive ladder at Reed International.

Others deserted a Britain hit by recession and hyper-inflation. Throughout the 1970s, Britain witnessed a 'brain drain' as many of the brightest and best took off to countries like the United States, Australia and Hong Kong in search of greater opportunities and a freer enterprise culture. In Britain, there was simply little chance for a poor person with a good idea to become rich.

The City of London became traumatised by a succession of disastrous events. First came the collapse in the commercial property market, sparked off by Anthony Barber's tax on unrealised capital gains on property; the property collapse precipitated the fringe banking crisis, which in turn sent the stock market tumbling. Soaring inflation and interest rates crippled the economy. Then as the *coup de grâce* came the oil crisis, the three-day week and finally the return of a Labour government with only the most precarious grip on power.

In 1973, some 102 companies including the mighty J. Sainsbury, had floated their shares on the stock market. By the following year, the number had fallen to just 14 and throughout the late 1970s hardly any new companies were launched on the stock market. Only the biggest and best-capitalised blue chip companies could raise expansion funds from the City in the form of new shares.

Between 1975 and 1980, the financial institutions in the City put an average of just £1 billion a year into British industry. In the early 1980s, confidence revived and the City re-established itself as a source of funds for expanding companies. In 1987, fund managers and private investors put over £15 billion into corporate Britain. In 1986, the number of companies that floated on the stock market, which by then included the now thriving Unlisted Securities Market, nearly doubled from 80 in 1985 to 136.

During the late 1970s, many believed that Britain's entrepreneurial culture had been stamped out by economic events and the bullying tactics of powerful trade unions. But from beneath the gloom of Britain in the late 1970s a new dynamism was about to emerge.

A pointer to the changing mood was a big poster that appeared on the hoardings around the country in the late summer of 1978. 'Labour isn't working' was the simple slogan in bold capital letters over the head of a lengthy dole queue. It was an advertisement on behalf of the Conservative Party and its new leader Margaret Thatcher, a politician with no great experience of government but intent on becoming the first woman prime minister of Britain. Instead of turning to the great multinational American advertising agencies like J. Walter Thompson, or Ogilvy & Mather, she hired a small but dynamic and creative firm called Saatchi & Saatchi, run by the two, now famous brothers, Maurice and Charles.

The advertisement was lethally effective: it got straight to the heart of Labour's failure. Here was a government dedicated to full employment and social welfare, yet it was painfully failing to deliver the goods. By 1976 unemployment had risen to a post-war peak of 1.3 million and during the 1978–9 'winter of discontent' the government's relationship with the trade unions – traditionally the mainstay of its power – broke down. Rubbish littered the streets, the dead went unburied and hospital strikes brought parts of the National Health Service, that classic post-war Labour institution, perilously close to breakdown.

If the country wanted to restore its economy, which had been in relative decline for decades, it was clear that it needed new strategies.

It was the start of an economic counter-revolution, in which a new generation of entrepreneurs, utilising the financial power-house of the City of London, would emerge to revitalise and take control of some of the country's largest industrial and commercial assets. It was the start of a period in which Britain's booming service industries, represented by Saatchi & Saatchi itself, founded just nine years before, would emerge as the most vibrant and dynamic sector of the economy, as the traditional British manufacturing industries contracted. Of the eleven individuals in this book, it is significant that seven are in service industries, while only John Ashcroft and Nigel Rudd have built empires from a manufacturing base.

Thatcher capitalised on the discontent and insecurity, and offered a way out. 'Profits are the foundation of a free enterprise economy. In Britain profits are still dangerously low,' said the 1979 Tory manifesto. 'We need to concentrate more on the creation of conditions in which new, more modern, more secure, better paid jobs come into existence.' Thatcher pledged to 'restore incentives so that hard work pays, success is rewarded and genuine new jobs are created in an expanding economy'. The message to would-be entrepreneurs was clear: Go forth and make money.

The economic climate got worse before it got better, as the country painfully shifted itself away from state control towards the free market. Exchange controls were abandoned and high interest rates and a strong pound followed as part of the campaign to curb money supply and reduce inflation – then running at well over 20 per cent and rising. The first privatisation did not come until 1981, when British Aerospace was brought to the stock market. And though big business intellectually approved of the introduction of market disciplines into the economy, captains of industry still complained about the nasty taste of the medicine. The *Financial Times* index of 30 leading shares hit a new peak of 558.6 on 4 May 1979, the day after the convincing election victory, but then went into a rapid decline – falling 26 per cent in just seven months to end the year at 414.2.

For British industry, bloated by inertia and crippled by over-powerful trade unions, the combination of a high pound and high interest rates was extremely uncomfortable.

The corpocrats objected vehemently. Sir Terence Beckett at the Confederation of British Industry warned the government it would face a 'bare knuckled' fight if it persisted with its policies, while Imperial Chemical Industries, that bellwether of the economy, cut its dividend. 'We like a bracing climate but we are dying of pneumonia,' said John Harvey Jones, the chairman, in a speech that was warmly received by his fellow industrialists.

The government remained impassive. The stark alternatives for company managements were either to become efficient or to die. Where older managers proved unequal to the task, new, younger brains were brought in or emerged from the ranks. Vast numbers of under-utilised workers were sacked, swelling the numbers of the unemployed. At last, dragging behind its competitors in Japan and Europe, British industry was pushed into taking advantage of the extraordinary advances in technology. Old plants were closed and money reinvested in labour-saving machinery and modern management systems. Some of the basic engineering and other manufacturing industries simply ceased to exist in this country. It was cheaper to buy elsewhere.

Gradually, the economy began to respond to this tough medicine, and gross domestic product bottomed out in May 1981 after the Chancellor of the Exchequer, Sir Geoffrey Howe, produced one of the most restrictive and deflationary budgets of the post-war era. In the words of *The Times* on March 11, it was 'a harsh budget designed to take from individuals and give to struggling business'. Interest rates were cut by 2 per cent to 12 per cent but there was no help on income tax. Indirect taxes on items such as petrol, drink and tobacco rose sharply.

The industrialists continued to bleat but the stock market, anticipating events as usual, started to grasp the true significance of the Thatcher regime. There were hiccups. In the autumn of 1981 interest rates started climbing again and the market fell by

30 per cent in the space of five months. But the City's nerve soon recovered and between October 1981 and the crash of October 1987, share prices barely paused for breath in what was the longest and most sustained bull market of the twentieth century.

The big pension funds and insurance companies, gorged on huge inflows of cash as the growth of contributory company pension schemes and personal investment products accelerated, had to find an outlet for their funds. They discovered that there was a new breed of young entrepreneur queuing up for their money. At first they were suspicious, but as these businessmen began to prove themselves, the City institutions backed them with increasing enthusiasm. Alongside the well-known companies mentioned regularly in the financial press, unfamiliar names, such as Williams Holdings, F.H. Tomkins, Amstrad and Coloroll, began to appear. These were young, fast-growing, aggressive groups headed by hungry young men and women, bent on fortune but also with an eye on posterity.

There were a number of role models who had flourished during the previous boom of the mid and late sixties and had survived the rigours of the seventies. Gerald Ronson, the head of Heron, had kept his property business alive because he built a petrol retailing empire alongside it, providing the cash flow to pay the interest bills when the property crash hit in 1973. In the mid-sixties a Mr James Hanson, the scion of a wealthy Yorkshire family whose transport business had been nationalised by the post-war Labour government, arrived in the City as a protégé of the legendary Slater. When he and his partner, Gordon White, took control of the tiny Wiles Group, Hanson was better known as the one-time fiancé of Audrey Hepburn. But he was to build a reputation as one of the country's most astute takeover specialists. Stanley Kalms had built an electrical products chain called Dixons from his father's one photographic shop. Then there was the thoughtful Sir Owen Green, who took over the reins at a tiny company called British Tar and Rubber and began to transform it into a major industrial conglomerate. In 1983, his £600 million hostile takeover bid for Thomas Tilling, made against the wishes of the incumbent management, ushered in the era of the 'megabid'. Along with others, like Sir Nigel Broackes, the chairman of Trafalgar House, and Sir Jeffrey Sterling, of P&O, they survived to become the elder statesmen entrepreneurs of the Thatcher era.

The sometimes stormy partnership between the City and growing companies is crucial to the entrepreneur, particularly those who expand by taking over other companies. In America it was the junk bond, a high-yielding form of debt, that fuelled the takeover ambitions of corporate raiders like Sir James Goldsmith, Carl Icahn, and Ronald Perelman. From tiny beginnings these men were able to assault and take over some of the sleepy giants of America like Revlon, TWA and Crown Zellerbach using vast quantities of debt finance. In Britain, it was equity rather than debt that fuelled the takeover boom of the eighties. Ordinary shares became the takeover weapons of charismatic men who convinced investors they could extract greater value from their target companies than the incumbent directors.

Once the bull market was under way, there was no shortage of fee-hungry investment bankers and stockbrokers willing to marshal the domestic and overseas money pouring into the City and put it at the disposal of the ambitious young businessman or woman with a convincing story to tell. As the stock market took off in the early 1980s, a new aggressive mood swept the corporate finance parlours of the City of London. Banks that had been relative minnows in the previous takeover boom in the late sixties began to thrust themselves forward.

Leading the way was Morgan Grenfell, very much a second division player at the turn of the decade. But, under the leadership of men like Graham Walsh, George Magan and Roger Seelig, the corporate finance department set out to climb the league tables. By 1986 it was the leading merchant bank in terms of the number and value of deals done. Along the way it reshaped large chunks of British industry. When 'merger mania' reached its peak in the spring of that year, with £10 billion of takeover bids on the table in the battles for Distillers and Imperial Group, it was Morgan Grenfell that was at the heart of the action.

Young corporate finance teams at the subsidiaries of the clearing banks, such as Samuel Montagu and County, used their parents' vast financial resources and international contacts to muscle their way onto the takeover scene. Without the long lists of blue chip clients boasted by Cazenove, S.G. Warburg and their ilk, the only way to compete was to take aspiring business builders and power them forward.

Observers compared them to Drexel Burnham Lambert in New York in the late 1970s. Just as Drexel, a tiny minnow alongside the giants of investment banking like Goldman Sachs and Morgan

Stanley, used junk bonds to claw its way up the Wall Street league tables, the aspirant takeover stars of the City used shares. Just as Drexel pulled in the funds of the savings and loans societies in the United States, Samuel Montagu and County utilised the cash flow of the pension funds and insurance companies. Aware, too, of an increasing move towards 'globalisation' in many industries, including their own, the younger banks began searching for acquisitions abroad. The United States, the biggest market, proved to be a treasure trove. The new wave of entrepreneurs became their clients.

In a seminal series of articles in the *Financial Times* written in the summer of 1988, John Lloyd defined them as the 'Disestablishment', rebels and outsiders challenging the cosy world of the Establishment. Lloyd wrote:

> Britain is no longer run by an Establishment. In its place is a Disestablishment comprising men and women whose values, assumptions and habits are those of outsiders.
>
> Often they still perceive themselves as outsiders, radicals, anti-Establishment figures but that is increasingly a pose. They have successfully dethroned much, though not all, of the old Establishment and in many crucial centres of power have taken its place. . . . The values transmitted by the Disestablishment are materialistic, efficient, demotic, hedonistic, internationalist and rule breaking. These contrast sharply with the ambient values of the old Establishment, which was, if not anti-money, certainly not for it, amateurish, even sloppy, in style. . .

Lloyd wrote of the intellectual pioneering of polemicists like Sir Alfred Sherman, Sam Brittan and Lord Harris and their attempts to elevate the market as the most effective means of determining the use of resources within a society after the social democracy of the Wilson and Callaghan years.

> Crucially, they enthroned the figure of the entrepreneur. Adam Smith, whose glory they exhumed and burnished, had excused the 'butcher, the brewer, the baker' – in modern parlance, the entrepreneur – from the exercise of any more than his self-interest. That strain of thought, so beguilingly modest in its first springs and now such a broad flood, has met its acme in Alan Sugar, of Amstrad, the quintessence of the Disestablishment of the market place.

Lloyd pointed out that his Disestablishment business figures had merely done what businessmen have always done – found markets and served them. 'The differences', he wrote, 'are:

they see themselves as clearing away dead practices, old attitudes, restrictions of class and habit, inhibitions imposed by governments and unions. They are fanatically anti-corporatist. They are extolled by, and extol, the Prime Minister and the Thatcherite ministers – especially Lord Young.'

In a sense, Thatcher provided the ultimate role model: the grocer's daughter from Grantham who fought her way up the greasy pole of politics to become Britain's first woman prime minister. There had been other outsiders who had reached the top of British politics but these were on the Left, the natural home of the outsider until the 1980s. Not since Disraeli has an outsider emerged to lead the forces of the Right as leader of the Conservative Party, and Disraeli, like Thatcher, was a radical.

She has sold the idea of the 'American dream' – whereby anyone can 'make it' if they are diligent and reasonably intelligent – to a highly sceptical British public. Thatcher had a vision of how she wanted to transform the face of British society, abandoning the comfortable post-war social democratic consensus and replacing it with the more bracing disciplines of the market. The young entrepreneurs who so admire her and have a place at her table have succeeded by showing foresight and creativity in their exploitation of that market. And just as she is now so admired and respected internationally, so too is the new breed of British businessman.

The men and women who form the Disestablishment come almost exlusively from backgrounds that made them feel in some way special or different. 'We were Italians, we served in our parents' café, we always knew we were different,' says Anita Roddick. Even an apparently blue-blooded pair like John and Peter Beckwith, the old Harrovian brothers who created London & Edinburgh Trust, one of the leaders in a new wave of actively managed property companies, suffered a feeling of being on the outside looking in as schoolchildren. It is this feeling of being different by way of race or social standing that so often inspires individuals to prove themselves – to prove that they are every bit as good as, if not better, than the Establishment yardsticks against which they judged themselves.

This insecurity shows itself early in an intense competitive drive, manifested most frequently in sport, less often in academic achievement. Later, life becomes a scoreboard where pound notes and accolades are the points. Capital – or 'fuck you money' in the words of Peter Beckwith – spells, for the socially insecure, control of life and power. That thirst, not necessarily for the cash itself, but for the power that stems from running a major public company, can be insatiable.

When Alan Sugar of Amstrad was asked in a television interview in 1986 to name the moment when he felt he had 'made it', he replied that it had been when the company floated on the stock market in 1980, a flotation that valued his holding at £2 million. In the autumn of 1988 when asked the same question he replied, 'It was when the company became worth £1 billion.'

Sugar is an opportunist. His twin skills have been, first, to spot a market and dramatically increase that market by cutting product prices through shrewd purchasing; and secondly to appeal to the consumer by simplifying a complex product. He took the hi-fi – a typical middle-class product in the 1960s and early 1970s – and transformed it into the Tower system. The combination of a few simple design changes and miniaturisation cut the cost of the product to the point where the market staged a quantum leap in size. After the hi-fi came the Amstrad personal computer and, most successful of all, the word-processor.

Alan Sugar's story has caught the public's imagination, partly because he still owns nearly half the businesses, making him personally worth over £400 million, but also because, overnight, word-processing, hitherto the preserve of the elite, was available to the masses for the price of a washing machine.

Other young businessmen and women have created equally dynamic companies with the help of the stock market in the last ten years. Some have transformed the size of the markets in which they operate, catching the waves of technology or fashion. Others have pulled together fragmented industries to become the dominant force in that field.

In retailing, a relentless 40 per cent surge in consumer spending in the first eight years of the decade prompted spectacular changes in our high streets, while growing car ownership has fuelled out-of-town shopping centres and parks. One result was the formation of new, large groupings through takeovers; another the birth of new shopping concepts.

One man led the way in what rapidly became the City catch-phrase, 'specialist shopping'. His name was George Davies.

Davies profoundly altered the way women shop when he created Next. He spotted that women aged between 25 and 40 were poorly served by the existing fashion outlets. At one end of the spectrum were stores like Top Shop and Miss Selfridge which focused on the teenagers and under-25s. But for the young professional woman wanting to make a statement about how well she was doing, their clothes were too frivolous and of poor quality. At the other end were the department stores like House of Fraser and the chains like Marks & Spencer and British Home Stores. At M&S, a company much respected by Davies, there was the quality but, at that time, little style or flair. Davies had noted what Sir Terence Conran had done for furniture with Habitat. He saw the future in offering professional young women a product that had quality, was well designed and, above all, could be coordinated easily with other items in the shop.

For a time he seemed unstoppable. But Davies made three costly errors: he failed to keep tight financial controls on the group; he failed to communicate effectively with his fellow directors, who turned against him; he failed to buy a significant holding in the company during the early days. Davies' avowed aim was to become the Marks & Spencer of the 1990s. But his autocratic style proved unsuited to running the big company he had created and was his undoing.

At the other end of the high street, Gerald Ratner used his poorly regarded family firm, Ratners (Jewellers), as the base for his bid to transform the selling of jewellery in this country. Ratner, like Davies, is the ultimate competitor and, goaded by his friend Charles Saatchi, he determined to build for himself a major retailing empire. His idea was simple but revolutionary: to recast jewellery as a fashion industry. The jewellery establishment had for years sold jewellery as an investment – although the underlying value of precious metal within a piece of jewellery is tiny compared with the retail cost of any item. Ratner slashed prices, and introduced huge numbers of lower-priced semi-precious stones below the diamonds and emeralds. Due to his influence and dominance, jewellery became the fastest-growing retailing sector from 1987 onwards.

Jewellery and clothes were existing speciality formats crying out for fresh ideas and imagination in an increasingly design-conscious era. Davies and Ratner answered the call. But as living standards rose, so did the realisation that design and flair could be profitably grafted onto basic products – historically found buried away in department stores. They could then be sold in conveniently placed, stand-alone outlets. Richard Branson's Virgin Record shops and Our Price Records (sold to W.H. Smith in 1986) did it for music at a relatively early stage.

Traditionally, men and women bought their socks, tights and stockings at department stores. Supermarkets and corner shops sold limited ranges of tights but were usually at the bottom end of the market. That was until Sophie Mirman dreamed up the idea of the Sock Shop. Mirman, who had trained in retailing at Marks & Spencer after a spell as Lord Sieff's secretary, had tried to buy a pair of white woolly tights to keep her legs warm one cold January day. None were available. She took the idea of a shop dedicated solely to hosiery to her bosses at Tie Rack. When they dismissed the concept, she and Richard Ross, then the finance director of Tie Rack, decided to set out on their own.

Another woman who has brought a new dimension to shopping is Anita Roddick. Before the Body Shop there was just one place, apart from the department stores, where the average woman could buy her cosmetics and skin care products – Boots. Once inside its doors, the new breed of woman (who might be buying her suits at Next and her tights at Sock Shop) was faced with expensively packaged dreams, promising unattainable youth and beauty. Roddick produced a range of no-nonsense but attractive products in colourful and sweetly scented surroundings at reasonable prices. She tapped into a growing environmental awareness by forbidding animal testing in the making of her products and by using natural ingredients like herbs, plants and fruit.

While retailing is our most basic service industry, increasing affluence and advances in technology have powered forward the creative businesses. Maurice and Charles Saatchi were the pioneers, showing that a people-based creative company could be expanded into a multinational empire. Michael Green, the chairman of Carlton Communications (the television and video group), is a classic service industry entrepreneur – and a close friend of the Saatchis. He had watched them carve out a big business from the ephemeral world of advertising and communications, and decided he could apply their strategies to video.

Like British advertising before Saatchi, British television in the early 1980s comprised big institutions and small creative outfits – known as hotshops. Whereas the institutions of the ad world were the multinational agencies, mostly American in origin, the institutions of television were the network contractors whose entrepreneurial drive had been destroyed by the luxury of local monopolies over advertising – and by restrictive labour practices only topped by those of the newspaper industry.

Green decided to add business disciplines to creativity and, within a few years, the formula enabled him to emerge as the largest player in the industry. Such was his City reputation by the autumn of 1988, a year after the crash, that he could attract funding for the takeover of the American-owned Technicolor, one of the most respected international brand names in the screen world.

But without doubt the boldest conquest of an American business institution came in the summer of 1987 when Martin Sorrell, the Saatchis' former finance director, conquered the J. Walter Thompson advertising giant on behalf of his company WPP. Two years before, WPP, or Wire & Plastic Products as it was then known, was a tiny manufacturer of supermarket baskets.

The bid for JWT turned the tiny WPP into the world's fourth-largest ad agency – almost overnight. Sorrell, the financier, is a new type of adman, a number cruncher willing to trade in an industry in which the key income earners can walk out of the door and in which intangibles like creativity are the keys to success. Tony Berry's experience in taking over Manpower, where the franchisees revolted and its former head is now in charge of Blue Arrow, shows what can happen if you get it wrong.

Tony Millar, a shy accountant, trades in the more tangible area of fruit and vegetables. But like Green and Sorrell he spotted a market ripe for change. Like them, he took a previously parochial and fragmented industry and built a global business servicing supermarket chains around the world. Millar, who had already built up a cleaning business before it was taken over, realised first that the distribution of fruit and vegetables was destined to be one of the growth markets of the 1980s and, secondly, that it was wide open for penetration by larger and more efficient groupings.

As living standards rose and foreign travel increased, the public's appetite for healthy and varied eating grew rapidly. The increasingly dominant supermarket chains began to demand a much broader, more exotic range of products from around the world in order to provide all-year-round supply.

Home furnishing was also a fragmented industry in the early 1980s, offering great opportunities for a would-be business builder. So thought John Ashcroft, whose Coloroll group won the *Sunday Telegraph* Best Young Company award in 1980. Ashcroft had become managing director of Coloroll in 1978 when it was a sleepy, family-run wallpaper business. His ambition was simple: to become the largest and most comprehensive manufacturer of home fashion products in Europe. Sales in 1978 were just £6 million but Ashcroft's target even then was to build a company with turnover of £500 million. Sales in 1988 topped £550m.

In 1987, Ashcroft had tried to buy his old company, Crown Paints, but he was beaten by a company called Williams Holdings. Williams is the quintessential creation of the Thatcher bull market. At its helm are two accountants, Nigel Rudd and Brian McGowan, who installed themselves in the boardroom of the company in the spring of 1982, when it was known as W. Williams & Sons. Williams was then a tiny Welsh engineering company with a market value of under £1 million and losing money fast. Rudd and McGowan had always wanted to create a major public company, but they determined to avoid the mistakes of men like Jim Slater. They recognised that their own skill was in deal-making, and they employed strong managers to run their creation.

In 1987, when the *Sunday Times Magazine* listed those people it reckoned would be the leaders of society in the next decade, it described Rudd as a potential Lord Hanson of the 1990s. Another man who sees Hanson as an aspirational model is John Beckwith, the chairman of London & Edinburgh Trust (LET), the property and financial services group. In 1983, after a decade of stagnation following the 1974 property crash, John and his brother Peter launched their company on the stock market. It was far from being a traditional property company. The Beckwiths were aggressive in competing for large development schemes, innovative in the way they raised money and used shares to acquire buildings, and daring in their use of architecture.

The Beckwiths spotted that deregulation in the City, allowing foreign institutions into the London Stock Exchange, would create new demand for accommodation. They researched other major international centres, noting the new emphasis on architecture, on attention to detail, and on giving the client what he wanted. The result was a company ideally placed to win some of the prize projects in the City's more relaxed planning environment.

But by the end of 1988 the Beckwiths showed that their ambitions went beyond property. They diversified first into financial services and then into retailing through the purchase of the Owen Owen department store chain, and they began to speak more openly about using property as the base from which to build a powerful conglomerate à la Hanson.

The men and women who succeeded in the 1980s have all started with a vision, whether it was to be able to buy a decent selection of tights and stockings in one shop, or to open up the market for high-technology products to the masses. They have also possessed enough drive, marketing and management skills to create a sizeable company from that vision. In the process they have become men and women of influence. Their success is measured in different ways. In market capitalisation terms Williams Holdings is four times the size of Body Shop. But Williams is unknown outside the City while Body Shop is a household name. In terms of personal wealth, there are huge variations. Coloroll and LET are roughly the same size, but the chairman and deputy chairman of LET are worth over £60 million between them, while John Ashcroft's shares are worth barely £1 million. Perhaps one of George Davies's mistakes at Next was that he never owned a significant part of the business, something he intends to put right in his new venture.

What unifies them is that to some extent they were all outsiders who have come inside, nobodies whose influence is now felt in the highest places, employees who have become substantial employers, ordinary people who are now millionaires. They are the New Tycoons.

THE
SHOPKEEPERS

Name: *Anita Roddick*

Title: *Managing Director, Body Shop International*

Born: *1942, Littlehampton, Sussex*

Education: *Local state schools, Littlehampton and Worthing; teacher training, Bath*

Qualifications: *7 'O' levels, 3 'A' levels*

First Job: *1963, primary school teacher*

Family: *Married Gordon Roddick in 1968; they have two daughters*

First Business Venture: *1970, bed and breakfast hotel*

Opened First Body Shop: *March 1976 in Brighton*

First Openings Abroad: *1978 in Belgium; 1980 in Canada; 1983 in Australia; 1988 in the USA*

Made First Million: *In 1984 when Body Shop floated on USM*

Awards/Honours: *1985, Veuve Cliquot Businesswoman of the Year; 1987, Company of the Year*

Most Exciting Moment: *Opening first shop*

Hobbies: *Travel, anthropology, the environment, work*

Latest Salary: *£145,000 (1989)*

Personal Stake: *15 per cent; worth £58 million*

Latest Company Statistics: *1988–9 – sales: £55.4 million; profits: £11.23 million*

Chapter II

Anita Roddick
BODY SHOP INTERNATIONAL

'There's not a lot of difference between entrepreneurs and crazy people.'

As a teenager, Anita Roddick wanted to be an actress. Today her business, which sells lotions, potions and soaps from Dubai to New York, provides the perfect stage for the non-stop Anita Roddick Show.

'I realised right from the start that you didn't need to advertise, you just had to do your own PR, you get far more column inches that way,' she says, gazing wide-eyed over her horn-rimmed spectacles.

Roddick – tiny, tousle-haired and packed with energy – opened her first shop in a Brighton side street in 1976. She set up in minute premises squeezed between two funeral parlours.

She pinched the name Body Shop from a car repair business she had seen while drifting around the United States in her 'hippie phase'. But the funeral businesses thought this was the height of bad taste and attempted to put pressure on her to change it. Roddick was on to the local paper in a flash, a damp cloth over the mouthpiece. 'I told them these mafia-style funeral operators were threatening a poor little housewife who was struggling to set up her first shop, selling face-cream.' The resulting publicity brought the customers streaming into the shop and gave her the first lesson in public relations.

In October 1988, when she opened the first three shops in the United States in an operation called 'Hello America', she notched up two lengthy and glowing feature articles in *Life* magazine and *MS*.

At the end of 1988, there were 400 Body Shops, 290 of them overseas, selling over 1,000 product lines, keeping as close to the natural ingredients of plants, fruits and herbs as commerce will allow. None of them are tested on animals. 'How can you kill an animal or cause it pain for something as trivial as a moisture cream,' she says scathingly.

What distinguishes Body Shop International from other retailers is that the majority of the shops are franchise operations. One of the reasons for Body Shop's success, where so many franchise operations fail, is that the demand from potential franchisees is so great that Roddick can pick the most talented and committed. Meanwhile, the company's control of the products and the way the shops are run is obsessive down to the last detail.

Anita Roddick and her husband, Gordon, own 30 per cent of Body Shop, which by early 1989 made them personally worth £114 million. It also makes Anita the fourth richest woman in Britain. Their sleeping partner, Ian McGlinn, a Littlehampton garage owner and close friend, must rate as one of the luckiest men in the world. He lent Anita Roddick around £5,000 in the very early days, and as a result he, too, owns 30 per cent of the company.

Anita Roddick was the third daughter of Gilda and Henry Perella, Italians who had settled in the sleepy seaside town of Littlehampton. Gilda was born and grew up in Italy, but Henry was a first-generation New Yorker. Littlehampton – incongruously for an international company with sales of over £40 million a year – is still the headquarters for Body Shop. British Rail does not rate Littlehampton as worthy of a fast train service – the train from Victoria is mostly empty and stops at every station along the way.

There was a little group of Italian immigrant families in Littlehampton after the war, explains Roddick. One family ran the ice cream factory, and Henry, her father, ran the local café. 'We always had the stamp of being different, of being special,' says Roddick. Childhood incidents emphasised the point. 'We were sent to school in trousers and sent back home by the nuns.'

When she was 10 her father died suddenly. If she hadn't already got the message that working hard was essential for earning a living, she got it then. From then on, all the children helped their mother out in the café after school and at weekends. 'I realised that you do not get anything in this life without working for it,' she says. 'People tell me I'm a workaholic, but it's just that I was never trained to know what to do with leisure.'

It sounds a pleasant enough life, but the family was far from well off. 'I thought anyone who had pelmets over their curtains or who went away on holiday was rich,' she explains.

Her relationship with her teachers is one which she regards as crucial in her life. In the convent she remembers being cosseted and clearly not taught an awful lot. It was something of a shock when she found herself in the local secondary modern. Luckily for her, in the 'O' level stream where she landed, the teachers concentrated exclusively on non-science subjects and worked hard to get the bright pupils of the school through their 'O' levels. Roddick adored her teachers, 'They are still my true mentors,' she says. The feelings were mutual. Roddick's exuberant enthusiasm would have endeared her to the stuffiest of teachers. She excelled in the arts subjects, and went on to the local grammar school in Worthing, along the coast, to take her 'A' levels in History and English. At that stage she was having a love affair with the English language, something that is still reflected in the copious Body Shop literature. 'I was just fascinated by the power of words.' It was then that she tried unsuccessfully to get a place at the Central School of Speech and Drama.

Instead, she went on to teacher training college in Bath, which she enjoyed because she was allowed scope to develop some of her more imaginative teaching ideas. 'Teaching was pure theatre for me,' she says. When she taught the history of the First World War she made her pupils watch the film *Oh What a Lovely War*, and played music from the era during lessons.

However, she was only 21 and it was the early 1960s, an era of great change and new freedoms. 'I wanted to suffer,' she explains with an apologetic giggle. So off she went to Paris on the pretext of needing to buy Lawrence Durrell's *Black Book*, which was banned in England at the time. She stayed a year, working in the archive department of the *New York Herald Tribune*, and spending her evenings in cafés and jazz clubs and meeting cult heroes, like James Baldwin.

After a brief spell back in England teaching in a secondary modern in Southampton, Roddick took off again, this time for Geneva where she bluffed her way into the United Nations.

She had none of the qualifications for secretarial work but she promised she would prove herself if they would just give her a chance. 'And by God I worked hard to prove myself,' she says. It was at the UN that she developed an interest in third world countries and two years later, still only 25, she and a boyfriend decided to travel the world.

Roddick believes she is a natural anthropologist with an insatiable curiosity about how people in other cultures live. Part of the tour included three months in the Polynesian Islands, where for the first time she noticed primitive women using basic ingredients on their skin. 'I wondered how with all that sun and water they all had skins like velvet. They just scooped up raw cocoa butter and used that.'

Finally, the nesting instinct set in and she returned to Littlehampton. 'I was 27, I was Italian and I wasn't married. I wanted to have kids.' Just at that moment, as in all good fairy-tales, along came Prince Charming, in the shape of Gordon Roddick, who at the time was writing novels. It was love at first sight. 'We just knew,' she says simply. 'Our courtship lasted about four and a half minutes.'

Domesticity set in with Roddick having their first child, a daughter whom they named Justine, after one of Durrell's characters.

Right from the start she wanted to work with her husband and, after some thought and some time 'doing hippie things' in America, they decided to set up a bed and breakfast hotel. The second daughter, called Samantha, was born. Running the hotel worked well while the children were still toddlers. But after a while Roddick's almost inexhaustible supply of restless energy began to fuel her ambitions again and they decided to open a restaurant, which they called Paddington. It was the Roddicks' first real business success. They started it as a wholefood restaurant, 'but after three weeks we were going bust so we went for pasta and steaks.' Running the restaurant was clearly great fun. It was the early 1970s, the decor was mainly wood and there was lots of rock music. The money came rolling in. But it exhausted even Roddick. At the end of three years Gordon Roddick was hankering for some fun and adventure, while Anita decided that her idea of heaven would be to have a tiny shop that only opened from 9 to 5. Her husband Gordon felt that this was 'all too cissy' and decided to slake his wanderlust by riding on horseback across South America for a couple of years.

It was at this time, left alone with little money and two small children, that her passion for messing about with raw materials and what turned out to be an outstanding retailing flair came together in a dramatic way.

One day it dawned on her that she could go into a greengrocer and buy any amount of apples or broccoli that she wanted. Likewise she could go into the sweet shop and buy two gob-stoppers if she felt like it. 'But I couldn't buy moisturiser and cleanser in small sizes.'

She approached Boots about supplying her with basic ingred-ients. She admits this was a naive move in retrospect and, not surprisingly, they were not remotely interested in providing the small quantities she was after. Neither had they heard of most of the basic raw materials that fascinated her. She was talking about cocoa butter, aloe vera and jojoba oil, and in 1976 they were unknown in Britain. Finally she tracked down a herbalist who shared her interest in natural products and, so the story goes, he just happened to have an uncle who owned a chocolate factory and had access to the magic cocoa butter. She and the herbalist concocted a grand total of twenty products. They did them in five sizes because she felt strongly about giving customers choice, but also, she admits, because it made the shop look full. Roddick says now: 'If the shop didn't survive we didn't eat.'

She and some friends decorated the shop themselves. She claims that all the features that are now so familiar to users of Body Shop came about through having to improvise because of lack of money.

'We used green on the walls because it hid the damp patches so well, used garden trellis work and fencing for our displays.' They also handwrote the labels and, because her concoctions were all new and so different from what women were used to finding on the cosmetic and toiletry shelves of the major stores, she decided to write an information card to be displayed by each product. The other major idea for which she has become famous was that of refillable bottles. Sadly for the environment, the service is only taken up by around 7 per cent of customers. Today those features have become the hallmarks of Body Shop even though there are now over 1,000 product lines.

The Body Shop hit the spot with women, particularly younger women. They were bored with expensive, fancily packaged products the contents of which were a mystery. At Body Shop, the atmosphere was homely, the staff friendly, and the smell from the concentrated scents used was wonderful. Not only that, there was information on exactly what went into the simple plastic bottles with their jolly labels.

The first shop had a target breakeven point of just £300 a week. But the contretemps with the funeral parlours and the subsequent feature article in the *Brighton Argus* ensured that this modest target was beaten right from the start. It also taught Roddick that to spend money on advertising was unnecessary. She had the Body Shop name on the van she used and it was on all the products. 'I'd have even put the name on my eyelids if I could have got away with it,' she laughs.

By the time Gordon Roddick returned from his travels, she had opened a second shop in Chichester and the product range was expanding. He began to find the business interesting and an outlet for his financial skills.

The idea of franchising was born out of straightforward demand; Roddick's customers were so enthused by the concept that some of them wanted shops of their own. Then a close friend persuaded Roddick to let her open one in Bognor. As the Roddicks were having trouble persuading the banks to lend them any more money for expansion it seemed the perfect solution. In the early days, the Roddicks helped with everything. 'We'd go in there, do the painting, write the labels and deliver the product.' They also sold items not really connected with the basic theme. 'We sold anything to survive,' she says now.

They began franchising in a serious way, seeing it as a relatively risk-free way of growing abroad. Gradually the company grew. They began importing items like soaps and started their own bottling plant.

One day in 1981 they had a visit from Brod Munroe Wilson, one of the wilder characters from the City of London, who had noticed the shops. Munroe Wilson had been with the merchant bank Hill Samuel but he had broken free to form his own mini merchant bank called Munroe Corporate. In his spare time he was, and still is, a jockey, owning and training horses, as well as a dedicated polo player. In background and culture Munroe Wilson could not have been more different from the easy-going, sixties-oriented Roddicks. But his interest and enthusiasm intrigued them, particularly when he asked: 'How would you like to be millionaires.' Munroe Wilson was looking for companies he could float. He had spotted one of Body Shop's early branches in Cheapside in the City of London, noticed it was always full and thought the company would be an ideal candidate for public flotation on the stock exchange's junior market, the Unlisted Securities Market.

Roddick claims she was not the least bit interested in being a millionaire; in fact she thought the notion was slightly obscene. It had always been ideas, rather than money that had driven her and Gordon Roddick forward. But it did set them thinking.

When the first shop opened there had been no problem at all about getting small retail units in good positions on Britain's high streets. In fact landlords were only too delighted to find tenants. But by the early 1980s 'niche' retailing was beginning to catch on, and with it the demand for the smaller outlets. 'We were fighting for places on the high street and we needed a higher profile, particularly among the property developers and pension funds who owned the shops. They simply were not taking us seriously,' says Roddick.

Munroe Wilson decided not to launch the issue single-handedly, but brought in the stockbroker Capel-Cure Myers, which had built up a reputation for bringing smaller companies to the USM. It is the same firm that, three years later, launched Sock Shop.

In retrospect, the brokers drastically underpriced the issue, floating 1 million of the company's shares at 95p, which soared to 160p the same day. After a £10 million share placing and a share split, the shares were selling at 440p, valuing the company at £380 million in mid 1989. Ever since the flotation, the Body Shop price/earnings ratio, the key measure of how attractive a share is to investors, has been way above that of its competitors. This is partly because the demand for the shares has always been greater than the supply. The Roddicks and Ian McGlinn hold 70 per cent, leaving only 30 per cent of the shares on the free market.

Another reason is quite simply that there is a lot more to go for. 'The scope for profit growth over the next ten years is enormous, both from expansion in existing markets and even more so from the entry into the US and Japanese markets,' says Andy Hughes, a retail analyst with Hoare Govett, the stockbroker. Unwittingly, Anita Roddick had hit on a formula that travels the world as easily as a tooth-brush. And it is one of the few franchise operations, along with McDonalds, that really works. Hughes, who follows the company closely, points out that, because it is a franchise operation, Body Shop is insulated from the rent increases that have been eroding margins at most other retailers. It is the franchisees who have to cope with the higher rents. Body Shop is also, despite the phenomenal growth, still a small company. Thanks to Anita Roddick's publicity machine, the size of the company's profile in the public mind is much larger than the reality.

The Roddicks' reasoning that the move to becoming a public company would help the growth along, proved well founded. Since the company floated in 1983, sales have risen from £2.1 million to £55.4 million in the financial year ending February 1989. Profits have risen from just £202,000 to £11.23 million. The company has changed its year-end from September to February.

The formula works because the Roddicks still manufacture 30 per cent of the products, mainly the moisturisers and other skin care products, and strictly supervise the rest. 'It is a benign dictatorship,' she says, 'and by God is it controlled.' Franchising, she claims, provides a well of energy for the franchisees to tap. But it is sometimes a struggle. 'No books are written on how to control a company growing at 70 per cent a year,' she points out.

Roddick herself has an impassioned but chaotic air about her and doesn't, for example, know off the top of her head how many square feet of warehousing there are in Littlehampton. She sees her job as the product and the ideas. She spends several months each year travelling round the world, picking up ideas, and talking to suppliers and potential suppliers in the third world. 'I also spend a lot of time just talking to women in various countries about their lives and their ideas.'

The partnership between herself and her husband appears to work very much in the same way as that between Sophie Mirman and Richard Ross at Sock Shop. There is little conflict because they are both involved in totally different aspects of the business. He looks after the finances and the management, while she addresses the product and the sourcing. 'My delight is research, but', she confides, 'I am also a shit-hot trader.' Gordon Roddick also sifts and refines the myriad ideas that come pouring out of her head every week. She is grateful for the discipline that he brings to the business. 'He can spot a core idea and turn it into something wonderful.'

Her own ideas quite often veer off into the whacky. One of the more recent projects is the development of a 'do-it-yourself' soap-making machine in the shops, 'You have a vat of liquid soap which you ladle into little moulds. Put in the perfume and colour, bung it in the fridge and hey presto,' she says, breathless with excitement. 'It's something tacky for those dull winter days.' However, there are a few technical problems to solve before the experiment becomes a reality.

But the overall operation itself is immensely slick and disciplined. The reception area of the company is tranquil, cleverly removed from the warehouses, which have their own entrance. It overlooks a fountain and a sculpture of a small boy, while near the road is another sculpture of a family around the letters BODY SHOP. It is the work of a family friend. Into the calm comes a mother looking for information for her daughter who is undertaking a business project at university. She is presented with a project pack within two minutes of asking. A few more questions and some financial statistics are added. Body Shop is unique in that it is the only wholly British retail success story that is a franchise. Tie Rack is much smaller. Body Shop's success abroad has surprised many. The history of most major retailing groups in this country is littered with tales of disaster about when they attempted to export the concept. Habitat had a terrible time in Europe initially, and even the great Marks & Spencer has found the going costly, slow and tough. George Davies at Next went into mail order rather than attempt to venture seriously overseas.

But Body Shop appears to have almost universal appeal. As early as 1978, the first Body Shop opened outside the United Kingdom, in Belgium, and other European outlets followed. France has always proved the toughest, most unwelcoming market for foreigners and, interestingly, even Body Shop has only two outlets there. But there are over eighteen in Germany, and twenty-five in Sweden. In 1980 came the first shop in Canada. Australia had to wait until 1983. But the biggest potential market of all, the United States of America, has only just been invaded. Have the shops been in any way modified for the American market? 'Not a bit, it's just like walking in off the Kings Road,' says Roddick firmly. That may be true of the decor, but the Roddicks do pay attention to the skin type of the host nation. The colder the climate, and the drier the typical skin, the more oil versus water in the product.

One of the keys to Body Shop's success is that, although the basic product range remains the same, there are constant additions and innovations. In September 1986 Body Shop formed a joint company with make-up artiste to the famous, Barbara Daly. Body Shops now sell an unusual and colourful range of cosmetics appropriately named Colourings, vaguely reminiscent of the Biba make-up in the 1960s. It has been a good financial performer, producing an extra 10 per cent of sales from a mere 8 square feet of selling space in the shops. Later that year came the 'Mostly Men' range, which is doing well. As one observer pointed out, the level of gift buying alone in the Body Shop, especially around Christmas, should ensure a good level of sales.

Roddick applied the 'lateral thinking' she is so proud of to the male market, which has proved so difficult for the cosmetic houses who have tended to go for fragrances. 'I do not believe men want to smell like women. We think that the market must be approached through shaving,' said Roddick at the time of the launch. 'Men know nothing about their skin type, but they do know about their beard type.'

Body Shop has had possibly more than its fair share of accolades and awards since the flotation. At the end of 1986 the new 80,000 square foot warehouse at Littlehampton was opened by the Prince of Wales. In 1984 Roddick won the Businesswoman of the Year Award, sponsored by the Institute of Directors and Veuve Clicquot, for which she privately had little regard. But in 1987 Body Shop won the Business Enterprise Company of the Year award from the Confederation of British Industry. After being presented with the award by the Governor of the Bank of England, the gentlemanly Robin Leigh Pemberton, she launched a savage attack on British industrialists, saying she had never met a captain of industry who 'makes my blood surge'.

It was a brave speech – and also one which guaranteed the headlines. Privately it is clear that Roddick does have a high regard for some of her fellow entrepreneurs. 'George Davies has that drive, that great sense of derring do,' she said, before his departure from Next.

Keeping up with the expansion is one of her problems. Her ideas spring forth quicker than the facilities to make them happen. There is a 'Mother and Baby' range on hold until the new warehouse is built, a carrot range, a passion fruit gel, not forgetting the soap-making machine.

The American venture is only just beginning and, until they see how well it works, the Roddicks have decided to manage the shops themselves rather than franchise. While franchising is a fast and low-risk way of expanding, it is not the most profitable. Because it is such a huge potential market, it may be that the decision will be to grow more slowly there, with managed shops. They are treading warily, despite the wave of publicity that greeted the New York opening. By the end of 1989 they hope to have fifteen shops along the eastern seaboard. Meanwhile Roddick is already working on skin products to suit the Japanese market.

There is not a chance of them buying another kind of chain. Roddick is not about to make the mistake of diversifying away from a winning formula. 'I just want to carry on doing what we are doing, but better.'

As the company grows, and a thousand shops by the early 1990s look possible, control becomes more difficult. The main board of directors is small. Along with Gordon and Anita Roddick is Stuart Rose, an accountant, and Jan Oosterwijk, who runs the European operations. But there are also young, enthusiastic people coming up. The distribution manager is in his early twenties, as are a number of key personnel. She clearly enjoys nurturing young talent.

'We have a young man here who wouldn't have stood a chance anywhere else, as he is always irritating the life out of us with new ideas. You have to learn to love the anarchist, as he will be the one to push you and your company further,' she maintains. Roddick's grounding in literature and the arts makes her a great communicator. She does not pay professional fees to the marketing companies, because she is the company's own marketing machine. Ironically, the marketing magazines and marketing pages of newspapers can't get enough of her.

She has grasped the secret that it is necessary to communicate within the company as well as outside. Part of keeping control as the company grows, she recognises, is giving the shops a feeling of belonging to the same company. Just as in Coloroll and Next, the workforce and the franchisees, although spread over thirty-five countries, are made to feel appreciated. Every month a video of the company's latest projects is sent to every shop. They have punchy names such as 'The Right Stuff', borrowed from the title of a book by Tom Wolfe, the American cult journalist. She is shameless about borrowing ideas. 'Entrepreneurs are doers and dreamers, they march to a different drumbeat,' she says.

There is also a newsletter called *Talk Sheet*, which highlights, not just the business events and achievements within the company, but also the social aspects. Issue number 11, for example, flags the American launch, 'Hello America' on the front page, but the main story is about a charity knock-out event that 'raised the incredible sum of £10,000 for Great Ormond Street Hospital for Sick Children'. Anita Roddick actually led one of the teams. The *Talk Sheet* has plenty of news about the shops in other parts of the world, but the overall style is of parents talking to children. An effusive thank-you to everyone involved in the charity-raising is signed: Anita and Gordon.

Desk-top publishing is quite a serious sideline at Body Shop and the company brochures and wide range of leaflets, all made from recycled paper, are well designed and carefully thought out. The ideas may be eclectic but the Roddicks have the ability to add a freshness and originality to them. Roddick would like to produce a magazine aimed at the young teenage market, which she believes is largely neglected. 'There are taboo subjects that need to be tackled, like date rape. It's about time someone gave power back to youth,' she says, harking back to the 1960s.

Roddick loves to talk about 'values'. She affects a disdain for profit, which is hardly consistent with the financial performance of the company. 'The bottom line should stay where it is, at the bottom,' she states firmly. Critics point out that this is a strange remark coming from a woman who is personally worth over £50 million and who was paid a salary of £145,000 in 1989, a hike of 73 per cent on 1986. Gordon Roddick, as chairman, got roughly the same. As earnings per share, which is what shareholders care about, have risen sharply, such a salary rise is more than deserved and at the lower end of what top executives of retail companies get. But it is hard for outsiders not to be cynical about her alleged lack of interest in money.

One of the secrets of their financial success is that Body Shop as a company is really a wholesaler rather than a retailer, in the same way as Alan Sugar's Amstrad is a wholesaler rather than a manufacturer. It supplies the products to the franchisees, who then sell them at a price fixed by Body Shop. As the manufacturing and purchasing capability of the group has increased, so too has the profit margin. In 1987 the group's pre-tax margin (the profit before tax but after interest, divided into the sales figure) was 21.1 per cent compared with 9 per cent in 1983.

But while Anita Roddick may be cool towards the City, particularly speculators who just want to make a quick profit out of dealing in her shares, the City adores Body Shop. Because the individual outlets take a few years to begin to produce worthwhile profits, analysts like Andy Hughes see the pattern of growth ahead. The number of shop openings in the recent past means he can confidently predict strongly growing profits and earnings for the next three years. But those amazing profit margins have probably got as high as they can go, so the next phase of growth will have to come from new shops.

The current view is that there is probably room for another 150 or so in the United Kingdom while in Germany there is plenty of scope left. But while Roddick hits the headlines with talk of opening in Japan and Russia, America is clearly the biggest potential profit earner.

While Gordon Roddick and Stuart Rose work away on the numbers and the nitty-gritty management, Anita Roddick is pushing the 'honest, non-exploitative and holistic' philosophies of the group to an increasingly receptive modern audience, which includes the Royal family, who are, naturally, her favourite customers. 'Prince Charles understands our philosophy more than anybody. He lives and breathes what we are doing,' she told *Life* magazine.

One of her links with Prince Charles is her keen sympathy for the environment. Body Shop is a corporate member of Friends of the Earth and believes in using recycled materials where possible. The products tend to use ingredients as close to their natural state as possible. None of Body Shop's products is tested on animals, quite simply because she sees the practice as unnecessary and cruel and feels that with growing technology there are many alternatives to animal testing. And yet she is far from being obsessed. Is she a vegetarian? 'Er, well, I don't eat red meat but I love chicken and fish,' she says, rushing round her warehouse chatting and waving to everyone in sight. And are her clothes natural fibre or man made. 'Mmm, I don't know – actually I couldn't give a stuff.'

To give her credit, Body Shop products are simple and straight-forward, claiming simply to cleanse, polish and protect. There is no promise of eternal youth or sudden beauty. The approach is practical and quasi-scientific. There is even a company brochure explaining about the skin and just what effects products can and can't have on it. Charles Revson, the founder of Revlon, said: 'In the factory we make cosmetics, in the shops we sell dreams.' Roddick is fundamentally opposed to that stance, preferring the Quakers who made profits out of honest policies and products. '*They* make my blood surge,' she declares. She does admit, however, that the Quakers did not seem to have a lot of fun. She, on the other hand, is committed to fun.

She is genuinely fascinated by the third world, spending several months a year there. Her method of helping poorer nations is realistic and not charity-oriented.

The Roddicks heard about an ex-monk called Joe Homan in Southern India who had taken destitute children and set about teaching them some rural skills and trades. He opened up a chicken farm and today there are eleven farms, called Boys Towns. The Roddicks put forward the idea of teaching them to make a simple wooden foot massager called a footsie roller. Homan, who is a firm believer in the phrase 'trade not aid', was enthusiastic. The Roddicks pay the boys what the same product would cost to buy in Europe and last year 89 boys made £100,000. 'Our relationship with the Boys Town is a partnership. We are giving them trade: they are making products for us to sell. They want work, not to be patronised,' says Roddick. Body Shop has schemes like this in several places in the Third World. In Tibet she has helped set up a paper-making plant using pineapple and banana leaves under the guidance of a Canadian crafts specialist. She believes that a business is a rich neighbour and should behave in a neighbourly way.

Although Anita Roddick loves travelling to strange places and discovering new ingredients and sources of supply, Body Shop is concerned with poverty and hardship in Britain as well as the third world. Gordon Roddick also gets involved in the social aspects of the company. When Anita had the idea of putting a soap-making plant in an underprivileged part of Glasgow called Easterhouse, it was Gordon who suggested putting 25 per cent of the profits back into the community.

The Roddicks and outside observers agree that for the foreseeable future there is no need for any diversification. The new companies that have been formed, such as Colourings and Jacaranda Productions (which makes corporate and training videos), are logical extensions of the existing business. There are separate companies for trading in Europe and in the United States.

Since 1985 Body Shop has run a training scheme for young people, attempting to inject some of the vital Roddick enthusiasm.

The Roddicks' home life is comfortable. They live in a large house and employ a full-time couple to see to the chores. 'It's a very normal house, very lovely. Incredibly boring.' Anita enjoys gardening and Gordon still has his passion for horses and plays polo regularly – an interesting pursuit for an alternative environmentalist.

The two daughters, like their parents, travel a lot and the younger one helped set up a manufacturing project in Nepal in 1988. The elder one took a trip round the United States before starting college. Because they both travel extensively on business, holidays tend to be in Britain, mainly in their house in the Highlands of Scotland. 'We can have 20 people to stay and just relax and do a lot of walking.'

'After work we might go for a drink in a local pub with the heads of the departments and sometimes we will go to a movie.'

They also bought a mews house in central London, near the Body Shop training school, in late 1988, for occasions when they need to be in the metropolis.

There is little life away from the business and that appears to be the way the Roddicks like it. 'All my friends are in the company and share the same values. They are the people I feel comfortable with,' she says firmly.

City investors have shown signs of becoming slightly wary of Roddick's increasing preoccupation with the third world, although a recent placing of shares to finance the new warehouse was snapped up quickly enough. So far there is no sign that projects to recycle paper or make products in distant parts of the world are based on anything other than sound economic sense. And as the Western economies become more aware of 'green' issues over the next decade or so, the Body Shop's products will appear to be in tune with events. Roddick appears to have no doubts about the future.

'The shop is a global product, there is no other company that has that. We have an international network of good, honest, anarchic fun. I think it's unstoppable.'

Name: *George Davies*

Title: *Managing Director of the George Davies Partnership. Former Chief Executive and Chairman of Next*

Born: *1941, Netherton, Lancashire*

Education: *Netherton Moss Primary; Bootle Grammar; Faculty of Dentistry, Manchester*

Qualifications: *6 'O' levels, 3 'A' levels*

Family: *Married Anne Margaret Allan in 1965. Married Elzbieta Krystyna Szadbey in 1985. He has five children*

First Job: *1961, stock controller, children's ankle socks, Littlewoods*

First Business Venture: *1972, School Care, a mail order venture in school clothing, set up with £15,000 of personal money*

Joined J. Hepworth & Son: *In May 1980, by invitation, as merchandise director and assistant managing director of new ladies venture*

Most Exciting Moment: *January 1988. The secret reception by everyone at Next after being awarded Retailer of the Year*

Awards/Honours: *1985, Guardian Young Businessman of the Year; 1987, Retailer of the Year; Fellow of RSA; 1988, Marketing Personality of the Year; Senior Fellowship of the Royal College of Art*

Hobbies: *Tennis, golf, watching most sports, doing up houses*

Drives: *Audi Quatro, Range Rover, Bentley*

Latest Salary: *1988, £561,000 at Next*

Chapter III

George Davies

NEXT

*'I've always learned most from
adversity and once you get to a
position where you could pay them back,
there doesn't seem to be any point anymore.'*

One mild December evening in 1988, George Davies and his wife Liz were summoned to the City offices of the company solicitors Slaughter & May and fired. The board of Next, the company Davies had revived from obscurity to be a revolutionary force in the high street, was unanimous that he should go.

The news was splashed across newspaper front pages in the next few days, signalling that, during his time at Next, Davies had achieved the kind of a folk hero status accorded to men like Richard Branson and Sir Clive Sinclair. Next's share price may have fallen, but Davies' image had never been stronger.

The coverage of the Next bust up, which extended to television and radio, swung public opinion firmly behind Davies and away from the quiet man who had masterminded his destruction, David Jones the head of Grattan, Next's mail order arm.

But four months later, when he announced the formation of the George Davies Partnership with his wife Liz and a new venture with Asda, the superstore group, the reaction was less than ecstatic.

Davies, a volatile, talented Liverpudlian, had dreamed up the idea of Next – initially a small, well-designed shop offering women middle fashion coordinated clothes – sometime in 1980. On that idea had been built a £1 billion empire, where profits had climbed from just £8.6 million in 1983 to over £90 million in 1988.

That December night, just after 11 p.m. the man who pioneered 'specialist' or 'niche' shopping in Britain found himself on the street in EC2, after three minutes' explanation from the board of Next. His title of Chief Executive was taken by Jones. The role of chairman, which was also his, had gone to Michael Stoddart, an eminent City fund manager and the previous chairman.

The only thing that was clear to the public and City investors was that there had been a breakdown in communication between Davies and his fellow directors.

The flashpoint occurred one Monday in late October 1987 when Davies flew in the company helicopter to see Jones at the Grattan headquarters in Bradford. He wanted to move the merchandising and warehousing of Grattan down to the Next headquarters in Enderby, near Leicester, to be under the supervision of Liz, the product director of the group. Jones fiercely opposed the move. Not only would it cost 237 jobs in Bradford, but he claimed that Enderby simply did not have the capacity to absorb the Grattan operations.

The row that Monday shows that the downfall of George Davies was not merely a disagreement over policy, strategy or management style. It was also an old-fashioned power struggle between Davies and Jones – men who had told the City that they had a unique complementary relationship.

'There had always been a culture clash between Enderby and Bradford,' says Nick Bubb, the top retail analyst at Morgan Stanley, the investment bank. Jones had enjoyed a relatively autonomous power base at Grattan, the mail order company bought in 1986, and saw the move as destroying it.

During that autumn, it had also become clear that the borrowings at the group had escalated out of control. Davies was all for firing Peter Lomas, the finance director, originally from Grattan. Supporters of Lomas say Davies would never sit down and talk about the finances for more than five minutes at a time. Whether that was true or not, the reality was that debt levels were over 120 per cent of shareholders' funds, more than double what is regarded as prudent.

Jones pressed Davies to sell the Zales and Collingwood stores which had been acquired when the company bought Combined English Stores. Reluctantly Davies agreed, and Gerald Ratner (head of Ratners, Britain's biggest jewellers) had the pleasure of buying the stores that Next had beaten him to over a year before. The package went to Ratner for £150 million, considerably cheaper than if he had won originally. Davies was on the run.

When it came to the final showdown, that Thursday in December, Jones sincerely believed that he was acting in the best interests of the company. 'George was brilliant at certain aspects of the business – he was magic with the shops – and I thought he should concentrate on those,' says Jones. He claims to have tried a compromise solution. One was that Davies and Jones would become joint managing directors. Strangely, that was what Davies had suggested to Jones when Next merged with Grattan. But at this point it was clearly not a solution that Davies, with his sizeable ego, could possibly accept.

A power struggle does not erupt without cause. Davies had fallen into two classic traps of the successful entrepreneur. He had been beguiled by the euphoric publicity he had received on the way up, and his management style had failed to grow with the company.

Rather than delegating more as Next mushroomed in size, he insisted on having a say in the key decisions of every division. And he increased his power by taking on the chairmanship as well as the chief executive's job in 1987. Liz Davies, too, had become unpopular within the company and had been adamant that the Grattan operations should come under her control. Ironically, Jones had sponsored her appointment to the board, impressed with her flair for merchandising and her attention to detail and quality control.

The coup at Next was not the first time Davies had been ejected from a company he thought he was running. In 1980 another power struggle saw him pushed from his job as managing director after he had pulled round profits at Pippa Dee, a quoted clothing company. The major shareholders sold the company, against his wishes, to a company called Amber Day.

David Jones joined the group when Next took over Grattan in a friendly merger in 1986. He maintains that he is still fond of Davies and would like to be friends again in the future. But it is unlikely that Davies will ever forgive the man who persuaded even his traditional friends and supporters that he had to go if the company was to survive.

'I thought that if the alternative to George going was Next and Grattan splitting apart, I had to vote for him to leave,' said one non-executive. The corporate director, John Roberts, a man whose career success owed much to the personal backing of Davies, also voted against him. Another to vote against Davies was Brian Marber, the independent financial technical analyst who had become a non-executive director as a result of his friendship with Davies. 'It was the most painful thing that has ever happened to me apart from bereavement,' said Marber.

George Davies never made any secret of his aggressive personality – if anything he gloried in it. 'The whole of life is a fight. At the end of the day fighting becomes an instinct,' he said prophetically during an interview in 1988. At the time he was sitting securely in his airy, futuristic office in Enderby.

At that interview Davies described himself as a British bulldog. He certainly has both the physique and the character – stocky, tough and determined. Like a lot of other dogs, a bulldog is aggressive, but more important as far as Davies' description is concerned, once he gets his teeth into something he won't let go. 'If there's a problem, I have to crack it,' he said chirpily in his Liverpudlian twang over tea and toast in the Enderby office. At the time he was in the middle of 'cracking' the problem of high borrowings.

His problem in 1989 was to extricate himself from Next with what he regarded as fitting financial remuneration after a suit for wrongful dismissal. It became a long, unpleasant, drawn-out affair.

Whatever his flaws, he was the undisputed creator and the public face of Next, and, until the last year of his reign, he was considered one of the success stories of the Thatcher era.

He is highly regarded by fellow retailers like Geoff Mulcahy of Woolworth, now called Kingfisher, and by Sir Terence Conran, with whom he developed an extraordinary love-hate relationship when they were both at J. Hepworth & Son. They back him, partly because of a sense of identification, but also because there is much genuine admiration for his vision, his flair and what Anita Roddick of Body Shop calls 'his sense of derring do'. His public persona is one of great personal warmth, good humour and charm. He also appeared to care genuinely about individuals in the company, particularly the young.

The City, which dislikes public displays of enmity, would have preferred Davies managed, rather than sacked. 'They have thrown the baby out with the bath water,' said Nick Bubb firmly. They have also made Next a bid target.

But, intriguingly, not one of Next's professional advisers re-signed in protest at his treatment. The merchant bank Lazard Brothers, two public relations firms, the company lawyer and the stockbroker all opted to stick with the group, privately admitting that they found Davies difficult to deal with. Some resented it more than others. 'He's a bit of a bully-boy; he pushes and needles people until he gets what he wants,' says one. Others are kinder: 'He's got plenty of bullshit and bluster,' says Roger Seelig, the former Morgan Grenfell corporate financier and a friend, 'but he knows what he wants and will try everything to get it. He's a closer.'

George Davies' most important claim to fame is that he single-handedly changed the way women buy their clothes. The growth of Next is one of the most astonishing success stories of modern retailing; combining vision, pioneering and, above all, timing.

As recently as 1981, Next was just an idea in his head. At that time Davies was virtually unknown, even in the world of retailing. By the mid-1980s he had become prime feature material for the Sunday newspaper colour supplements and television, as well as the financial pages of newspapers. Next grew into a company with fashion shops for men, women and the home in every major high street in the country.

Davies learned a lot from the sports field where, as a child, he became a star early on. 'I wasn't really interested in anything else but sport until I was 15,' he admits. In the playground too, he learned tactics for life. Never very large – as an adult he is around 5'7" – he was a natural target for bullying. Those who tried got as good as they gave. Listening to him one gets the impression that it was then that he learned how to bully the bigger boys. He simply fought back harder. He also responded with a determination to 'show them' by excelling at sport, especially soccer.

But he also has a softer side, something David Jones still points out, despite the bust-up. 'George could be very considerate with the staff. He has a very happy knack of remembering people's names and the nasty things that happen to them,' he said.

Davies would never have turned his dream into reality had he not been ousted from Pippa Dee. When the directors of J. Hepworth & Son, then a traditional menswear retailer in desperate need of some new blood, heard that he was free they invited him to join the board. Davies was the transfusion J. Hepworth needed.

The original Next concept, of presenting good-quality, well-coordinated, middle fashion clothes for the working woman between 25 and 40, spawned many imitators, but in the high street Davies always managed to stay ahead of his competitors. As the company grew, he diversified the Next name into men's clothes, fashion accessories, underwear and home furnishings.

After the merger with Grattan in 1986, Davies set his heart on creating a new kind of mail order catalogue. In early 1988 it emerged as the Next Directory, something he and Jones worked on together – and reasonably amicably. 'George would come up with ten ideas and I saw it as my job to pick up the one or two that were viable,' says Jones.

Although the shops dominated the corporate image, by 1988 over 60 per cent of the profits came from mail order – another reason why David Jones felt that Davies should be more democratic in his management style.

The Next headquarters at Enderby remain Davies' creation, reflecting his fertile mind. The design is light and futuristic, with polished wooden floors and elegant railed walkways. The colour blue dominates. An open spiral staircase leads from the ground floor to the managerial offices above. It is as different from the civil service type atmosphere of most big companies as it is possible to be. Part factory, part showroom, part office, it hums with activity. The atmosphere is relaxed, enthusiastic and professional. Being whisked round in the summer of 1988 there was no visible sign of discontent. Davies was continually greeted by cheery staff: 'Hi George,', 'Hello George'. Apart from Davies himself, no one seemed much more than 25 years old.

At that time, Davies claimed that he had enough humility to recognise that the company had to be able to operate without him. But, despite the outward show of friendliness, there had long been unrest. 'Everyone was petrified of him actually,' commented one less friendly observer. 'The staff played up to his mood when he was sweeping visitors round playing the beneficent boss.' It was certainly convincing at the time. The women particularly seemed to like having Davies around.

'I have to admit that I find most women attractive,' he said, smiling his lopsided smile. His eyes twinkle. Most women also find George Davies attractive. He is cuddly and tough at the same time; he's in control yet poses no real threat. Women relax with him and he makes them laugh. 'These guys who look like Adonis never have to bother developing a character,' he said.

Davies always gave a lot of credit to his wife Liz, who became product director in early 1987. 'She initially refused, feeling it could embarrass George, but the fact is she is there entirely on her own merit,' said Jones in an interview in 1988. Which shows just how things can change. Liz followed Davies from Pippa Dee where she had been an assistant buyer to Hepworth. Polish by birth she has a reputation as a stickler for detail and quality. Davies credited her with technical knowledge which he felt he lacked. 'She brought the missing x-factor to the business.'

Davies had long respected Marks & Spencer, Britain's leading clothing chain store. 'When I was at Littlewoods, everyone was neurotic about Marks & Spencer. I knew it was simply a case that they had better people.'

In the early days of Next, Davies astonished the retailing world and affronted M&S by declaring he wanted it to become the Marks & Spencer of the 1990s. Davies' obsession with Marks & Spencer was always in evidence, references to the company cropping up regularly in his conversation. He even boasted that Next was attracting staff from M&S. During 1988 he pointed out that if Next could grow at 25 per cent compound over the next ten years (less than its average over the previous five) it would be 50 per cent bigger than M&S. 'It's tough, but it's possible,' he said. Ironically, by the end of his reign, even M&S top management acknowledged his achievements.

Davies believed in finding young people and took pride in recruiting from the Midlands and the North. 'Our great opportunity is being able to get people in when they are young.' What he apparently failed to do was to give them sufficient autonomy and responsibility.

Davies may have been autocratic, but he was against any kind of bureaucracy. There was a very free egalitarian spirit at the Enderby offices. Everyone ate in the same airy, pleasant self-service restaurant and everyone from the ladies serving up the meals knew Davies by his first name. 'I saved you a nice piece of haddock, George,' said one, beaming fondly at him.

George Davies was born in a Lancashire village called Netherton. His mother's parents were farmers. It was a two mile walk to school down country lanes, with his sister Pam, who is eighteen months older than him. Davies loathed it. School was pretty much a battleground. 'I was a tough lad, always in fights,' he laughs.

The work ethic was strong in the Davies household. His father worked all hours for the local pie and sausage factory and ended up running it. 'My father gave me balance, he believed in the true things of life.' His father was also his introduction to sport, and played football for Everton and Blackburn Rovers. But it was his mother who had the real drive and ambition. Enlisting the support of her children, she persuaded her husband to move to a better area. When Davies was 16 years old they moved to Crosby, just outside Liverpool.

His mother tried to persuade Davies to go to Merchant Taylors, the local public school, but Davies preferred to stay at grammar school despite the rough and tumble. 'They had really tough guys there,' recalls Davies. But he survived through sport. 'If you can do something really well, that counts for a lot.'

By the age of 12, he was an advanced golfer and he was accepted by the local golf club. There he fought a different kind of battle, against the snobbery of the local public school boys. But adversity seemed to suit Davies. 'Inside I always felt, I'll show them.' At one stage his handicap was six.

When the time came for Davies to leave school, he had no clear idea of what he wanted to do. His mother, however, had her heart set on him becoming a dentist and he duly went off to dental college in Birmingham.

But he quickly got bored and applied for a job at Littlewoods. Starting off as a stock controller in ankle socks, he stayed at Littlewoods for nine years, learning all aspects of the business.

At the age of 29 he decided to break away and start his own business. It was the turning point. He managed to raise £100,000, which in 1970 was a substantial sum. He put in £15,000 of his own money, made from building his own house. Around £50,000 came from the Hollas Group, a small public company, and the rest from various sources. 'I must have been very convincing,' he laughs. 'All I had was a concept.'

That particular concept was to specialise in selling schoolwear by direct mail order. Called School Care it had promise, but after an initial success it foundered. Sales hit £1 million in the first year but the company was under-financed. When the mid-1970s' banking crisis came along some of the backers pulled out. It taught Davies some valuable lessons. First, he realised that you had to be able to trust your backers, and, second, that without a stable financial structure a company cannot survive when the going gets tough. 'Banks have no heart; you don't expect them to understand that you have had to shell out for research and design. They are more interested in personal guarantees.' It is a lesson he appeared to forget once Next became successful. School Care was never liquidated, but Davies ran the operation down. One day he received a phone call from Pippa Dee, then a publicly quoted clothing company. He was invited to bring his operation and team down to Burton on Trent.

Davies mentally wrote off the £15,000 he had lost personally and prepared to start again. Unhappily, things did not go as he had hoped. Within three months Pippa Dee plunged into losses and its share price fell to 4p. The managing director was fired and the board asked Davies to take over and make an almost instantaneous presentation to ICFC, the venture capital organization, which held 29.9 per cent of the shares and which was attempting to raise some support finance.

'I was very good up front,' says Davies, who is well aware of where his talents lie. The situation was so bad that it would not have been possible to trade out of it. Selling the main business seemed the only answer.

But Davies had another idea, which in its small way was a forerunner of Next, and he sold the doubtful directors of ICFC on it. It was selling coordinated fashion by 'party plan'. The concept was to sell women's clothes through house parties, very much like the famous Tupperware parties. It was ideal for housewives with young children. After the presentation ICFC agreed to back him and the atmosphere on the train going back to Stoke was jubilant.

The plan worked, profits began to climb again and by 1980 the shares were up from 4p to 28p.

Then Davies came up with a brainwave. 'I suddenly hit on the idea of making everything match.' That resulted in the value of each 'party' rising on average from £70 to £90. The banks were delighted with the sales figures coming through, and everything looked set fair.

Seemingly overnight, a classic boardroom power struggle erupted. One morning a rumour spread round the company that Jim Ingles, the chairman and a major shareholder, was planning to appoint a new managing director. Davies found out that the candidate was someone called Mark Dixon, who was at United Drapery Stores, or UDS as it was known. Davies confronted Ingles, told him that in his opinion Dixon had an uninspiring track record and demanded that the appointment was put to the entire board of directors. Most of the other directors were furious with Ingles and at the next board meeting they voted for his resignation seven to two.

But Ingles was in a powerful position. He owned 20 per cent of the company, which he tried to sell to clothing manufacturer Amber Day. Ronald Metzger, the chief executive of Amber Day, went to see Davies to persuade him into formally recommending shareholders to approve a takeover. Davies, displaying his bulldog spirit, refused and thought – perhaps naively – that he had seen the last of Metzger. But three months later Ingles and ICFC, with a total of 49.8 per cent of the shares, both irrevocably accepted a takeover from Amber Day.

There was nothing Davies could do. Ronald Metzger wanted to bring in Mark Dixon. It was clear that the two sides could not work together. When Davies refused to give long-term commitment to the company, he was fired. He never sought revenge. 'I've always learned most from adversity and once you get to a position where you could pay them back, there doesn't seem to be any point, anymore,' he says.

Later that same day Davies received the phone call that was to change not only his life but the face of the British high street. County Bank's thrusting young corporate finance team, which was only beginning to be treated seriously in the City, had advised Pippa Dee in the negotiations with Amber Day. One of its other clients was J. Hepworth & Son, the menswear group, then chaired by Sir Terence Conran. Hepworth had a good name, but it had failed to move with the changes in retailing. Burton was forging ahead under the new leadership of Ralph Halpern. It was homing in on specialist markets, and taking chunks out of Hepworth's market share every week.

At County's suggestion, one of the Hepworth directors rang Davies and asked if he would be interested in joining the company. Hepworth was in the early stages of buying Kendalls, a company with 78 shops in high streets. But Hepworth had realised that they needed someone like Davies to develop them, and even went so far to say that they wouldn't go through with the deal unless Davies joined.

He was asked to research the group thoroughly. 'I was a free agent for a month,' says Davies. During that time he visited 50 different towns. 'I spoke to everyone I could to get a feel for each place. I chatted them up in the supermarkets, in the pub, anywhere.'

Then he wrote the Next concept. 'I did it very professionally. The ghost of School Care was was still very much with me,' he recalls.

When he made the presentation to the board it was highly detailed, down to having swatches of the types of fabric and colours that would be used that coming season.

In February 1982 the first Next shop was opened. 'If Ronnie Metzger hadn't bid for the company I would never have started Next,' he smiles.

The Next concept was an overnight sensation. The *Daily Mail* reported: 'From day one, stock just walked out of the shops.' So successful were the early shops that the opening programme had to be slowed down, as supply could not keep pace with demand. Within a year there were 120 shops. To give him his due, when Sir Terence Conran resigned in June 1983 to pursue full-time activities at Habitat, he said that George Davies was the only man at Hepworth capable of bringing flair to the menswear shops. Davies was then just 41.

When Next shops first began springing up on the high street it was the beginning of the craze for niche retailing. Suddenly City investors didn't want to know about large stores; a wave of specialist shops sprang up in many different product areas. Our Price, Body Shop and more recently Sock Shop and Tie Rack were among the more successful. But Davies was the first to go nationwide and he expanded at breath-taking speed.

Five years on, he had seen saturation coming and was focusing on mail order and larger stores. The first Department X, his concept for bigger stores, opened in London's Oxford Street in the summer of 1988. It is completely unlike any other department store; all the goods are on display, with many of them moving round the store on moving rails.

Davies travelled a lot in the cause of fresh ideas. He understands that it is essential to keep abreast of the market. Fashion, like so many other things, has now become a global business.

Davies always worked hard and expected his staff to do the same. The Next day started at 8.30 in the morning and Davies was often working at 8 or 9 in the evening. He believed in 'getting things done and getting them done right'. In retrospect, it seems he rode roughshod over too many people's feelings, too often.

The Enderby headquarters provided a 'think tank' as well as an office. On the ground floor were ten or more shop prototypes for showing new ranges and developing new concepts. Here, Next Too and Next Accessories were first tried out.

Davies is a compelling salesman. But although the fortunes of Next have been built on the vogue for design, the one thing he is not is a designer.

Sir Terence Conran, on the other hand, is Britain's best-known designer and was also the non-executive chairman of J. Hepworth when Davies joined. Their disagreement, soon after Next became an established success, was Davies' first public fight at the company. There is confusion over the details of the row, but it centred on who should take the credit for Next. Conran liked Davies' idea of a specialist shop for a certain type of woman and his design subsidiary Conran Associates came up with the design of the shop and the distinctive Next shop front. Conran felt that he did not get enough credit for the Next idea and Davies understandably became extremely irate.

In the event, Conran left Hepworth and Davies became chief executive. At the beginning of 1986 he changed the name of the company to Next. It was, perhaps, a signal that there would never be room for another strong character besides him in the business.

Although there has always been a churlish mutual respect, the two men never really got on until the Next boardroom coup when Conran publicly spoke out in support of Davies. While they may not work well together, Conran too has had his share of boardroom strife and clearly identified with Davies.

By the end of 1983, Davies had tasted stock market success. The shares had doubled in less than a year and every retail analyst in the City was hailing him as the new messiah of the high street. The retail analysts saw him as an original thinker. 'He has tremendous enthusiasm and new ideas all the time. He can take something very obvious and make it into something original,' comments one. When he won the Guardian Young Businessman of the year award, in 1985, he was described as having a 'charming ability to combine modesty with ruthless bull-headed conviction'.

It is perhaps this early adulation that made the City's subsequent disaffection from 1987 onwards so difficult for him to bear.

As onlookers realised that Davies had unleashed a real winner, the bid rumours began to fly. Hepworth was at that crucial stage where a predator might think he could still buy the group cheaply and reap the fruits of continued recovery. There were approaches, but Davies wasn't interested in any so-called 'friendly' deals, and he was moving too fast for a hostile predator to catch him. Davies consolidated his position early in 1984 by demonstrating that he could take unpleasant decisions too. He announced the closure of sixty Hepworth stores. What was unusual was that he invited managers of most of them to take over the individual stores, offering financial help along the way.

By June 1984, Davies had become joint managing director of what was still J. Hepworth & Son, with an agreement that he would become the chief executive at the beginning of 1985.

In the August, Davies took the plunge into menswear. Eighteen shops under the banner Next for Men were opened virtually simultaneously, decorated with cosy wood-panelling, using American cherry with marble facing. 'We are after the male partner of the Next woman,' declared Davies at the time. They found him. Next for Men rapidly became as much, if not more, of a runaway success than the women's shops. Suddenly, the younger City gents were to be seen wearing the Next baggy-trousered suits cut, some speculated, to reflect Davies' own teddy bear shape.

Meanwhile, newspapers and retail magazines never tired of writing about Next. Imitators like the Solo chain began to spring up. Sir Terence Conran revamped Richard Shops, while Burton Group opened Principles to compete in the same market. Most significantly of all, Marks & Spencer began to show signs of unease about the competition and put one of their top directors, Alan Smith, onto the job of giving its women's clothing a new look.

Davies loved it. By the end of 1984 there were 180 Next shops, and 41 Next for Men. Then at the beginning of 1985, when he stepped into the role of chief executive, he launched Next Interiors, a soft-furnishings chain. That was intended as the place where Mr & Mrs Next bought their curtains. Somehow it has not quite hit the spot, possibly because others like Laura Ashley were there before him in the area. It remains a relatively small part of the total business.

The shares surged on, earning the company the status of 'glamour stock', being valued at more than the double of some of their mundane counterparts in retailing.

Davies dabbled in Germany, but at home began to develop the idea of a mini-store housing several Next formats under one roof. In the group's financial year to August 1985, profits cruised through the £20 million mark. Around a quarter of that came from Club 24, the group credit card business.

Davies was beginning to look at the takeover market. Between 1984 and 1986 'merger mania' gripped British business, reaching a peak in the spring of 1986 when Dixons, the giant electrical retailing chain, launched a hostile takeover bid for Woolworth. Davies believed he could apply the Next formula in department stores. His problem was the lack of the right kind of big stores in which to do it.

He talked to the Egyptian Al Fayed brothers, who had become the proud owners of House of Fraser, about buying all the stores apart from Harrods – but nothing came of it. He made do with piecemeal acquisitions like 100-odd shops from the ailing fashion chain Raybeck, but he knew he was on the profits treadmill. To keep City investors happy he needed something bigger to power the group forward, but he shied away from the expense and drain on management resources of hostile bids. All the department store groups seemed impenetrable. His break came when he went to see David Jones at Grattan who was at the forefront of the new ideas in mail order. A deal suited both of them and at the time the two men seemed to complement each other. 'It took us two seconds to decide how we would relate,' remembers Jones. 'George said, shall we be joint managing directors. And I said, no, you be boss and I'll be your deputy.' The £300 million agreed bid for Grattan was announced on 1 July 1986. For two years it looked like a perfect alliance and laid the foundation for the Next Directory. 'If I couldn't expand with further shops, I had to think of something else,' Davies said shortly afterward.

The deal was greeted with euphoria in the press, but all that year there had been rumblings that the original chain was running out of steam. In mid-August, Davies split the concepts into Next Too and Next Collection and upgraded the quality, shortened the time-scale each line would be on sale for, and launched some stunning new designs. Less than a year later he was on the acquisition trail again, and outbid Gerald Ratner for the Combined English Stores group with over 900 shops, comprising the jewellery shops Zales and Collingwoods, Salisbury's the handbag chain, Paige fashion shops, and Allens the chemist.

At that stage, it seemed that Davies could not stop spending, and many thought he had taken leave of his senses when he announced the purchase of 270 newsagent shops under the name of Dillons. The idea was to provide a distribution network for the Next Directory, but it has not worked well.

By 1987, Next had made it into the league of big retailers. Davies was mentioned in the same breath as Sir Ralph Halpern of Burton, Stanley Kalms of Dixons and Conran. And like so many before him he made the daunting discovery that to travel hopefully is often so much better than to arrive.

Like a lot of entrepreneurs who came from ordinary backgrounds, Davies found the City hard to understand. The row at the time of his annual results announcement in the spring of 1988 was typical of his communication problems with young investment managers. The Next Directory had just been launched amid an enormous wave of publicity but also considerable scepticism.

Davies knew his annual profits were going to be good, so he had arranged to fly a group of stockbroker's analysts up to Leicester for the day, and present the figures to them while showing them the new formats.

At one point he started talking about his concept for a much larger store. The idea, he explained, was to take a much bigger space than he had hitherto used and create something revolutionary. 'Would the sort of stores that BHS had be the right kind of size?' asked one of the analysts. 'Absolutely right,' replied Davies, buoyed up with confidence and a dash of mischief. It rebounded on him.

The following day the shares in Sir Terence Conran's Storehouse shot up on rumours that Next was thinking of making a bid. Ironically Next shares fell slightly as investors worried whether he would be able to handle such a big prize. Davies was livid as he saw his plan to improve his share rating backfire.

He has said that, in a sense, the City helped him, because it built up his aggression. 'That anger comes out in creativity,' he claimed. But although he used the City to fuel the growth of Next, he, like so many businessmen, was irritated by its capriciousness. Twenty-five-year-old fund managers, who one month can't get enough shares, can turn cold overnight. It is hard for a man like Davies to understand that a fund manager may be more concerned with the three-month performance of his fund than the long-term ambitions of the companies in which he invests. It was also difficult for him to understand why for three years he could do no wrong and for the last couple, as the profits came through, the shares started underperforming the market.

'He always took criticism of Next personally, as if someone was injuring him,' says David Jones.

But the City was proved right. His headlong dash for growth had resulted in the debt piling up and his fellow directors, particularly Jones, were putting pressure on him to do something. From the early days of the Next–Grattan merger, Jones had seen that below the surface rhetoric lay serious weaknesses in the area of financial controls. The worst problem was the Club 24 credit card operation, which sold its services to other store groups like Dixons. In the consumer boom, Club 24 had taken on far too much business from naive young consumers unable to cope with their credit card bills. By 1988, the bad debts were piling up, resulting in hefty write-offs.

Both Davies and Jones began to talk to advisers separately. Davies consulted his bankers Morgan Grenfell and also called up his former adviser, Roger Seelig, who had also been approached by Gerald Ratner, who was still looking for more outlets in the UK.

Seelig hit on a way of solving both their problems. It was to sell 450 of the former Combined English Stores shops, including the jewellery chains Zales and Collingwoods and the Salisbury handbag boutiques, to Ratners for £150 million.

It showed the City that he was a realist, but there was still unease. The whole retail sector was being squeezed by soaring rents and rates and rising interest rates were punishing those with high borrowing. But, when Jones and fellow board members pressured him to appoint some new non-executive directors to give some balance and wisdom, he chose Brian Marber, one of the controversial breed of City chartists. It was an intriguing move and Marber was much flattered and almost as bemused as everyone else. Davies did heed Marber's advice on currency. 'He's got a mind like a steel trap. I had casually remarked that he need only start worrying about sterling if it went over 3 Deutschmarks. The moment it did he rang me to say he'd covered the company's position.' However, Marber was not the steadying influence for which the rest of the board was hoping.

Davies never admitted to any business heroes or role models, preferring men from the world of sport. They include Stanley Matthews, George Best and, above all, Arnold Palmer. 'He is the sort of person who will play a difficult shot with a driver.

That sort of player is thrilling to watch,' he says. Sport remains his great love. He played soccer for England Schoolboys and was a keen golfer and squash player from the age of 11. 'Sport teaches you a lot about business,' he maintains.

At Next he worked punishing hours, but found time to play tennis twice a week on his own courts, which he has floodlit so he can play any time (he often plays at around 9 at night). Golf suffered during his years at Next, but the last reports were his handicap was heading back towards its peak of six.

Davies has three daughters from his first marriage. In May 1988 Liz presented him with a baby girl, called Lucia, rapidly followed by Jessica in June 1989. He has a strong sense of family. His father's death at the time of his bid battle for Combined English Stores affected him deeply. So impressed was he by the treatment his father received in the Leicester Royal Infirmary that he donated a substantial sum towards a lithotripter, a highly sophisticated piece of equipment that uses ultrasonic sound to break up gallstones.

He and Liz also enjoy doing up their house and grounds. In 1985 he bought a six bedroom mansion in 12 acres of ground in Leicestershire. He has been influenced by Liz, who had a long-standing interest in antiques. Together they have furnished the house in an individual style and planted over 5,000 trees. They also own a house in Chelsea, which has become a weekday base since their departure from Next.

The ousting of Davies has, if anything, raised his profile. He and Liz have become minor celebrities since then, seen at the best parties dining with cabinet ministers and frequently attending the opera at Covent Garden.

Davies clearly enjoyed being rich – although with only a few thousand of the company shares he did not become a millionaire on the back of Next – yet his total assets probably add up to over £1 million, including the undisclosed settlement following his departure from Next. However, if his claim against Next for £5 million compensation is met, he will, ironically become seriously rich for the first time. His lack of share ownership was another Davies mistake. It made his sacking easier. Conran owns 7 per cent of Storehouse and the possibility that he might sell that to a predator would make fellow directors think twice before contemplating a coup. The problem was that he behaved as if the company was his. 'I feel that Next is mine, even though I don't own it,' he said in mid-1988.

At that time he talked of providing for his succession. But while he may have liked the idea, he was not keen to put it into practice. Davies was convinced that he was at his peak, like a good sportsman – 'You hit the peak but you are still good for a few years,' he said. At the time, the remark smacked of someone justifying his position, but one senses he is someone who will never willingly share power. The more than doubling of his salary in 1988 to £561,000 seems to confirm that he believed he was the best man for the job.

Ever since the coup, Jones has been careful never to malign Davies personally, maintaining that he is still fond of him. He claims that he used to enjoy Davies' line in practical jokes. After Next announced it was buying the Dillons newsagent chain in 1987, Jones was left to explain the logic of the fashion group going into newsagents to an astonished and sceptical press. After a gruelling day, he headed for some relaxation on the golf course, taking his portable telephone just in case. He was just approaching the eighteenth hole when the phone rang and a French voice asked him if he would be interested in buying some French newsagents. It was Davies.

Jones also remembers that Davies could be patient. One time when they were playing golf, Davies spent one and a half hours painstakingly teaching Jones a golf shot.

Jones was regarded as the steadying influence on Davies. 'David spends quite a lot of his time digging George out of pits he has dug himself into,' said one adviser before the break.

Whether Next can remain a significant retailing force without Davies is still open to question. It was Davies' ideas which gave the company its originality, and his power and drive which kept it moving forward.

Whatever his sins at Next, fellow retailers and City analysts believe Davies still has plenty to offer by way of original ideas and design and marketing talent. Almost immediately after the coup, Davies began working closely with Roger Seelig, the merchant banker known for his acquisitive flair at Morgan Grenfell before he was forced to resign for his role in the Guinness scandal. Their original idea of finding a small public company that Davies could buy into using money from the institutions was abandoned in favour of forming the George Davies Partnership, a consultancy group.

The Partnership's first venture – to take over the design, purchasing and merchandising of the Asda Superstore's clothing and footwear ranges – hit the headlines at the end of April 1989. Asda is taking a 20 per cent share in the George Davies Partnership, which includes Davies' wife Liz, while the Partnership will be paid 25 per cent of any profits it makes from business above the original Asda targets.

Davies and his wife, who are also in the process of writing their own account of what happened at Next, believe that the difficulties facing the high street groups in the late 1980s whose margins are being squeezed by soaring rents and higher rates, should provide a lucrative market for the Partnership.

Sophie Mirman with Richard Ross

Name: *Sophie Mirman*

Title: *Chairman and Joint Managing Director of Sock Shop*

Born: *1956, London*

Education: *French Lycée*

Qualifications: *Baccalauréat*

First Job: *1976, joined typing pool at Marks & Spencer*

Family: *Married Richard Ross in 1984; they have two children*

First Business Venture: *1981, setting up first Tie Rack shops*

First Sock Shop: *April 1983, in Knightsbridge underground station*

Made First Million: *In May 1987, when Sock Shop floated on USM*

Awards/Honours: *1988, USM Entrepreneur of the Year, Veuve Cliquot Businesswoman of the Year, Marketing Woman of the Year*

Hobbies: *French, babies, skiing, tennis, waterskiing, riding*

Drives: *Range Rover*

Latest Company Statistics: *1988–89 – sales: £32.2 million, pre-tax profits: £2.4 million*

Latest Salary: *1987 – £50,000*

Personal Stake: *40 per cent, worth £10 million*

Chapter IV

Sophie Mirman
SOCK SHOP INTERNATIONAL

*'It is quite extraordinary that it is
considered more natural for a woman
to control the destinies, both
financial and otherwise, of a nation,
than it is for a woman to control a
business.'*

Sophie Mirman was still in the Marks & Spencer typing pool when
George Davies was experimenting with coordinated clothes at
Pippa Dee. But she was only two years behind the first Next
opening in starting the Sock Shop chain.

Davies had caught the wave of specialist or 'niche' retailers with
the precision of a champion surfer. And for the early and mid 1980s
these companies became the darlings of the stock market. Davies
was perhaps the first to prove conclusively that people preferred
shopping in small, attractive environments that didn't dazzle the
consumer with choice. Body Shop, Anita Roddick's natural
beauty products concept, was already in existence in a small way,
while Our Price records had turned what used to be a Saturday
afternoon pastime for teenagers into a wildly profitable business.

Like Body Shop, the Sock Shop began as one tiny shop based on
one good idea. There was no big company backing and no City
finance. Other retailers, banks and venture capitalists all gave the
idea the cold shoulder. Finally, a government-aided loan saved
Sophie Mirman and her idea from obscurity.

From the day the first tiny shop opened its doors in Knightsbridge tube station it was a far greater success than either Mirman
or her husband and business partner, Richard Ross, had thought
possible.

The stock market flotation in May 1987 was also a sell-out, with the offer for sale over-subscribed 53 times, valuing the company at £27.5 million. Once dealings started a few days later, the shares more than doubled from the 125p offer price.

By mid 1989 there were 103 shops all over Britain, and 33 in America and France, all selling an eye-catching range of tights, stockings and socks for women, children and, most recently, men. The potential for overseas expansion made them change the name to Sock Shop International.

The company history includes true love, a flight from un-happiness, a stock market quotation and public acclaim when in February 1988 Sophie Mirman won the Businesswoman of the Year award, sponsored by Veuve Clicquot and the Institute of Directors. All this, and substantial personal wealth at a very young age. In mid 1989, after a difficult six months, Sock Shop was valued at £25 million on the stock market, the smallest company in this book. But Mirman and Ross, both born in 1956, own 80 per cent of it.

They both pooh pooh the idea that their success comes from driving ambition or was in any way planned.

'When we started, we thought we would aim at four shops,' says Mirman. 'Then we thought we might as well go for ten. It just mushroomed.' Listening to them, it sounds as if success and fame took them by stealth. But in fact Mirman was always ambitious, even though initially she was unsure in which direction to go. She is the optimist of the two and her original business ambition was to become the first woman director on the board of Marks & Spencer, the UK's biggest retail chain in terms of profits. Being a pioneering woman entrepreneur has not got in the way of family life. Since Sock Shop floated its shares on the Unlisted Securities Market, Mirman has had two children.

How does she cope with overseeing all the buying, mer-chandising and design of the company and have time for a family with two children? After all, Anita Roddick, whose children are now grown-up, says: 'Any female entrepreneur who has two kids is thwarted by the fact that the kids are the weak link in the chain.'

One of the differences between them is that Mirman was already very rich, while Roddick was still relatively poor when her children were young. The other is a matter of temperament. 'I cope by being very calm,' Mirman says with a mischievous smile. She is also good at organising those who work for her, both at Sock Shop and at home.

She does indeed exude a well-ordered serenity – an example of someone who can keep her head in the midst of chaos. While the office she and Ross share in the crowded company headquarters is relatively peaceful, it is surrounded by frenetic activity. Nestling inside the Nine Elms industrial estate in Vauxhall, the offices are teeming with energetic youngsters rushing in and out, delivering orders, supplies, messages and bills.

Mirman was born in central London in 1956, the only child of French parents, Simone and Serge, who had eloped and settled in England to escape the disapproval of their families. They were both successful in their own sectors of the fashion industry.

Mirman was brought up in a comfortable, international atmosphere in Belgravia with a cocker spaniel for companionship. Her father was the vice-president of Christian Dior in the United Kingdom and introduced the first Christian Dior hosiery licence here. Her mother started off in England as a milliner in the famous Italian house of Schiaparelli, but set up on her own after a while to become a highly regarded royal milliner with a shop for many years in West Halkyn Street. It was a reasonably affluent childhood, although the family fortunes tended to ebb and flow with the fashion business.

When Mirman's father died in 1980, finances were difficult, and as Sock Shop prospered they have been able to put some money into Simone Mirman's business, which is still thriving.

Educated at the French Lycée in London, Mirman left school at 17 intending to take up her place at university a year later. But typically, so as not to waste her spare year, she took a secretarial course and finally decided that a degree in Russian and economics was not really going to help a business career. Instead, she decided to join Marks & Spencer because it had a good reputation in training. She began work in the typing pool but rapidly progressed to become secretary to Lord Seiff, who was then the chairman. It was a post that most of the girls were nervous about applying for, but Mirman went for it.

'I was 19, and a lousy secretary; to add to the problem, Lord Seiff smoked large cigars whilst dictating his letters.' Despite all this they hit it off. Now retired from Marks & Spencer, Seiff has become a non-executive director of Sock Shop, something which clearly delights Mirman.

'He influenced me tremendously,' says Mirman. 'He had immense self-discipline and knew how to get the best out of everyone.' She confided to him that her ambition was to become the first woman director of M&S. Lord Seiff took it very seriously and advised her to work in a variety of departments and then decide where she wanted to start as a management trainee.

Mirman experienced delights such as booking in the foods from the delivery lorries at 6 in the morning and sweeping the shop floor. 'It was marvellous experience,' she claims. But her ambitions became frustrated as she began to realise just how long it might take to get to the top at M&S. There still is not a woman director at M&S.

After four years working in different stores around the country and in Paris and Brighton, she had been appointed manager of the the large food section in the Croydon Marks & Spencer. It was good going but decades away from a seat on the board.

It was then that a friend introduced her to Roy Bishko, a South African who was starting up a new chain of shops, specialising in ties and scarves, called Tie Rack. Although she lacked experience in opening new outlets, she impressed him so much that he offered her the job of general manager. It was too tempting to turn down. Leaving Marks & Spencer, she says, was one of the hardest things she has ever done. 'It was terrible going up in the lift to tell Lord Seiff; I'll never forget it,' she shudders.

Richard Ross was born and brought up in North London. His father owned and managed a hotel in Knightsbridge, while his mother was a housewife.

He claims that he did not take to school and was particularly bad at maths. Nevertheless he passed the entrance exam to Merchant Taylors' public school in Northwood, Middlesex, although he hated the experience of being there.

'I was not very good at school and I didn't want to go to university,' he admits. But he realised that he was undisciplined in his approach to life and decided to study accountancy to give himself some focus. The experiment worked, and he quite enjoyed his years at Stoy Hayward's West End practice, whose clients were mainly hotels, restaurants and shops.

But once he had qualified he looked around for something more challenging and replied to the advertisement for a financial controller for Tie Rack, which was just starting up. There, in 1981, he found Mirman busily opening shops. They were both 24 years old.

It is a measure of Mirman's quiet ability to make things happen that, after joining the company in the October, three Tie Racks were open by the December. 'I had never done any buying, recruitment of staff or dealt with shop fitters and architects,' she says. 'But you have got to get on with things.'

Although the Mirman–Ross team soon proved itself a great success, with Mirman becoming managing director and Ross finance director, they fell out with the backers. Both of them disagreed strongly with the management style and felt ill at ease with the tactic of expanding through franchising. 'The whole atmosphere was very aggressive,' says Ross. They were thrown together in their discontent. 'Unhappiness draws people together,' explains Ross. Romance and a business partnership blossomed.

Eighteen months after Mirman joined they broke with the company. 'We didn't leave because we were fantastically ambitious; we left because we were miserable and we wanted to be happy,' says Ross.

Mirman had the idea for Sock Shop one cold January day in 1982 when she wanted some white woolly tights to go with an outfit. They were not to be had. She became annoyed and then intrigued. It turned into a quest. In the end she claims she went to every department store in London without finding any.

She went right back to Tie Rack and suggested the idea of a shop specialising in tights and stockings to Roy Bishko. But although they were having tremendous success with Tie Rack, he and his colleagues dismissed Mirman's idea as silly. It was the final straw.

Mirman convinced Ross that the idea of a specialist shop selling nothing but high-fashion stockings and tights was a winning idea and they set about looking around for backers, while they were still at Tie Rack.

It is a chastening story. They had £1,000 each and needed £45,000 start-up money. 'Richard wrote a very comprehensive business plan with five different sets of forecasts and I typed it', says Mirman.

They should have presented a tempting team for venture capitalists. Mirman had considerable retail experience from four years with Marks & Spencer and Ross was a qualified accountant. And they had short but crucial experience of niche retailing through setting up Tie Rack.

They were prepared to give away 49 per cent of the company for that £45,000. Had anyone been brave enough to put up the money it would have been worth £30 million by the end of 1988. It was a perfect example of how the so-called 'risk-takers' in the City can sometimes be way out of touch with what is happening in the real world. They have become twice as rich as they might have been if an outside investor had been prepared to take the risk.

Venture capital house after venture capital house turned it down. Nobody wanted to know. 'They just couldn't grasp it,' says Mirman.

In the end they negotiated a loan under the government's Loan Guarantee scheme through their local bank manager at Barclays. Even that was tricky, because so many companies funded by government loans had gone to the wall.

After the third amended application Ross became so impatient that he threatened to take his business elsewhere if the loan was not processed immediately. 'I've since discovered that the golden rule of banking is not to judge a venture by its viability, but to judge a client by his durability: if he threatens to leave – lend.'

They then set about looking for premises for the first shop. Because they were still working at Tie Rack, Ross went property hunting using a pseudonym. Finally Peter Thomas of property agent Edward Erdman came up with tiny premises, just 110 square feet in Knightsbridge tube station.

Mirman and Ross were ecstatic. But then they discovered that Tie Rack had also expressed interest. It was a difficult few days. Ross insisted that they could not snap it up for themselves while they were still directors of Tie Rack. Fortunately, Tie Rack decided against taking the premises.

They both left in the March after considerable bad feeling. Weeks later, one Saturday in April, she and Ross opened the first Sock Shop in Knightsbridge. 'Richard and I were absolutely terrified. We had no idea what kind of response we would get and we couldn't even work the tills properly,' Mirman remembers. Ever since they had had the idea people had tried to convince them not to do it. 'Everyone laughed, including investors, manufacturers and potential landlords,' says Ross. But they were all wrong.

Success was instant. On that first day they took £632, much more than they had ever dared to hope for. They went home and got 'absolutely drunk'.

The novelty of having a successful business kept them busy to begin with. The name Sock Shop was devised by both of them 'just playing around with words'. 'Hosiery is a dreadful word, stockings smack of Ann Summers and tights just are not very nice,' says Ross. Sock Shop was unthreatening, a slightly silly fun name that appealed to a public just emerging from the worst recession since the 1930s.

The early days were clearly a lot of fun. 'We used to have our business meetings in the photo kiosk in the tube station,' recalls Ross. The shop was tiny and very hot in the summer. Mirman claims that the only real arguments over business they have ever had were over who worked in the 'sauna corner'.

There was no room in the shop for spare stock, so they kept it in the basement of Mirman's mother's shop. Mirman would collect it every day on her bicycle. But one day the bike was stolen so they scraped up enough money to buy a car.

Expansion was painfully slow to begin with. It took another six months to open a second shop and around three years to get to ten shops.

Ross admits to being a terrible pessimist. He never believed that the idea could work outside London. When that theory was proved wrong with a widening network of provincial shops, he was very chary of going to the US. Here he was proved right, and a number of the shops in Manhattan have hit problems

Meeting Mirman, she seems practical rather than creative, but those who know her – like Bob Lederman, of the stockbroker Capel Cure Myers – have been impressed by her flair.

She has a knack of turning everyday occurrences into business opportunities. Just as the original idea stemmed from her own need, the expansion into children's socks arrived shortly after her own children. 'When my daughter was born, I couldn't find any coloured socks.' The solution was obvious.

Mirman never actually designs anything herself, although she reckons she has a good eye. 'She is outstandingly talented with merchandise,' says Ross. 'She just knows what will sell.' Mirman's own appearance, apart from the latest pair of outlandish tights, worn one suspects for P.R. rather than personal preference, is muted and conventional. She does not wear make-up and turns up for lunches in the City wearing a blouse and jacket with a calf-length skirt. She is quietly spoken, but combines a cool confidence with a quick wit.

Her speech has the slightest hint of a foreign accent, often noticeable in those who are bilingual, although she claims she couldn't speak French as an infant.

Crucial to the success of the business is the relationship between Mirman and Ross. They were married in October 1984, by which time the company was flourishing.

Although Ross's financial ability has been fundamental to the group, he is quite happy to let his wife enjoy the limelight. She is the one who is feted and constantly badgered to make speeches and presentations. 'Behind every successful woman is a man without a chip,' he is fond of saying. He does, however, admit to bristling slightly when he is called Mr Mirman.

One reason the alliance works so well is that they have totally different functions within the company. Ross looks after finance and property, while Mirman is in charge of the buying and the design.

'We have never argued about a business decision; we feel exactly the same way about things,' says Mirman. They claim they can walk into new premises and know instantly what the other one thinks about it. They live together, also work together, and quite obviously love every moment. 'We try to switch off at home, but quite honestly I think there would be something wrong if we could,' confides Ross.

Sock Shop has constantly and rapidly outgrown itself. After six months Mirman's mother decided that enough was enough – something triggered by a large delivery of stock coinciding with a royal customer – and that she would like her basement back. So they moved briefly to a squalid office in the Fulham Road, which was so damp that the paint never dried on the walls.

Taking a deep breath they rented 1,000 square feet in Kensington, but within a year they were bursting out of that. Finally they moved to Nine Elms, near Victoria, initially taking 15,000 square feet although another 8,000 was added later. Towards the end of 1988 they realised that they could no longer have all their operations in central London and signed the lease on a 60,000 square-foot warehouse just outside Cambridge.

As the success of the group has increased, so has their ambition. Unlike the case of Next, there are still plenty of high streets in Britain without a Sock Shop, indicating considerable potential growth. Experience also shows that a really busy shopping street can support several Sock Shops. Oxford Street in London has seven.

Mirman's horizons expand almost with every day. In 1987 she was talking in terms of the United Kingdom being able to absorb

150–200 shops, while at the end of 1988 she was predicting as many as 500. But a combination of the hot summer, high interest rates and the transport strikes brought growth to a halt in 1989.

During the first few years of the company's life, the London stock market was enjoying its most active time for many years. When takeover bids were not centre stage, company flotations were and niche retailers were the latest craze. It seemed sensible to take advantage of the mood and 'go public'. Anita Roddick's Body Shop, a franchise operation, had been an outstanding success with the City, but Mirman and Ross were not convinced.

They were told by their accountants, Stoy Hayward, that a stock market debut would entail six months of being 'out of the business' and be sheer misery, since flotations involve a large amount of detailed and tedious legal work. But they needed to raise capital for expansion and there is nothing like a public quotation to aid in negotiations with landlords and suppliers. Stoy Hayward introduced them to Bob Lederman and John Gregory at Capel Cure, which had built up a reputation for floating smaller companies, often on the junior Unlisted Securities Market. Lederman and Gregory had also developed experience in the retail area by floating Body Shop. More recently they launched The Reject Shop.

The clincher was the success they had in New York in 1986, where they opened three shops in three weeks. If they were serious about expanding internationally, then they needed to be public. 'But we were not out of the business for six months and we had fun,' says Mirman firmly.

Lederman and Gregory had been almost instantly won over by Mirman's charm and enthusiasm. Ross was slightly wary in the early days and his pessimism emerged not long before the company was due to make its stock market debut. He realised that Sock Shop would be arriving around the same time as the Rolls-Royce launch and he felt that no one would want to know about a company as tiny and frivolous as Sock Shop.

But investors viewed the two companies as totally different and not the least bit in competition for their money. In fact, Sock Shop got the rave reviews and the share offer was over-subscribed a staggering 53 times. That meant that nearly £260 million was chasing just £5 million of shares. 'Forget Rolls-Royce. The prize for provoking an investors' stampede last night went to Sophie Mirman's Sock Shop,' wrote the *Daily Express*.

Then, a few days later, dealings in the shares began. They soared from the issue price of 125p to 295p, more than doubling the worth of Mirman and Ross's shares from £22 million to over £50 million in minutes. It was the height of the bull market, just two months before the stock market hit its all-time peak in July. Amid the euphoria there were sceptics, who pointed out that the Sock Shop shares were backed by assets of only 15p a share and, even at the issue price of 125p, they were selling at over 24 times the yearly earnings. There were also doubts about the ability of the management (Mirman and Ross) to handle the growth of the company. By 1989 the shares had come back to a more sensible level and, while Mirman and Ross have been recognised as able managers, they are not expected to be immune from a downturn in consumer spending.

Since 1985, operating profits grew from £216,000 to £2.6 million in the year to September 1988, on sales up from a tiny £613,000 to £25.8 million. In the year to February 1989, after a change in the year end, profits fell slightly.

What the sceptics failed to take into account was the value of Mirman's years at Marks & Spencer. Not only had she watched Lord Sieff at very close quarters for a year and a half and was an able pupil, but she had spent four years as a manager at M&S. Ross, meanwhile, has proved to be that rare breed, an accountant with imagination.

They both realised that at some stage they would have to start delegating, and Sock Shop now has a strong management team. They have developed management systems, controls and philosophies that will enable the group to become a much bigger company without a lot changing. 'We used to do everything ourselves, but the flotation forced us to expand the team,' says Mirman. By the summer of 1988 they were employing over 800 people.

The bottom line of the management philosophy is the product. 'We are a product-driven company,' explains Mirman. 'We believe if we get the product right, the staff and the management right, the profits will follow.' Sock Shop started with a few jolly designs. Today there are over 300 different styles of tights, stockings and socks in several different colours. Mirman is also keen to undercut brand names with their own label. In 1988 Sock Shop launched the City Slicker range of plain black tights, selling at £1.99, while the nearest competitor sold at £2.25. It rapidly became one of the best-selling lines. Mirman is also zealous about quality control. 'We have the best quality controller in Europe,' says Mirman. The quality control manager had fourteen years' experience before joining Sock Shop and he works closely with suppliers. 'He sometimes knows better than they the latest types of manufacturing machinery on the market.' It is a way of working directly with suppliers, culled from M&S, which is famous for its sometimes controversially close relationships.

Mirman would like everything Sock Shop sells to be made in Britain. In reality, around 60 per cent is the best she can manage. She feels that British manufacturers can be very stubborn when asked to try something new. And, as an English woman born of French parents, she is very conscious of the contrast in approach. 'The difference between the English and the French is that a British company will automatically say no to a new idea, while a French company will say yes, but then fail to deliver. The Japanese, of course, say yes and they also deliver.'

In Britain, Sock Shop's main competition is, Mirman believes, the department stores. And the department stores clearly feel the same way. Even when they opened the first tiny shop in Knightsbridge, Harrods' management was furious and tried to prevent the shop opening.

The most telling sign of Sock Shop's influence is in any hosiery department in London today. A galaxy of patterned tights will be prominently displayed. But Mirman is confident that the convenience factor will win out. It is just so much easier to buy stockings and tights at the station on the way to work, or in the high street, than to slog round a big store.

Mirman has deservedly won a reputation for knowing what the customer will want and she is constantly working to keep ahead of trends. In the Sock Shop headquarters, the design staff beaver away on new patterns, constantly perusing the work of freelance hopefuls.

'My goodness, what is that,' exclaims Mirman at a particularly garish effort for children's socks. 'Don't worry, we're not having it,' grins the executive.

Mirman may lack the charismatic approach of some of her peers. Nevertheless, watching her in action, she appears coolly in control. 'She leads by example,' says Bob Lederman.

She and Ross both believe in recruiting management from within the company where possible. 'Of our nine area managers, seven have grown with us,' she says. The senior management all have share options. The aim is to give opportunities to as many as possible. And home-grown executives have already absorbed the product-led, self-critical culture.

Mirman is well aware that pausing to congratulate themselves on their success could lead to disaster. Nevertheless, difficult trading conditions in 1989 found them partially unprepared.

One step they have taken is to employ a full-time training manager. Clearly this is the Marks & Spencer influence at work again. 'Yes, but it is also common sense,' says Mirman.

The early comparisons of Sock Shop with Body Shop foundered when Mirman and Ross decided against the franchise route. When they had just six shops they were approached by a would-be franchisee. They decided to go ahead but, although it worked financially, they didn't like the lack of control over the staff and merchandising and felt that the image of the group as a whole might suffer from shops that were not being run according to their high standards. 'We have a great deal of respect for the Roddicks,' says Ross, 'but we didn't feel franchising was for us.'

Mirman works hard, but she is also well organised. She has plenty of full-time help with the children and the home. Unlike many entrepreneurial personalities, she also needs a full eight hours sleep a night.

Some days, however, are worse than most; like one in the summer of 1988 when they moved house in the morning, had a board meeting at lunchtime, met an American partner in the afternoon and Mirman made a speech in the evening.

Being one of the few successful women managing directors of a public company, she has created a lot of media interest and has to turn down quite a lot of requests for appearances and interviews. She claims not to have experienced any sexual discrimination, but then she is the type who is too concerned with getting on with the job to notice. 'Being a woman doesn't make any difference to me. I've never come across any discrimination,' she says firmly.

On the other hand, she laments the general lack of success of women in business. 'It never fails to amaze and concern me that the captains of retailing who guide their ships through a sea of predominantly female consumers do not have amongst their ranks a greater proportion of women,' she told the Institute of Directors in the autumn of 1987.

Sadly, she feels that discrimination is sometimes something women create themselves. As an example she cites the recent response to two job advertisements. One was for area managers, where 90 per cent of the response was from men and only 10 per cent from women. Another was for sales staff, where the percentages were reversed. 'Does this mean that the more senior a position the less capable a woman is of handling it? Or simply that women will not aspire to greater things?' she asks.

Assuming the problems of 1989 are overcome, there is still plenty of room for expansion, using the original concept. Apart from aiming at over 500 Sock Shops in the United Kingdom alone, business in the United States has potential. They have formed a joint venture company 85 per cent owned by Sock Shop and 15 per cent owned by Barney Goodman, the former director of Mothercare. Unfortunately, there have been initial problems with the locations of the shops. The Mirmans have decided against the scattergun approach towards international expansion, deciding to concentrate hard on America, because of the size of the market, and France, because that is where Mirman's heart is. And if she can succeed in retailing in France, she will have achieved something rare indeed. Hitherto, British retailers have had a nightmarish time in Europe, particularly France. So far the omens are propitious. After the second French shop opened in Marseilles, the sales figures for the first week were so high that they initially thought they were in francs rather than in pounds. So far Sock Shops have opened outside Paris, because within the capital the leasing laws make it very difficult for newcomers.

For Mirman, 1992 can only make life easier for both buying supplies and expanding across frontiers. She and Ross believe there is quite enough growth potential in the company without looking for expansion into other areas. City investors who like companies to be as tightly focused as possible will certainly be happy about that. And there is every reason why Sock Shops should flourish in Germany, Spain and Italy. But will Mirman and Ross ever retire and sell out? She shrugs as only a French woman can. 'It would be like selling a baby.'

Name: *Gerald Ratner*

Title: *Chairman of Ratners Group*

Born: *1949, London*

Education: *Hendon County Grammar*

Qualifications: *None*

First Job: *Ratners shop assistant*

Family: *Married Angela Trup in 1971; they have two daughters*

Joined Ratners: *In 1965*

Made First Million: *In 1986, due to the rise in Ratners shares*

Most Exciting Moment: *Negotiating the takeover of H. Samuel*

Awards/Honours: *1986 Retailer of the Year*

Hobbies: *Skiing, snooker, poker*

Drives: *Bentley Turbo, Renault Espace*

Personal Stake: *£2 million*

Latest Salary: *£495,064*

Latest Company Statistics: *1988–9 – sales: £635 million; profits: £86 million*

Chapter V

Gerald Ratner

RATNERS GROUP

*'It is only when you fear that everything could come
to an end that you really start to perform.'*

Gerald Ratner is one of life's rawest competitors. Money is important to him – he paid himself a salary of nearly £500,000 in 1988–9, and he lives in style in an early Victorian country house on the banks of the Thames at Bray. But more powerful forces than money drive the head of Britain's biggest jeweller and one of the country's most successful young retailers. Of the H. Samuel takeover, which provided the quantum leap for his family's business, he says, 'I would happily have taken a 50 per cent pay cut just to get it.'

Ratner's aggressive competitiveness is not to everyone's liking. He has more than his fair share of enemies in the jewellery industry: he has taken one of Britain's weakest retailing sectors and dragged it kicking and screaming into the 1980s. In the process, sacred cows – like the idea that jewellery is an investment – have been sacrificed. Pop music, loud posters and price-cutting offers have replaced the pomp of marble shop fronts and plush velvet. Many small family businesses, as well as larger companies, have been forced to throw in the towel, unable to compete with the radical price-cutting which has been the hallmark of the Ratner style since he first became managing director of Ratners in February 1984.

He can be brash – he once referred to his products as 'crap' during an interview with the *Financial Times* – and even rude to those for whom he has no respect. During one takeover battle, rival jewellers formed a committee dedicated to halting Ratners' relentless growth and lobbied hard, though without success, to persuade the government to call in the Monopolies Commission to investigate its growing market domination. Typically, Ratner, who has a mischievously dry sense of humour, took their bleating as a compliment. 'The day I heard about the committee was one of the most exciting in my life. It just showed what an impact we were making.'

But the Alan Sugar of jewellery retailing has made money for investors. When Ratner, at the tender age of 34, took over the helm of Ratners (Jewellers), as it was then known, the company was valued at just £11 million, had 130 shops and was losing money. Just before the 1987 October crash, Ratners' market value had climbed to nearly £650 million, the shares having risen more than eleven-fold. Ratner was well on his way to achieving his ambition of becoming not only the leading jeweller in Britain, but also the number one in the world, overtaking the then giant of his industry, the Canadian-based Peoples Jewellers, which controls Zales of the United States.

And the crash did nothing to curb the ambitions of the *enfant terrible* of jewellery. Within six months he was back on the takeover trail in America, adding family firms to the core of his American business, the Sterling chain, bought for $203 million in July 1987. In May 1988, the cream of the City of London and the retailing world gathered in the glitzy surroundings of an H. Samuel shop in Shaftsbury Avenue to watch Ratner open his thousandth outlet.

Ratner's emergence as a retailing superstar had no inevitability about it. For a while he looked like the epitome of the second generation of a business dynasty. Sons, so it is often said, rarely make a success of their fathers' businesses. Most tend to spend the money accumulated by the previous generation. And it is only in the last five years that Ratner has given any indication of being an exception to the rule.

The young Ratner, only son of the company's founder, Leslie Ratner, showed little sign of academic achievement at school, and dropped out of what was then called Hendon County Grammar at 15. 'My father said I was not doing much at school so I left with no qualifications whatsoever and went to work in one of our shops on the corner of Oxford Street and

South Molton Street.' His performance there was not much better than at school. He was quite good at selling, but was not really interested in the details of the business like doing the paperwork and cleaning the stock, preferring to spend his time gambling and gatecrashing parties. 'I had what you might call an unruly youth,' he later admitted. 'I was seen as the playboy son who had entered the business.' Marriage came early – at the age of 21 – to Angela Trup, a girl he had met on the North London social scene.

Ratner accepts that he played a part in the mismanagement which drove the business into loss. The company had benefited from the surge in the gold price in the late 1970s, which pushed profits to £3.44 million in the year to April 1980. 'It was very easy to make money on one's stock in those days,' he recalls. But the surging profits caused Leslie and his son to launch an ambitious move up market, tarting up the shops and making the products more expensive. A company that had always made money out of being cheaper and more cheerful than its great rival, H. Samuel, was putting on airs and graces. In the process, Ratners parted company with Terry Jordan, an ace jewellery buyer who set out on his own, with an independent chain called Terry's, to specialise in what his old employer was abandoning: cheap, fast-moving items like chains, earrings and rings.

In 1984 when Ratner took over as managing director, he saw he had to reverse the process. 'I could see that Terry was doing things the right way. Ratners, with its expensive merchandise and more spacious displays, was a disaster. The look made people think it was expensive. Terry's on the other hand looked like a place where you could get a bargain.'

Terry Jordan gave Ratner the trading strategy that was to transform the face of British jewellery retailing. Corporate strategy, comprising a wave of takeovers, came from Charles Saatchi, the recluse who with his brother, Maurice, built up Saatchi & Saatchi, and from Michael Green, founder of Carlton Communications, the television and video group.

Green and Ratner had been close friends from the age of 15. They had been part of the same St John's Wood circle of affluent Jewish establishment families. Green had always looked as if he would be successful. 'You always knew Michael was going to be a successful businessman,' says Ratner. 'Even at the age of 15 he seemed to know who everyone was in the business world.' At Carlton he demonstrated how a business could be transformed by takeovers. This was in sharp contrast to the history of Ratners, which had been based on a steady but slow store-opening programme. In its twenty-year period as a public company it had not made a single acquisition or issued any shares to fund expansion.

His friendship with Charles Saatchi came later – over the snooker table. Ratner, Green and Saatchi would play for hours in the basement of the Ratner family home in Regents Park. 'In the old days with friends, one used to talk about football or women, but with Michael and Charles it was different,' he says. 'They were always talking about money and business. Charles, for me, was another person to look up to. After all, Michael at Carlton had merely copied the acquisition strategy of Saatchi & Saatchi.'

The all-too-apparent success of both Saatchi and Carlton had, by the spring of 1984, given Ratner the competitive spur needed to release the workaholic businessman from the pampered playboy. 'I suppose I wanted to prove something to my father. People had always talked of me as "Leslie's son". Now I wanted to prove that I too could be successful. It bugged me that when we were playing snooker I had a business worth £11 million, while both Charles and Michael were running companies that were worth much much more. It was a competitive thing.'

Even after five years at the helm, he remains as competitive as ever with his two snooker rivals, if the evidence of the screen beside his desk in his restrained grey office in Great Portland Street is anything to go by. On the customised pages displaying share price information from the Stock Exchange he has assembled the major high street retail chains like Dixons, Next, Woolworth and Burton. But two other share prices are also on display: Saatchi & Saatchi & Carlton Communications.

In 1984, the base from which he hoped to build a major retailing group was not in good shape. Sales were poor and the company was heading towards higher losses in its traditionally weak first half. Predators had started to eye the chain as a potential takeover target, and the founding family, with just 12 per cent of the shares, was not in a good position to repel boarders. Says Ratner, 'We really had to do something dramatic. My back was against the wall and I was fighting. It is only when you fear that everything could come to an end that you really start to perform.'

The problem was in the Ratner buying department. Ratner knew he had to be competitive, but the company was buying jewellery that was too expensive. So he decided to pay a visit to Terry Jordan, then trading successfully under the Terry's (Jewellers) banner. At the time Jordan was in the middle of a divorce, and, as his wife had a stake in the business, he was looking for a buyer. Says Ratner, 'There I was trying to change my shops so they looked like Terry's. Why didn't I buy his company instead?'

Unfortunately it was not that easy. Having agreed to buy Terry's for £4 million, Ratner then needed to finance the deal, but the company did not have enough money or sufficient borrowing power. To compound the problem, profits in its traditionally stronger second half were heading downwards, hardly the sort of performance that the City would require to back the first purchase of a new and untested managing director in his mid-thirties.

Ratners' own stockbroker, Grieveson Grant, had little faith in the idea, believing the company was paying too much for Terry's. With little ceremony it announced that it would be unable to place the shares needed to fund the purchase and came up with an alternative proposal: the Ratner family shares be bought out by a Scottish property developer at 55p or 60p, a premium on the reigning market price of around 44p. 'At the start no one wanted to know Gerald Ratner,' says one adviser. 'They all stuck their noses up at what they saw as a clapped out little jewellery firm with no prospects.' In his despair, Ratner turned to Morgan Grenfell, the merchant bank, which succeeded in persuading his father that the deal was sound and knocking down the sceptical arguments of Grieveson Grant. In the end, Jordan took £1.5 million in cash upfront, all that Ratners could afford from its own resources, and a further mixture of shares and cash, based on profits performance. The show was on the road.

The deal, agreed in September, was finally announced on November 26, but, despite the delay, a critical five weeks of Terry's trading were included in the Ratners figures. More important, Jordan showed Ratner how to solve the problems in his own business. 'What I did was I went to the managers. My father used to tell them off if they questioned the business. I decided to listen to them instead and they told me what was wrong – little details about quality or salaries.' Surgery was required in some parts of the company. The jewellery factory in Camden Town was sold, the Dutch subsidiary, which had been losing money heavily, was also put on the block, as were the opticians' branches.w'z

Though painfully shy in his early months in control, Ratner learned from Charles Saatchi and Michael Green how important it was to cultivate the financial press and the broking community if he was going to build a major company. There had been some minor publicity following his arrival in the hot seat. But the opticians' disposal provoked the first real interest in Ratner. The first piece of stockbroking research analysis, produced by Buckmaster & Moore, in February 1985, although hardly ecstatic, was the first indication of outside interest. The investment view was to 'hold' at 47p. 'Although not outstandingly cheap statistically, the changes being made by the new generation of management have improved the profits outlook significantly,' was the verdict of Katherine Wynne and Jenny Nibbs in their annual directory of smaller retail companies. On March 3, a small paragraph in the *Sunday Telegraph*'s influential 'Market Miscellany' column advised its readers to 'Note the strength of Ratners shares at a four-year peak of 61p . . . They could have further to go.'

In July, Buckmaster & Moore, though still very much on its own, changed its recommendation to 'buy/hold'. The price having soared to 87p, Ms Nibbs wrote, 'The established business of Ratners is responding well to the trading formula . . . while expansion prospects have been enhanced by the growth possibilities of the newly acquired Terry's chain. On the back of this, plus the disposal of loss-making activities, Ratners should continue to grow at a rapid pace over the next few years.'

Inside the business Ratner's hunch about the attractions of lower-priced jewellery proved correct. The popular illusion that jewellery could be an investment was ebbing away as the tide of inflation receded in the early 1980s. Those jewellers that turned to selling jewellery as a fashion item would be the winners; those that chose instead to price their stock high and wait for the buyers would be in trouble. 'In 1985 the business did take off with genuine improvements on a like-for-like basis,' Ratner says. 'It made us feel a bit cocky, especially when we began to realise how easily the competition was giving in, particularly H. Samuel.'

On the buying front, Ratner had recruited his younger cousin, Victor Ratner. His task was to exploit the market power of the combined group to buy products at more competitive prices. Once in the shop they were sold through aggressive marketing and the use of devices like dual pricing. This involves the retailer putting two prices on a particular article with a slash through the higher one. An early experiment with diamond rings showed how powerful the new approach could be. Sales increased, more than compensating for any loss in margin, while stock turnover soared, enhancing returns on capital.

The shops themselves were designed with minimum frills. If anything, Ratner revelled in the sheer lack of style. He strove to keep the look of his outlets as far as possible from the traditional Dickensian idea of what a jeweller ought to look like, as well as what the new generation of retail designers might think was appropriate. 'Do not believe all the talk you hear about calling in design companies. If you do the opposite it might work. It is far better to listen to the grass roots,' he says. 'The managers and staff may have less sophisticated views but they are at the sharp end of things and tell you the truth. They are better qualified to tell you what is right or wrong with your business than the guys in the design and advertising agencies.'

Ratner's own management style was simple but effective. 'Gerald is one of the few businessmen I know who has nothing on his desk. He is a great delegator. He gets involved at the concept stage but is happy to pass on the details to his staff,' says one adviser. 'He motivates by a none too subtle blend of stick and carrot. He can be pretty bad-tempered, both with close colleagues and advisers. He gets through public relations consultants by the dozen. But he is quick to praise when things go well and is happy to reward his successful staff generously.'

The success with the Ratners and Terry's stores showed that Ratners had the capability of entering a bigger league, and the search for a second acquisition commenced in early 1986. At 36 and just two years after taking over as managing director of his family company, he decided it was time to transform it from an also-ran into the leader in high street jewellery sales.

The first priority was to get better financial advice. Ratner felt he was an outsider when it came to bids and deals. 'At the time, the City was like a club of which I was not a member, yet I wanted to be in it. I wanted to turn Ratners into a big business and if you wanted to be big you had to be with the right people whatever their fees,' he recalls. Alfred Davis, one of Ratners' non-executive directors, had criticised him for paying £50,000 of fees during the Terry's deal, but Ratner had come to realise that investment in a front-line merchant bank would pay off. 'Michael Green told me that if you start asking questions about the costs you end up not doing deals. If you want to do deals you have to pay for it, even if the costs are horrendous.'

His search led him to Roger Seelig, the Morgan Grenfell corporate financier who played such a big role in reshaping the face of Britain's high streets before he got caught up in the Guinness scandal. It was Seelig who built up Sir Terence Conran's Storehouse combine from Habitat, Mothercare, Heals, Richards and BHS. It was Seelig, too, who helped Stanley Kalms to victory in Dixons' bitter battle to take over its leading high street rival, Currys.

The candidate had to be H. Samuel, then the largest jeweller in the high street, with 350 outlets. Like Ratners, it had a family man in charge in the shape of Anthony Edgar, a descendant of one Mr H. Samuel. But, unlike Ratner, Edgar had not pushed up profits or wooed the City. Samuel's profits were poor and analysts were not pleased by the fact that the Samuel chairman turned up for one briefing with his wife. There was talk that Edgar senior had not seen eye to eye with his son and that Anthony had only returned to the business after his father's death.

Ratner reckoned that H. Samuel had lost its way. To the outside world, Samuel appeared to be doing the right sort of things. Rodney Fitch, the designer who had brought new life to stores like Burton and Top Shop, had redesigned the outlets to create a brighter and more congenial atmosphere, and the company had indulged in heavy television advertising. What it forgot to do, says Ratner, was to offer its customers the right products at the right price. 'The result was that morale was nil and motivation was nil,' he says. 'Samuel had made profits of £15 million in 1980, at the peak of the gold boom, but it had gone into decline. It had a huge portfolio of shops, probably worth around £100 million, yet these assets were producing profits of just £5.8 million. It was laughable.'

The problem for Ratner was that Samuel's equity was made up of a mixture of voting and non-voting shares. It was impossible to take over without obtaining the approval of the Edgar family. Edgar himself, along with his mother, controlled 43 per cent of the voting stock and Ratner made more that one attempt at negotiating an agreed merger. He had suggested a reverse takeover of Samuel, whereby the larger company would make a bid for Ratners but Ratner himself would end up in charge as managing director. Samuel was after all a much bigger company, with a market value of £90 million, against Ratners' £30 million. But

Edgar showed no interest. 'You are an unsuitable candidate to be managing director of H. Samuel,' he told the Ratners managing director, a man he appeared to regard as an upstart. After all, in the late 1970s Samuel had owned a big stake in Ratners and it seemed extraordinary that the tables should be turned on him.

Yet turned they were – for the simple reason that other members of the extended Edgar family became increasingly disenchanted with his stewardship and began looking for an escape route. Trading was not good, something the City was starting to recognise, and in April 1986 Samuel parted company with its chief executive, Tony Dignum. He had been regarded as the 'great white hope', but fell out with Edgar and chose to return to his old home, Stanley Kalms' Dixons.

On April 28, the *Daily Telegraph*'s 'Questor' column sounded an ominous note, which struck a chord with the Edgar rebels. 'Britain's best-known jeweller, H. Samuel, has lost contact with the City,' it declared. 'Even worse, it has lost its only executive director. It may even be losing money. Samuel has a terrible trading record. . . If the next set of results are as disappointing as some analysts fear, the pressure will be on for change despite the family grip.'

Ratner first knew that something was up, and that he might have a chance of achieving his long-held ambition, when he took a call from Andrew Coppell, a Morgan Grenfell corporate finance executive who later joined the Ratners board. Coppell had discovered that the Edgar family stockbroker, the Bristol firm of Stock Beech, was looking for a buyer for 27 per cent of the voting stock. 'My response was simple: I said, "Buy them at any price",' Ratner recalls.

The shares bought, Ratner had to court the man who just a few months earlier had said he was 'unsuitable' to run his business. Ratner had the eloquent Seelig to help him, but it was not destined to be an easy negotiation. Ratner had to use every ounce of charm and flattery he could muster to convince an extremely reluctant Edgar that there were benefits to a marriage between the two companies. Though he had little respect for the older man, Ratner persuaded himself that he would be content to be chief executive while Edgar could hold on to the title of chairman.

The H. Samuel chairman was hesitant. There were other predators eyeing his 350-strong portfolio of freehold and long leasehold high street locations, among them George Davies' Next and Murray Gordon's Combined English Stores. Yet Edgar knew he needed new management. Just a month before he had lost Dignum, and he was under pressure from his non-executive directors to reorganise the company and recruit new executives. He also knew that Gordon would not offer him the chairmanship if he chose a merger with CES, so he eventually agreed to pursue the idea of a Ratner takeover. It gave him more than 60 per cent immediate profit on the value of his shares before the bid and offered an honourable exit from hands-on management of his family company. On the evening of May 22, Ratner was summoned into Edgar's presence. Samuel was the jeweller that Ratner and his family had always looked up to, but this time Ratner was not going to pay obeisance to the management of Samuel. He was going to negotiate the details of an agreed takeover.

'I remember getting the good news on a Thursday. I got a call saying that Edgar would be calling me in 10 minutes. He said "Come over to my house". When I got there I said I would be managing director and he would be chairman. I said we would call the company H. Samuel Ratners. I said my father, my Uncle Jack and Alfred Davis would resign from the board to make way for representatives of H. Samuel. At that stage I was in a mood to agree to anything. I would have even jumped out of the window if he had asked me to. It was like a dream come true – after all I had been telling people when I was 10 years old that I wanted to buy Samuels.'

The City, both press and brokers, loved the deal, which pole-vaulted Ratners into unassailable leadership of the industry. The day it was announced, Ratner declared 'This is the happiest day of my life.' The transaction was presented as a merger, but it was clear whose culture would dominate. The company's name might begin with H. Samuel, but management of the larger company – led by its 47-year-old chairman – had abdicated in favour of Ratner. One more of the old retailing dynasties that had dominated Britain's high streets for decades had vanished.

Quantum Leap, an investment newsletter, wrote, 'Gerald Ratner has pulled off a remarkable coup in taking over much larger fellow-retailer H. Samuel. It gives him exposure on virtually every High Street in Britain at a time when he, and a colleague, Terry Jordan, are doing to jewellery retailing what George Davies of Next, Conran and Ralph Halpern have done to clothes retailing. We rate it as good as, if not better, even than the Dixons takeover of Currys.'

The problem for Ratner was that while everything was sweet-ness and light on the surface, his working relationship with Edgar got off to an awful start. Any fears he might have had about Edgar's behaviour were quickly realised. He had been warned that Edgar's presence as chairman might cause problems: just two weeks after the takeover had been announced the *Sunday Times* wrote ominously, 'Analysts are bearish [the City term for pessimistic] about the prospects for the combined group, and are not keen on Anthony Edgar, chairman of H. Samuel, who will hold the same position after the merger.'

Ratner recalls one meeting with Victor at which his cousin was told by Edgar to take his hands out of his pockets. More importantly, Edgar seemed to be criticising all his decisions. Ratner had forced his own family to accept sacrifices in order to complete the merger. Three Ratners directors had resigned to make way for Samuel representatives, and now it looked as if Edgar was out to challenge Ratner's day-to-day authority. At one meeting with store managers, his audience watched with horror as Edgar persistently interrupted him, undermining his authority and causing uncertainty among those who were waiting for action. Clearly things had to change, and in late August Ratner announced that his chairman was leaving the board with a record golden handshake, which eventually totalled £585,000.

With Edgar out of the way, Ratner set about reviving morale within the Samuel management. He recalls his first presentation to staff. '"Samuel," I said, "you were the number one but you have lost your dignity in the last few years. You did a good job in the shops but you have got the wrong merchandise." We then showed them how we wanted to change the stock and how we wanted to abolish all the stupid forms and book-keeping work that kept them away from the main job of selling. We also asked them for questions and we agreed to the proposals they made. The response was amazing. They started to clap and cheer and from that moment the business did not look back. Only by listening to your managers, the people who really know about your business, can you really do something.'

The new ranges combined with the new incentive schemes for staff pushed Samuel sales ahead. In earrings and chains, particularly, demand became overwhelming. In one shop 650 pairs of earrings were sold in a single week, against the Ratners shop record of 250. Staff who had felt neglected, like area managers driving battered old cars and store staff having to cope with worn carpets, were given a new lease of life. Says Ratner, 'There were no clever gimmicks about it. In many ways it was just normal textbook stuff.'

Textbook stuff or not, the combined group instantly made a big noise in the high street. The bid itself was partly financed by a large sale and leaseback operation in which £27 million of Samuel property was sold to financial institutions and then rented back. Meanwhile, inside the stores, crowds poured in, attracted by the lower prices. Jewellery was suddenly in the limelight, having for years been the dullest sector in the retail industry, after butchers and books. Ratner learnt well from the pioneers of the 1980s' retailing revolution like Sir Ralph Halpern at Burton and Dixons' Stanley Kalms: clear away the cobwebs. Music was introduced into the shops, while high-fashion items at very low prices were prominently displayed.

But more than flair was necessary to keep control of a retailing group that had exploded from 130 outlets in early 1984 to 550 outlets following the Samuel takeover and had a declared target of reaching 1,000 outlets within two years. Ratner needed systems. 'My father placed great reliance on systems. He knew that 70 per cent of sales came from just 30 per cent of the items one displayed, and that if one was out of what the customer wanted, one simply did not make a sale,' he says. He introduced a sophisticated electronic point-of-sale system which gave him daily information on sales. With an electronic finger on the pulse of the business, he was able to keep stocks in individual branches and the warehouse low, while meeting customer needs.

By 1987, what had been one of the most sluggish sectors of the high street had become the fastest growing according to government figures, almost totally due to the revolution that young Ratner had precipitated. It was causing his competitors considerable pain. Murray Gordon, the amiable chairman of CES, had, with Ratner, seen the profits to be made from modernising and rationalising an old-fashioned business, and had been attempting to build his own major group. In 1986 he trumped bids by both Ward White and a management buy-out team to buy Zales from its American parent and then shortly afterwards he added J. Weir. Ratner himself had turned down Zales, a move he says was 'one of the biggest mistakes I ever made'. But by early 1987, Gordon was not particularly enjoying the competition his outlets were facing from Ratner and there were rumours that he was interested in retiring, taking his profits on a company whose shares had recovered spectacularly from the recession.

'I remember an estate agent from whom I wanted to buy outlets telling me that Murray wanted to retire. I went round to see him and he said he wanted to sell his whole jewellery division which was finding it impossible to compete with us,' he recalls. 'The initial proposal was that he would inject his jewellery interests into Ratners in return for a 20 per cent shareholding. I said I was not interested but suggested the idea of Ratners buying his whole company. The idea of removing a competitor appealed.'

The takeover attempt started well enough. Agreement was reached on a price. But then news of the talks leaked out in a prominent article in the *Observer* in March 1987. 'Speculation swirls around the future of Combined English Stores, the £210 million, 950-shop Salisbury handbags, Zales jewellery and Allen's chemists combine,' it wrote. 'Late last week rumour had it that Ratners . . . was again on the acquisition trail and poised to bid £200 million-plus for CES.'

It was enough to scare Gordon off, and when talks were restarted the price had moved up. Even then Ratner could have been successful had he been able to buy the 26 per cent stake in CES owned by Warburg Investment Management, the fund management group. But that was impossible ahead of the announcement of the deal because such a transaction, at around £80 million, would have required shareholders' approval because it was more than 15 per cent of his company's net asset value. When on May 1 Ratner announced his £309 million offer, it was wide open to a counter-bid even though he had the backing of the board. Two days later Ratner read in the *Sunday Times* what he had feared. 'Next, the retailing group headed by George Davies, is this weekend considering entering the bidding for Combined English Stores,' the newspaper wrote. 'Davies . . . has been eyeing the high street assets of CES for some time and has made approaches in the past. He is anxious to find new outlets for Next, which is in the midst of an extensive diversification programme.' The following week Davies entered the fray with a £317 million offer.

Ratner tried to fight back. Following the announcement of his bid he was besieged by offers for bits of the CES group. Sears in particular was willing to pay £110 million for the Salisbury handbag chain and the Biba clothing outlets in West Germany, putting him in a position to threaten a counter-bid unless Davies agreed to sell him part of the CES retail portfolio. But the threats were in vain, as Ratners' share price drifted downwards making it more difficult by the day to turn to the City for funds for a new and higher CES offer. Davies was prepared to sell him some outlets but the sites were dreadful, in the sort of locations where it would be extremely difficult to make money. Eventually he decided to back off and let the Next deal go through. It did, after all, have its attractions. Davies wanted CES for its 950 sites, many of which were to be converted into Next shops. He proposed to take the Collingwood and J. Weir names off the high street, a move that would reduce the competition to Ratner. 'I was very upset, even though the exit of Collingwood and Weirs was a consolation prize. But I did learn some lessons – you don't hold a gun to a person's head, especially if it is George Davies. He was able to double bluff me.'

Revenge came 17 months later – and it came extremely sweetly – when Ratner was able to take advantage of Next's high borrowing levels, the product of expensive expansion, to snap up both Zales, which had 130 outlets, and Salisbury's with its 235 shops selling costume jewellery, handbags, briefcases, luggage and other fashion accessories, for £150 million. It was Ratner's first move out of mainstream jewellery. But in the spring of 1987 the deal was many months off, and Ratner's more immediate task was to rebuild morale after the defeat.

The share price had taken a big knock, which did not seem warranted by the underlying performance of the business, and Ratner wanted to show the City how quickly he could bounce back. In June he announced an £81 million rights issue, which would either serve as a war chest to buy stores off Next or some other retailing group, or be used to open more outlets. Ratner had entered informal talks with the Weinstein family, founders of the Ernest Jones retailing group, almost immediately after the CES deal moved out of reach.

More ambitiously, he began work on a plan to take the Ratners low-price, no-frills formula into overseas markets, in particular the United States – the biggest consumer market of them all, and one capable of putting the Ratners growth engine into a new and higher gear. America had been a nightmare for many British retailers, often proving a highly expensive graveyard for their ambitions. While businessmen in other sectors had demonstrated that Britain does have something to offer – the exploits of Lord Hanson and Sir Gordon White and Maurice and Charles Saatchi were the best-known examples – the country's retailers had, in general, found themselves up against great difficulties. Nevertheless Ratner felt he did have something to contribute, partly because the US jewellery market in many ways reflected the British scene before he had taken over the management of his family's company. Zales was the leading company, followed by Gordons and Kays, but the independents controlled 70 per cent of a market that was ripe for reorganisation into bigger groupings.

Ratner is an opportunist. 'I'm not one for scientific study. I'm one for gut feeling.' But he had done enough homework to be interested when a corporate financier from PaineWebber, the US investment bank, called to say that Kays could be up for sale. It turned out that the information was wrong, but Ratner's appetite had been whetted and he readily accepted PaineWebber's invitation to travel with cousin Victor to the US to visit a number of possible targets. One of these was Sterling, an 117-store group that had been the subject of an institutionally backed management buy-out in 1985.

Ratner liked what he saw. He immediately struck a chord with Nate Light, the company's chief executive, and came away impressed with Sterling's stores and its head office staff. On the buying side, the company had control of its diamond purchasing, sub-contracting out the manufacturing and thus enhancing its profit margins. Its in-house developed computer systems were outstanding. As one broker put it after a visit to the company, 'Sterling's computer systems rank as the finest operating systems for control over inventory and store functions we have seen.'

But Ratner knew that if he was going to get the business he would have to move fast. Light liked the Ratners' operation, but there were other bidders around. To add to the complications, Ernest Jones, the jeweller Ratners had been wooing in Britain, had entered merger talks with Next, although the Weinstein family still favoured a deal with Ratner – and Ratners still had its outstanding £81 million cash-raising exercise out in the market.

Miraculously, all the loose ends were tidied up. Ratner was able to announce both the £125 million purchase of Sterling and the £25 million takeover of Ernest Jones, to be funded by a new £122 million issue of shares on top of the earlier cash call, on the same day. The City was bemused. The influential 'Lex' column in the *Financial Times* sounded a sceptical note: 'When it comes to offering glitter at low prices no one beats Ratners. The question is whether Ratners' shareholders will regard yet another rights issue even before the last one has closed as cheap and cheerful, or cheap and nasty. . . Ratners itself must be taking quite a bit on trust, as well as paying a hefty price, and is in turn asking its shareholders to do the same.'

But the sense of the Sterling move gradually started to sink in. In August, John Richards, the star retailing analyst at Wood Mackenzie, one of Ratners' brokers, wrote of the two trans-actions, 'Today is the time to lay the foundations of tomorrow's growth. In the UK Ratners know the market and can be totally confident of turning an undermanaged company round; overseas that approach is arrogant and dangerous as many other UK retailers have proved. It is essential to buy good management and a sound base for expansion – Sterling is an excellent retailer and, while the entry price is therefore high, the potential is enormous. The US jewellery market is large ($20bn+), fragmented and undermanaged. Ratners has bought the No. 4 player and the most highly regarded company with the best operating ratios in the industry.'

Ratner himself made no secret of the fact that Sterling was an expensive purchase, but it did give a foothold into a market capable of giving his company sustained growth over many years. 'We did pay through the nose,' he says. 'But I could see that in time the UK might run out of steam. And it was a very good business. Its sales at $1 million-a-shop were higher than both Ratner and Samuel. We could have bought a cheaper business and tried to improve it but it might have been a big mistake, particularly in a country we did not know. Instead we choose to buy a fabulous business and expand it. The Sterling deal was our entry ticket.'

And, despite the market crash, Sterling proved to be a good entry ticket. Its diamond-buying skills were brought over to Britain with great effect, and in 1988 Ratner was able to offer 1 carat diamond rings for just £1,600 against a typical price from his competitors of £2,700. Equally importantly, he was able to add on other chains whose stores could easily come under the control of Sterling's headquarters management. Two months after the takeover, he snapped up one of Sterling's local competitors in Ohio, the privately owned Westhall chain, in a deal that was expected to leave Ratners with over 200 American outlets by Christmas 1987. In April 1988, he added another 56 outlets as a result of the purchase of Osterman's, another private jeweller, for $60 million. By the spring of 1989, Ratner had well over 300

US shops, or 2 per cent of the market, and had the stated ambition of taking that total up to between 1,000 and 1,500 shops by the year 2000.

Ratner is well aware that as his group grows the corporate culture of competition and incentive could be diluted. But he is determined to stay involved with the everyday concerns of his group, motivating his key staff with a skill that belies his brash public image. 'The deals have only been possible because the basic trading has been good. You have to have a good track record to raise money in the City,' he says. Each Monday morning, the weekly sales figures arrive in his spartan office in Great Portland Street. There at his desk, surrounded by pictures of his children, a graph of his share price, a few reference books like *Who's Who* and the *Retail Directory*, and a print of a Loire Valley chateau, he pores over the numbers, searching with an eagle eye for potential problems and emerging success stories. He painstakingly goes through the details of new window designs, incentive programmes and posters. Ratner has decreed that all diamond rings will be displayed 42 inches above the pavement as this is the most comfortable viewing height for the average woman. All the stores are designed at head office after ideas are gathered from the grass roots and each branch manager is then supplied with photographs showing him exactly how to lay out his shop. 'It is like painting by numbers,' explains Ratner. 'If I did not keep a watch over the day-to-day things we would not do as well.'

Ratner does not disguise his combative nature and has had his fair share of clashes along the way. He parted company with his wife in 1986 after fourteen years of a marriage which produced two daughters. Says Ratner, 'I guess I was a bit of an angry young man and the pressures of work were enormous.'

After he fell out with Anthony Edgar, Ratner faced an action replay when he took over Ernest Jones in 1987. Little more than two months into the agreed takeover he and the Weinstein family parted company. There had been a furious row over Ratner's description of the Ernest Jones chain as 'a mess'. The Weinstein directors took Ratner to an industrial tribunal claiming unfair dismissal, while he was left ruminating over the continual search of jewellers for 'respectability'. 'There is a jewellers' disease which appears to affect about 70 per cent of the industry. They like prestige and image, and believe the only way to succeed is to go up-market and install things like marble shop fronts. They hate the pop music and the posters and think Ratners is a five-minute wonder.'

His ambition is to take his company into the big league of British retailers, made up of companies like Marks & Spencer, Storehouse, Woolworth, Burton and Sears. The crash may have slowed him down by limiting his abilities to raise cash in the London stock market, but he is content to build gradually on a number of fronts. The US remains a big opportunity, as does Salisbury in Britain, and further diversification into mail order is a possibility. 'We were rather lucky in 1987,' he says. 'I am not in a hurry in the US and am quite prepared to build the business gradually over five years.'

In the spring of 1989 Ratner reported that his annual profits had climbed from £53 million to £86 million, and City analysts were predicting another rise to around £117 million for 1989–90. This puts him in a position to overtake companies like Dixons and Storehouse. His business philosophy is simple: 'Do not do the same things that everyone else is doing. When everyone tells me I am doing the wrong thing, I know I am doing the right thing. Ratners is not the story of a financial magician. What we have done is to go back in time and return to the basics of how things should be sold.' His drive is based in part on material hunger. 'When I took over the business from my father, I had £200,000 of shares and an £80,000 loan and a mortgage. I guess that if my father had given me his shares I might not have been so hungry.'

But equally important is a competitive drive whose source goes beyond materialism. Ratner sees the retail industry as a league table he desperately wants to climb, and reckons business is the ultimate intellectual challenge. 'There is no better platform than business. There is no better game than something where you are using all your skills. Everything after business has become mundane to me. I often get home at night and find my brain is still racing from the excitement of a deal. You just can't put it down.'

THE PEOPLE
BUSINESSES

Name: *Martin Sorrell*

Title: *Chief Executive of WPP Group*

Born: *1945, London*

Education: *Hasmonean; Haberdashers' Aske's School; Cambridge; Harvard*

Qualifications: *8 'O' levels, 6 'A' levels, Economics BA, MBA*

First Job: *Marketing trainee at Glendinning Associates*

Family: *Married Sandy Finestone in 1971; they have three sons*

Joined WPP: *In 1985 when he took a major stake with a partner*

Made First Million: *As finance director at Saatchi & Saatchi*

Most Exciting Moment: *The night that JWT agreed to be bought*

Awards/Honours: *None*

Hobbies: *Skiing, cricket*

Drives: *Ford Scorpio*

Personal Stake: *£6 million*

Latest Salary: *1988–£505,000*

Latest Company Statistics: *1988-sales: £547 million; profits: £40 million*

Chapter VI

Martin Sorrell

WPP

'It's nice to do the impossible.'

On the morning of Tuesday, 23 June 1987, Martin Sorrell left his Manhattan hotel and took a Lincoln town car twenty blocks downtown to the headquarters of J. Walter Thompson. The diminutive bespectacled finance man strode through the grand atrium, with its indoor trees, chrome and glass, and took the lift to a third-floor conference room. Assembled around a long, thin table were the top managers of JWT Group Inc, the parent company of the world's best-known ad agency. Their chairman, Don Johnston, was one of the doyens of Madison Avenue.

The atmosphere was icy. Sorrell's tiny company, WPP, which two years before had been an insignificant maker of supermarket baskets, was in the middle of a hostile $500 million bid for the American ad agency group, ranked number four in the world. When the bid was announced, Madison Avenue asked 'Martin who?'. American advertising executives knew he had been finance director of Saatchi & Saatchi, but beyond that they were mystified. Here was a mere finance man, who shunned the flamboyance of advertising and was content to describe himself as 'boring', taking on the Madison Avenue establishment. A businessman, who exuded conservatism and convention and who had never written an ad in his life, was doing something completely unconventional. The risks of the bid were enormous:

JWT was a 'people' business, whose assets, if they wanted to, could literally walk away.

Wall Street knew Sorrell a little better. It had been Sorrell who had come with his employer, Maurice Saatchi, to New York in the early 1980s to educate American fund managers in the virtues of investing in advertising agencies. They reckoned he was the best financial brain in British advertising, but they still gasped with amazement at what was the most audacious and extraordinary move made in the history of advertising. An unknown company, valued at just £130 million, was bidding for the 'university of advertising' (so-called because of the quality of its ads and the weakness of its profits).

The offer was bitterly resented by Johnston, who told friends he did not think it was possible. But on that June morning WPP's $50.50-a-share offer was sufficiently high to be taken seriously. Johnston may have been contemptuous of the Englishman and his plans, but, as his financial adviser, Morgan Stanley, reminded him, he had a duty to his shareholders to consider the offer. With more than half the shares in the hands of Wall Street speculators anxious to take their profits and run, Johnston had either to accept the bid, or find a higher and more acceptable offer.

Sorrell and his finance director, Robert Lerwill, were ushered in to two seats on one side of the table, almost opposite Johnston, and asked to make a presentation. The message was simple: to explain what WPP was and what its skills were, to talk about JWT's problems, and to say why a merger of the two companies could make good sense to both sides. After that, Sorrell answered a few questions from the JWT executives, and the meeting broke up in a little under an hour. 'I think they wanted to make sure I did not have two horns and a tail,' Sorrell recalls.

For the 42-year-old graduate of Cambridge and Harvard, it was the climax of his two-year stint at the helm of WPP, whose transformation from being Wire & Plastic Products, an unknown maker of wire baskets, into Britain's second biggest marketing services company after Saatchi has been one of the most dramatic business success stories of recent years. Sorrell, who combines professional toughness with a mischievous, almost schoolboyish, sense of humour, recalls the emotions he felt as he stepped off the pavement into the JWT lobby. 'It was a thrill,' he admits. 'Less than three years before we had walked into Wire & Plastic Products, in Dartford, to meet the directors to ask them if we could invest in their company. Now we were standing in a magnificent Lexington Avenue atrium about to meet the board of JWT. It was awesome.'

His former employers, Charles and Maurice Saatchi, had spent seventeen years building their agency into a business of world scale. Founded in 1970, the company obtained its stock market quote through a merger with the larger Garland–Compton group in 1975, and had waited until 1982 before making its first takeover on Madison Avenue, the world's advertising capital. Yet Sorrell swept onto the world stage within a matter of months of buying into WPP, and did it by the high-risk means of a hostile takeover on Wall Street. If he won he would be crowned in glory, but if he lost, his small company would be stripped of the image of success and enterprise that it had fostered in the City over the previous two years.

Six days before his meeting at JWT, Sorrell had breakfasted alone with Don Johnston at the exclusive Sky Club at the top of the Pan American building, which straddles Park Avenue. Decorated in the subdued but expensive style of an investment bank dining room, it was a fitting setting for the confrontation. A haunt of some of America's top industrialists, bankers and lawyers, the private Sky Club is the classic power breakfast forum.

Sorrell had met Johnston just once before, but that had been in 1984 when the American had invited him to New York to discuss the possible purchase by Saatchi of part of JWT's European network, and the two men must have made an odd pair. Johnston, at 60, was one of the patriarchs of American advertising, after more than a decade at the top of JWT. Yet years of advertising management had left him devoid of interest in finance. Sorrell, on the other hand, was cast, particularly in the American media, as the hard numbers man, the former finance director, who would, if he gained control of JWT, slash costs to improve financial performance. One of his London stock market followers, Neil Blackley, of James Capel, the stockbroker, said, 'He is the Karpov of the financial community. He sees at least six moves ahead. What sets him apart is his combination of financial and strategic acumen.'

It was an inconclusive confrontation. When Sorrell had announced his first bid at $45 a share on June 10, Johnston had told him on the telephone he would not meet with him, and made no secret of his reluctance to discuss the subject at the Sky Club breakfast. After some small talk, Sorrell made his pitch, but

Johnston stonewalled. He warned the Englishman of the dangers of proceeding with his bid and showed his anger at WPP's plan to bring Jack Peters, JWT's former president and chief operating officer, back into senior management. Johnston himself had fired Peters just a few months before the bid after he had attempted a coup alongside Johnston's heir apparent, Joe O'Donnell.

Yet it was on Wall Street that the battle would be decided, and when Sorrell made his second offer the JWT chairman had to concede that his days of independence were numbered. An auction, to be conducted by Morgan Stanley, was launched. Besides WPP, the bidders included a team headed by Bob Jacoby and John Hoyne, two former directors of Ted Bates, the agency that had been bought for $450 million the previous summer by Saatchi. As chairman of Bates and its biggest shareholder, Jacoby had been paid $110 million for his shares, and had then collected another $5 million in a breach-of-contract case after he fell out with the Saatchi brothers just five months into the takeover. Their adviser was Lazard Freres. A management buy-out team backed by Merrill Lynch was in the running, while Wall Street gossip suggested that MCA, the West Coast entertainment combine, and a group backed by Rockefeller family interests might also bid.

Bidders were asked to have their offers in by 6 p.m. New York time on Thursday June 27. The previous Sunday, Sorrell and Lerwill had met at WPP's offices, then a tiny basement below a car park, in Lincoln's Inn Fields, to plot their strategy. Thanks to the sophistication of modern telecommunications, an international conference call linking up Bruce Wasserstein (then the takeover king of First Boston), Rupert Faure Walker, of Samuel Montagu, and representatives from WPP's law firms in both London and New York was arranged. Says Sorrell, 'No one was trying to score points. It was a great team of people, each of whom had an input.' The strategy which evolved on that transatlantic telephone line was that WPP was going to bid again at $55.50, a deliberately odd number. 'We chose $55.50 because people tend to fasten on round numbers and there was the chance that one of the other bidders would come in with the same figure. By adding the 50 cents we would be offering just a little bit more,' he explains.

The strategy worked. At 6 p.m. on the 27th, Sorrell and his advisers were assembled in Wasserstein's Park Avenue office when a call came through from Peter Kellner of Morgan Stanley: $55.50 was the right price and it was time to negotiate the details. For the next five hours, Wasserstein and Kellner negotiated by phone, with the appointment of Peters emerging as the one serious sticking point. Johnston was affronted by the suggestion that the man he had fired for attempting a boardroom coup earlier in the year should return in triumph thanks to an unwanted takeover. The impasse was only resolved when Sorrell agreed that Peters would not return unless the JWT management committee voted in favour.

At 11 p.m., Sorrell decamped to the offices of Sullivan and Cromwell, JWT's corporate law firm, and spent the next eight hours drawing up the papers. 'After that,' he recalls, 'I went back to my hotel, shaved and showered and went to meet Johnston at his office at 10 a.m. I said congratulations to him but he did not return them. At the end of our conversation I asked him how we were doing, and he said he didn't know and I had better talk to Terry Martin, the chief financial officer.'

Thus ended one of the boldest takeovers on Wall Street. It may have been dwarfed in size by the megabids for companies like RJR Nabisco, Federated Stores and Revlon, but as an example of giant-killing it is without parallel. The following day, *The Times* wrote, 'When it is completed next month, Mr Sorrell will have pulled off arguably the most spectacular business deal in memory by a British businessman in America. JWT is a corporate prize few but Mr Sorrell believed was there for the taking. . .To win, Mr Sorrell and his Anglo-American banking backers defeated four rival offers from corporate America's most powerful companies. In the lush atmosphere of Madison Avenue, heart of New York's advertising industry, they thought Mr Sorrell was joking when he made his first offer for JWT less than three weeks ago.' Says one banker, 'Martin has all the makings of becoming one of the country's most important industrialists in ten years' time. He has had lots of luck but his timing has been excellent and he is a tough character. He gets what he wants through persistence and determination. Sorrell looks after staff and advisers who do well, displaying a warmth that belies the figures man myth, but he expects total loyalty and commitment in return.'

The scourge of Madison Avenue was born on St Valentine's Day 1945, the son of Jack Sorrell, a prosperous Jewish electrical retailer, and his wife, Sally. An only child, young Martin was the object of a great deal of love and concern. His father was the managing director of the J. & M. Stone and Broadmead, the largest radio and electrical retailer in the country, the Dixons of its day, and Sorrell grew up surrounded by some of the brightest business brains in the country. His father was a methodical executive who worked hard at keeping good control over his sprawling retailing group in an age innocent of computers. Sorrell recalls how each weekend his father would take reports from his regional controllers and record their detailed sales data in his Filofax personal organiser. It was decades before the personal organiser became a fashionable product, yet the young Sorrell received a Filofax as a bar mitzvah present.

Stone was owned by Charles Hayward, the industrialist who developed Freeport Grand Bahama, and Sorrell remembers tramping through Hayward's estate at Haywards Heath, talking about the future with his father's boss. 'He asked me what I wanted to do and I said I wanted to go into business,' Sorrell recalls. 'He told me that I ought to go to Harvard Business School.' Another early influence on the young Sorrell was Sir Jules Thorn, one of Stone's biggest suppliers. 'I got to know Sir Jules quite well. He was never too busy to chat for half an hour.'

As the son of religious parents, his first school was Hasmonean, the Jewish school in Hendon, North London, but at the age of seven he moved to the more cosmopolitan environment of Haberdashers' Aske's School. He won a place at Cambridge to read economics, but was not particularly academically gifted – he left university with a lower second degree. However, he did demonstrate an interest in things both creative and financial. In his leisure time, he wrote for *The New Cambridge*, a paper which had just been launched by Bruce Fireman (who became a founder director of the *Independent* newspaper). Under the pseudonym of Harpagon – a Shylock-like character from Molière's *The Miser* – he wrote a financial column, and also ran an investment club. 'We each put in 6d a week and bought stocks, most of which plunged disastrously.' In 1964 he went to the US to cover the Atlantic City National Democratic Convention, which selected Lyndon Johnson as its presidential candidate, and used his time in the States to visit the admissions tutor at Harvard, saying that he intended to apply in 1966. 'If you express an interest in something people will appreciate it,' he explains.

Between Cambridge and Harvard, Sorrell decided he wanted to do some freelance journalism and applied to Robert Heller of *Management Today* for a summer job. Heller refused to employ him, but said that if he came up with a good article he would happily pay for it. The result was an article which eventually appeared in the December 1966 edition of the magazine. It was a critique of undergraduate recruitment by major British companies – the so-called 'Milk Round' – and an analysis of why Britain's brightest and best ended up in the professions, research or the Civil Service rather than where they were most needed – in industry.

The article took about eight weeks to put together, after which Sorrell took off for Harvard, an establishment that turned out to be far more to his liking than Cambridge. 'Academically the people were not the most brilliant, but they were ambitious and well directed,' he recalls. 'It was a trade school, so you could see that a little bit more of what you learned at the time would be of immediate value.' Sorrell now admits the value was a little illusory. 'You come out of Harvard thinking you can run things because a lot of the teaching is about the role of the company chairman or chief executive. That is why Harvard MBAs tend to go into investment banking or consultancy, because from a young age they get to grips with major strategic problems, instead of joining a company at the bottom of the ladder.'

Sorrell himself chose to get on the bottom of the ladder by joining Glendinning Associates, the marketing consultancy founded by Ralph Glendinning, inventor of the promotional game and the pioneer of modern sales promotion. It was the perfect place to learn marketing. Sorrell did a mixture of brand consultancy and acquisition work, concentrating on marketing rather than financial opportunities. Besides Glendinning, whose business Alma Mater had been Procter & Gamble, inventor of mass consumer marketing, the company employed Joel Smilow, the man who went on to take over Playtex, the lingerie company, and in the process earned himself the title from *Fortune* magazine of one of America's most feared bosses.

'Glendinning was the classic manager turned entrepreneur,' says Sorrell. 'He loved early morning meetings. If you uttered an ill-considered thought you were crucified. You therefore thought very carefully before you opened your mouth. He was a tough boss and working at Glendinning was hard work full of intensive deadlines.'

From Glendinning, Sorrell was head-hunted by Mark McCormack, the man who taught the stars of sport and entertainment how to make real money – and hold on to it. The task was to set up a London operation on behalf of his group, then known as International Management Inc. The two men had met at Harvard, when McCormack had been one of the case studies in a course called 'The Management of New Enterprises'. Remarks Sorrell, 'McCormack is an entrepreneur *par excellence*. He has a very flat organisational structure. He is also highly organised – I remember him showing us at Harvard how he kept all his notes on 4in by 2in cards which he would keep in his top pocket. I still do that today.' His time with McCormack taught him the importance of quick decision-making. 'It is often better to make a bad decision on Monday than a good one on Friday. One should not let things drag on.' McCormack also instilled in Sorrell the importance of detail. 'I remember him telling me that he did not mind ringing up to get a pair of shoes for Arnold Palmer, and that doing that was as much a part of the business as the more glamorous things. His message was that one must do the menial things well as well as the bbzig things.'

Yet McCormack lacked structure. Everything revolved around him, which was hardly the base for building a really big business. Sorrell learned the secret of combining the personal touch with the structure and systems that could form the basis of a big business from his next employer, James Gulliver. The Scottish retailer had just sold his Oriel Foods company to RCA and was looking for a personal assistant to help him invest the proceeds in new ventures. Gulliver wanted to set up his own mini-investment bank to take big stakes in companies and then help them grow. Comments Sorrell, 'Gulliver was a managerial entrepreneur who could deal with the problems of size. His great quality was that he had strategic vision combined with an attention to detail. He proved to me that it is possible to run a large company in a highly personal and effective way without too many layers of management.'

One of the investments made by Gulliver was a shareholding in the Garland–Compton advertising agency. Compton had gone public by selling itself to a tiny public company which had originally been a crematorium operator. (In stock market terminology it had 'reversed' itself into a 'shell'.) Within months of Gulliver's arrival it began talks about a merger with a small but ambitious advertising agency called Saatchi & Saatchi. Sorrell remembers an early lunch meeting with Maurice Saatchi when the young adman shocked Gulliver by taking off his jacket. Gulliver was not at home in the racy world of advertising and after the merger was consumated he sold his shares, thus missing out on one of the investments of the decade. By 1985 the Saatchi shares had risen 2,000 per cent. He was happy with the earnings of the merged company: at the launch price the earnings multiple was a modest four, but the fact that the Saatchi brothers received a cash payment as well as their shares meant the asset value of the business virtually vanished.

Sorrell was much happier in the world of advertising, and in his later years with Gulliver he did a lot of consultancy work for Maurice. One particular problem for the Saatchis was the presence of Compton's former US parent, Compton Advertising, on the Saatchi & Saatchi share register, with a 19 per cent shareholding. As a passive investor Compton might not be a threat, but if it took exception to the brothers' growth plans it could do a lot of damage. It was Sorrell who came up with the plan of forming a new parent company. This would then launch a share-for-share purely paper takeover bid for the agency. He hoped Compton in the US would decline the bid, preferring to keep its stake in the advertising agency which it had once owned completely, rather than own a stake in the Saatchis' new holding company. As luck would have it the American company did just that, leaving Charles and Maurice with a much larger stake in the new public company. Without the reconstruction it would have been far more difficult, if not impossible, for Saatchi & Saatchi to take over the much larger Compton Advertising in 1982.

Sorrell and Maurice Saatchi also shared a common interest in financial management, an alien concept to most advertising men. After the original Garland–Compton merger the paperwork within the business had been in a shambles and together the two men introduced controls and systems all the way up from basic book-keeping to sophisticated budgeting and planning. Says Sorrell, 'I was fanatical about cash. Advertising is the sort of business, like retailing, where if you manage the payables and the receivables then you can grow. Gulliver's great success at Oriel had been based on managing his payables and getting better and better terms out of his suppliers.'

One of Sorrell's recommendations was that the reconstructed Saatchi & Saatchi should have a finance director, so Brian Burwash, one of that select band of top head-hunters, was sent out to find the right man. Initially, the trawl was made in Fleet Street, but no suitable applicant emerged. Maurice told Burwash he wanted a man like Martin Sorrell, to which Burwash replied 'Why don't you ask him?' On 1 October 1977, Sorrell became finance director of Saatchi & Saatchi, a job he held until 17 March 1986.

At Saatchi he continued to improve financial systems and became one of the principal negotiators in the acquisitions drive that transformed the group into the world's leading supplier of marketing services and a major force in management consultancy. Trained in City communications by James Gulliver, he became Saatchi's principal link with London and overseas investors, particularly as Maurice gradually distanced himself from the day-to-day running of the business.

By 1985 Sorrell had started to develop itchy feet. He had played lieutenant to both James Gulliver and the Saatchi brothers and had had a business education that was a modern version of Eton, Oxbridge and the Guards. Now he wanted to build a business for himself. 'I wanted to do my own thing.' There had been provision in Sorrell's original agreement to become Saatchi's finance director for him to spread his wings: a company called Saatchi & Saatchi Developments in which Sorrell had a 20 per cent stake had been set up as a vehicle to take the group into non-media areas of marketing. It was to be Sorrell's way of returning to his Glendinning roots. 'But nothing became of it – I don't know whether it was my fault or Maurice's – so by 1985 I decided that if I was going to do something for myself I would have to move,' says Sorrell. 'Ironically, the day I told Maurice that I was going to move into a small engineering company and take a 15 per cent stake, he said that that was exactly what he and Charles wanted to do. This was the seed of their personal investments in NMC, the packaging company, and Ex-Lands, a leisure business.'

Sorrell says of his spell at Saatchi, 'I treated the business as if it was my own. Like Tim Bell (who also left Saatchi in 1985 to join Frank Lowe in what became Lowe Howard–Spink & Bell) I worked all hours on behalf of the company, coming in very early in the morning and often working until late at night. When Tim and I left, we both left a lot of ourselves in the company.' He retains a great admiration for the Saatchi brothers' achievements. 'Though perhaps not quite as good as Gulliver in managing size, they have tremendous determination, ambition and strategic vision. They taught me that you have to do two things to run a successful public company: design a strategy that will satisfy clients and will appeal to your shareholders. I remember Maurice being asked what business he was in and he replied that he was in the "coup" business. The brothers would focus on an objective and go for it, even if it looked impossible. They had a determination not to be put off – I suppose it is

Mrs Thatcher's greatest characteristic as well.' But admiration for the Saatchis did nothing to dampen his desire for a place in the sun.

His partner for his new venture was Preston Rabl, a stockbroker he had met through Bill Muirhead, a Saatchi executive. Rabl, a partner with Henderson Crosthwaite, combined an interest in the advertising world with a concern about the future of his firm in the City after Big Bang (the deregulation of the London stock market). Together they began their search for a suitable 'shell' company, as a launchpad for their corporate ambitions. The criteria were broad: ideally it should be valued at around £1 million so that the £500,000 they had to invest would give them a third of the enlarged equity; it should be a profitable business run by good, but ageing, management in a low-rated and low-technology industry, like engineering or textiles but with good asset backing. There were some abortive talks. Sorrell recalls the Scottish solicitor who told him on behalf of his tiny confectionery client, 'We do not see what you can do for the company.'

The duo eventually came up with Wire & Plastic Products, a company that made a £312,000 profit in 1984. Based in a factory at Dartford in Kent, it employed 200 people. Sorrell recalls the day he first made his way up a flight of wooden steps to a bare office above the Dartford works to negotiate his plan to use Wire & Plastic Products as his vehicle. 'I had just had a bag of chips on the way and I remember smelling of vinegar. The directors played it fairly cool but they were well aware how tough it was running a small manufacturing business, and they were not getting any younger. I think they were impressed that Preston and I were putting money into the business.'

In attempting to build WPP into a non-advertising marketing services group, Sorrell was returning to his emotional roots at Glendinning Associates. But he also had a strategic plan to build in a sector of marketing that was ripe for consolidation. 'The aim', he explains, 'was to find the fragmented areas of marketing that were large and rapidly growing outside advertising, where the cost of television time, declining television audiences and media fragmentation were all impacting on growth prospects. The non-media areas were characterised by high labour intensity and were not managed well by advertising agencies.' Initially, the plan was to build a dominant position in the UK and use that as a springboard to break into the US, whose marketing services industry was eight to ten times bigger.

The City loved it. In the first ten weeks after the announcement that Sorrell and Rabl were buying a 27 per cent stake at a cost of £516,000, the shares surged from 38p to 136p. Some of the directors and friends decided to take their profits in June by placing shares with institutions, but by the start of November the price had hit 170p and it went on to soar to 270p at the end of the month when it was revealed that Saatchi itself was investing £1.1 million in return for 10 per cent of the company. At the same time, Sorrell announced he was formally joining the board of the company, which would change its name to WPP Group, and revealed his first purchase, a small graphics company called VAP, bought in Saatchi style for a maximum of £2 million in shares, with the actual total related to profits performance over five years.

The share price performance sent the earnings multiple of WPP shares into the stratosphere, giving Sorrell the perfect platform from which to build a company. Because the multiple was so high, it made funding purchases by the issue of paper extremely cheap. Sorrell could outbid competitors in any auction, yet if he paid for the purchases with his highly rated shares he could well afford it. So long as he bought companies on lower price/earnings ratios than the astronomic ratio at WPP, the group's earnings per share would immediately improve, even without organic growth or cost cutting. It was a perfect virtuous circle: each deal enhanced WPP's earnings and lifted its share price, making it easier for Sorrell to move on to the next one.

Sorrell was surprised at the scale of the City's enthusiasm for a wire basket maker, but acknowledges the lift-off it gave him. 'One did feel put under pressure. You felt obliged to justify it,' he says. 'But the advantages outweigh the disadvantages. At the time there were no questions about the growth prospects of Saatchi & Saatchi, and we were seen as "the next Saatchi". It gave us a certain mystique.' At one stage the historic earnings multiple was an astonishing 139. The company had a market value of £100 million yet its earnings were virtually non-existent.

Financial Weekly asked rhetorically, 'Besides £1/2 million, what do you need to make a multinational company? You could start with ambition, vision, experience, a clear strategy and perhaps a reputation as one of the most brilliant financial directors known to the City. Martin Sorrell has all of these.' In March 1987, the *Wall Street Journal* turned its attention to the man who had been laughed at in 1983 when he told New York analysts of Saatchi

& Saatchi's ambition to become the world's largest agency. 'But no one is laughing now,' wrote the Journal. 'The financial community's infatuation with Mr Sorrell is so strong that at times it seems almost blind.' At the time, WPP's shares were trading at above 60 times 1986 earnings and 30 times the earnings expected for 1987, against an average for the market of ten.

After VAP, Sorrell added P & L International Vacationers, a creator of conferences, product launches and staff incentive programmes for major companies. Once again it was a performance-related transaction in the Saatchi mould. But Sorrell soon demonstrated that WPP was prepared to take a higher-risk approach to growth than his former employer, whose acquisitions were always friendly and always of private companies. This enabled the Saatchis to have a good look at the books and tie in the principals by staggering payment over a number of years.

In March 1986, he did what many people regarded as the impossible when he launched a £7.9 million hostile bid for a sales promotion company called Promotions House. At the time, it was conventional wisdom that one could not make an unwelcome offer for a stock market quoted business whose only assets were the people. What if they did not like it? Could not the key players just leave and set up shop around the corner? The move startled the financial press, particularly when the Promotions House managers said they would quit. 'Whatever is happening to Martin Sorrell?' asked the *Evening Standard*. It went on to say, 'In a "people" business, as they say, the assets "walk", and PH managing director Alan Taylor has now told stockbroker analysts of his intention to do just that if the bid succeeds. He also showed them a petition, signed by all his staff, which indicated that Sorrell had made their feet itchy, too.'

The secret was that Sorrell had been invited by a number of dissatisfied major institutional shareholders in Promotions House to make the bid and had a management team waiting to step into Taylor's business the moment he and his colleagues passed through the door; a team that in Sorrell's view was far more capable than the existing managers. The institutional shareholders of PH demonstrated what they thought of Taylor when they leapt to accept Sorrell's share exchange offer less than a month after the launch of the bid. Reassurance came a few days later when WPP announced it was in talks with David Evans, the chief executive of Grass Roots Partnership, one of the country's leading motivation consultancies. Evans stepped in to run Promotions House and three months later a full takeover of Grass Roots was announced. Sorrell had broken new ground: 'people' businesses could be 'put in play', and even taken over against resistance from management, provided the bidder had resources of his own and a reputation that would keep clients loyal.

Between April 1986 and June 1987, WPP announced fifteen acquisitions with a maximum value of £104 million depending on the profitability of the companies acquired. Sorrell expanded further into sales promotion, design and graphics, audio-visual and video equipment hire, and specialist advertising of the kind that would not compete with the television and press ads of Saatchi. In October 1986 he took his first move into the United States when he bought Pace Communications, a company providing ads for the property industry; he added financial communications three months later.

Although Sorrell at first avoided mainstream advertising, in most other ways he modelled himself on what he had learned at Saatchi & Saatchi. Maurice and he would scattergun the private companies in their industry with takeover approaches in the hope that some would respond, and he continued to do this at WPP. 'It may not have been conventional, but the process – it was sort of like sending one's calling card – had a lot to commend it,' he recalls. 'Sometimes one was met by derision initially, yet six months or a year later it would lead to a highly successful takeover.'

By late 1986, however, Sorrell had decided he should use his base in the faster-growing non-media areas of marketing for an assault on mainstream advertising. It was a more mature market but one where success could bring huge advantages for WPP's shareholders, of whom he was the largest. His initial £257,000 investment had swollen by Christmas 1986 to over £4 million. 'It would have been marketing myopia for us to have ignored advertising, just as it would have been for an ad agency not to go below the line,' he says.

The Pace purchase had been the first crab-like move onto the edges of Saatchi territory. At the time, Sorrell portrayed Pace as a specialist communications business. But it was, in essence, an advertising agency that made good profits from dominating a particular niche market – on a good week it places 25–30 per cent of all the property ads in the Sunday edition of the *New York Times*.

Even before Pace, Sorrell began to think seriously about bidding for JWT, a company with whom Saatchi had negotiated on a number of occasions. Saatchi could not make a move because one of JWT's great clients was Unilever, the arch rival to P&G, on whose adverts so much of the brothers' business had been built. Sorrell, with no consumer agency yet under his belt, had no such inhibitions in bidding for the company known as the 'university of advertising'. Sorrell had never been near an ad in his life, but if he could massage those profits up a little, while maintaining the quality, the impact on the tiny WPP could be enormous.

In September, Alan Gottesman, Wall Street's leading advertising industry analyst, introduced Sorrell to Bert Manning, who had just quit his job as vice chairman at JWT after failing to get the job as head of the main agency. Would Manning be interested, Sorrell asked, in returning to JWT? At the time, the idea of buying JWT was little more than a pipe dream, but events started to move in Sorrell's direction, events that would 'transform an outrageous idea into an opportunity'. Manning's departure showed that something was rotten within the JWT empire. Towards the end of 1986 the agency started losing money, then in January came the failed management coup by O'Donnell and Peters. Finally, Burger King signed JWT's death warrant when it announced that its $190 million account, the agency's second largest, was going up for review. From a 1986 peak of $40.50, the JWT share price sank to just $27.00.

'All these things made the bid possible. In August 1986 JWT was a long-term strategic opportunity to be watched,' comments Sorrell. 'What made it possible was the sequence of problems.' In December 1986 and January 1987 he made a couple of secret approaches through investment bankers, suggesting to the JWT board that he had financial expertise which could be used in its business. He tentatively floated the idea of an agreed merger, but both approaches were shunned.

In early 1987 Sorrell realised he would have to fight to get the American agency, and he appointed as his main British adviser Rupert Faure Walker, the corporate financier at Samuel Montagu who had led the abortive bid by his former employer, James Gulliver, for Distillers. Gulliver's Argyll Group had lost, but the 'giant-killer' tactics that Faure Walker had developed for Distillers were deployed in refined form for JWT. Faure Walker had learnt from the Distillers battle that, even if success-related payments were used to cover fees, the costs of a giant-killer bid could still decimate profits, and decimated profits were something Sorrell could not afford. In 1987, WPP made just £1.76 million, and was expected to make £7 million in 1987. Stage one was to build a stake using a joint venture company. WPP's assets were tiny, so it could not buy the shares itself without telling shareholders – and its intended quarry. In great secrecy the duo began building a stake, starting in March and ending two months later with a near 5 per cent holding, bought at an average price of $31.

Then Faure Walker began planning the underwriting for the share issue that would be used to fund half the cost of the bid. In the Distillers bid, only a core group of underwriters accepted success-related underwriting payments, but in the JWT offer some 250 City houses were persuaded to limit their fees to just 0.5 per cent of the money raised – if the bid failed. The result was that the cost of a failed bid would be zero, assuming that WPP would make a reasonable profit on its share stake by selling to the eventual winner in the auction. Meanwhile, the borrowings for the bid, initially $310 million, were arranged by Ernie Cole, a colleague of Faure Walker's at Samuel Montagu, well known in the City for ambitious 'cash flow' financing packages. And 'cash flow' was all that WPP would have if the bid succeeded: after writing off the goodwill associated with the purchase, its debts would exceed its assets by many millions of pounds.

In the first week of June, bid rumours began to spread. The American entertainment group MCA had, like Sorrell, been buying shares and the speculation surrounding JWT reached fever pitch. *Advertising Age,* the bible of the American advertising scene, mentioned WPP as a potential bidder, as did the *Wall Street Journal.* The following Wednesday a letter from Sorrell arrived on Johnston's desk at 7 a.m. asking for a reply by 4 p.m. to WPP's request for negotiations around an offer pitched initially at $45 a share or $460 million. Sixteen days later, a short period by both Wall Street and London takeover standards, the JWT prize was his.

In the weeks after the completion of the bid, much of the City and press comment centred on the high price that WPP had paid for its entry into the world advertising league tables. But Sorrell had been extraordinarily lucky. Two months after the takeover he discovered that JWT had within its property portfolio a building in the heart of Tokyo worth around $200 million. It had been valued by JWT at just $30 million in 1985 and it seemed that the old management had had no idea of its true value. Had they appreciated the building's significance they could easily have funded their own buy-out offer at a far higher price than Sorrell, an outsider, could have justified. It is perhaps the finest example of the lack of financial sophistication within the business before Sorrell mounted his bid.

WPP had less luck with the state of financial markets. By the time Sorrell had completed the takeover in July, world equity markets were starting to look overheated and in August there was a serious loss of confidence as interest rates moved up. Most attributed this weakness to the traditional summer blues, but the storm clouds, which finally broke with unprecedented violence on October 19 – 'Black Monday' – were starting to gather. Some astute international investors like the Kuwait Investment Office and Sir James Goldsmith started selling. WPP's £213 million rights issue to fund the takeover had been priced at 875p a share, against a price in the market of 1075p. But the shares started to fall heavily, particularly as news seeped across the Atlantic of a number of account losses stemming from a combination of anti-British feeling and JWT's underlying problems. The Saatchis, piqued at the success of the bid, did not make life any easier by selling their shares to raise £7.9 million, and by the time the issue closed the shares had fallen below the 875p offer price. Shareholders owning just 34.7 per cent of the stock took up their shares; the rest were left with underwriters.

It was hardly the best way to go into a market setback. On Black Monday Sorrell was sitting with a large chunk of his shares owned by underwriters who had no loyalty whatsoever to the company. In the panic that followed, WPP, with its debts of $266 million, its net asset deficiency of £100 million and its weight of depreciating dollar earnings, was bound to be savaged. Eventually the price bottomed out at around 300p. Ten days after the crash, *Financial Weekly* declared, 'If nothing else, last week's worldwide stock market dive will curb the acquisitiveness of some newly predatory British companies.'

In the event, the crash did nothing to curb Sorrell's ambitions for growth. Three weeks after Black Monday he extended his video interests by a small purchase. His debt package was renegotiated at lower rates through S. G. Warburg, and by the end of November he was back looking for bigger deals. Talks with the Henley Centre for Forecasting, one of Britain's best-known marketing consultancies, were started in November and eventually led to a deal the following March. In the meantime, he also snapped up Mendoza Dillon & Asociados, America's largest Hispanic ad agency (showing that he was still interested in pursuing interesting niches in the market as well as running a global grouping), Stewart McColl, the British design house, and Anspach Grossman Portugal, a leading US corporate identity consultancy. Comments Sorrell, 'One could have done JWT after October 19 because bids are about relative values, rather than absolute ones. Our share price would have been lower but so too would have been JWT's.' By the end of 1988 he had bought another eleven companies, committing a maximum of £135 million of WPP resources in the process.

There were problems along the way. Sorrell knew that taking over JWT had been a high-risk strategy. In a hostile bid, there is no opportunity to get inside a company, take a look at its books, and assess the state of morale. The predator has to make do with published information, and the gossip of former employees and competitors. Staff can be tied in with contracts and share options, but there is little to stop them defecting to other agencies if they really want to go.

On March 18, one of JWT's skeletons fell noisily out of the cupboard, capturing the headlines of America's business publications: six top executives, including the chairman, Richard Lord, announced they were walking out of JWT's highly regarded Lord, Geller, Federico, Einstein subsidiary to set up on their own. Lord had been fighting to break out of JWT long before the WPP bid and after the initial walk-out others followed to his new agency, backed by Young & Rubicam. The *Independent* commented, 'For Mr Sorrell the departure of the pride of LGFE, together with a host of key employees, ranging from secretaries to paste-up artists, was a bitter blow and a reminder, if he needed one, that in the advertising business your assets disappear down the lifts every evening and there is no guarantee that they will be back in the morning.' Inevitably, WPP's share price, already crucified in the crash, came under new pressure.

Sorrell, displaying a resilience that surprised both adversaries and observers, fought back. Though Lord and his team had gone down the lift, Sorrell was determined not to let them take clients with them. He found documentary evidence suggesting they had conspired to take clients and employees and thus force WPP to let them lead a management buy-out. Others might simply have let the defectors go, but Sorrell, back up against the wall, decided the matter should be judged in court. Within a few weeks he had won injunctions preventing his former staff approaching Lord Geller clients or hiring its staff. 'I could not let them get away with it,' says Sorrell. 'The way they decided to leave the company, causing chaos to clients and employees, was unacceptable.' Says one adviser, 'During the Lord Geller crisis he managed to keep a level head and still had the ability to see the funny side of it. Even with his back up against the wall he was never depressed. He is a real fighter, who can be cold as steel and almost brutal at times. Lots of businessmen flip in a crisis, but Martin certainly does not.'

Eventually Lord Geller's most prestigious client, IBM, put its account, worth $120 million or half the total billings, up for review, and decided to take the business away in September. Heavy staff cuts followed and morale sunk. By the end of the year the agency, strengthened by the arrival of new staff from Ogilvy & Mather, had started to win some new business, but Sorrell was clear that the road back to full recovery would be long and tough.

Apart from Lord Geller, the integration of JWT went better than Sorrell could have hoped, with margins moving up and debt – thanks to the Tokyo building sale – coming down much faster than had been expected. Burt Manning returned as chairman of the J. Walter Thompson agency, and began knocking it into shape, and, by the autumn, performance overall was starting to look up. When Sorrell announced his interim profits in September showing a rise from £3.3 million to £16.2 million, he was able to say that JWT's pre-interest profits had climbed from $13 million to $30 million, thanks to some new business gains (alongside the losses) and improved efficiency. Hill & Knowlton, the public relations subsidiary, was back in profit and Sorrell forecast that his target of 10 per cent margins, which he had originally said could take four years, might in fact be achieved by 1989. Six months later he was able to tell the City that 10 per cent margins had been achieved at the end of 1988, helping to contribute to a year-end profit of £40 million. Analysts quickly pencilled in £46–50 million as the target for 1989.

Sorrell is under no illusions that his self-appointed task of transforming JWT's financial culture while retaining its quality advertising is anything but a long-term project. 'JWT is a 125-year-old company and Hill & Knowlton is a 62-year-old company. This brings both advantages and disadvantages,' he says. His starting point is to work on the attitudes of JWT's clients and the attitudes of its staff. Reviving the morale of both clients and staff will produce revenue growth, and it is the task of WPP's financial management to turn that growth into enhanced profits and earnings per share. Already Burt Manning at J. Walter Thompson, Bob Dilenschneider at Hill & Knowlton, JWT's public relations subsidiary, and Frank Stanton at MRB, the market research division, are starting that process of revival. But Sorrell admits, 'We will not be able to see how successful we have been until three or four years have passed. After all we have taken over a $700 million revenue company and it takes time to change its financial approach.'

On 14 May 1988, WPP produced its 1987 annual report, a glossy solid-spined 120-page affair. It included a detailed analysis of the services sector and its prospects and argued 'the case for investment in the marketing services industry'. All the various subsidiaries, acquired in three hectic years of takeover activity, were outlined alongside photographs of all the key staff except one. Sorrell permitted no picture of himself in the annual report, and any references to him in it do not even disclose his first name. In vain did the reader search for the simple fact that Sorrell was WPP's chief executive. But the key facts were plain for all to see: 'M. S. Sorrell' was the biggest shareholder by a long way with over 930,000 shares and had a salary of £241,000, up eightfold on the previous year. The self-effacing figures man from North London had come an awful long way in a very short time.

Just how far he had come was clear less than two years after the JWT bid when WPP pulled off its second giant-killer takeover on Wall Street. This time the victim was the Ogilvy Group, a business founded by the legendary doyen of American advertising, the Scots-born David Ogilvy. Ogilvy was the man whom ambitious advertising executives on both sides of the Atlantic looked up to. He was the most influential figure on the advertising scene in the post-war television era, with as great a reputation as J. Walter Thompson had had a century ago. His *Confessions of an Advertising Man* became required reading for ambitious young advertising executives. But by early 1989 Ogilvy and its main subsidiary, Ogilvy & Mather, had lost some of its edge. Its profit margins were slipping, its financial management was unsophisticated, and its senior executives were in disarray, with rumours of boardroom rows rife both on Madison Avenue and on Wall Street.

For Sorrell, it was a temptation too great to miss. Though not in such a bad state as JWT, it could benefit from his management style, and it would also go a long way to fleshing out his worldwide advertising business. Where Ogilvy was strong, JWT was weak and vice versa. What is more, the two companies were both on the same side of two of the great divides of modern consumer advertising: they both worked for Unilever and Ford. Most importantly, Ogilvy was a great agency 'brand' with institutional strength. Indeed WPP's code name for its target was Sirius, the brightest star in the sky.

Sorrell began his pursuit of Ogilvy in the spring of 1988, wooing its chairman Ken Roman with suggestions of joint ventures in media buying. At the time WPP was not ready to make a bid, but Sorrell started to make preparations for the moment when he would have the financial fire-power. His JWT team was reassembled in the shape of Rupert Faure Walker at Samuel Montagu, Bruce Wasserstein, the First Boston man who had set up his own corporate finance boutique, Wasserstein Perella, and Ernie Cole, the Midland banker who specialises in debt finance for takeovers.

In the autumn WPP started to accumulate a share stake, although it stopped short of the disclosure levels required by the American authorities, and Sorrell returned to the negotiating table with Roman, this time proposing a full merger. The American was very hostile. He had no wish to be taken over by WPP and instead went on the offensive, taking the fight from Wall Street to London where he launched a noisy campaign against Sorrell's company. His calculation was that if he made enough angry noises he would scotch WPP's attempts to raise takeover finance. In the spring of 1989, the City was not in the mood to fund hostile takeovers of 'people' businesses on Wall Street. The Blue Arrow scandal had broken and its chairman Tony Berry, who had taken over Manpower of the US in the summer of 1987, had been evicted from his job, and the Saatchis had just announced that their profits were falling. For a while it looked as though Roman's campaign was working. The WPP share price fell by the day, while speculators pushed the Ogilvy share price to higher levels.

But once again the Madison Avenue men fatally underestimated Sorrell's determination, his tactical skills, and the willingness of the City of London to put its funds at his disposal. While investment analysts might complain, Sorrell's key bankers and his main institutional shareholders were willing to put up funds, provided the terms were attractive. When he did put a $45-a-share proposal in writing, Roman responded by publishing the letter and wheeling in David Ogilvy, then in semi-retirement in a French chateau, to attack the young Briton. Ogilvy certainly did his job well. When the *Financial Times* reported his remarks, it censored them, but what was printed was still remarkable in its rudeness. 'God,' he told the FT, 'the idea of being taken over by that odious little jerk really gives me the creeps. He's never written an advertisement in his life.'

The second part was true. Sorrell claimed no creative skills. But Ogilvy and Roman, though they may have written ads, seemingly knew nothing about how to fight a Wall Street takeover battle, even though they happily gained the benefits from having outside shareholders and being listed on the New York Stock Exchange. When they made Sorrell's offer public they played straight into his hands. They effectively put themselves 'in play', in Wall Street parlance, and within a couple of days more than half Ogilvy's shares had been sold by institutional shareholders to short-term arbitrageurs looking to accept any sensible takeover offer.

From that moment it was inevitable that Ogilvy would be taken over. The question was, by whom. Once again Sorrell took the initiative. He raised his bid to $50 a share, a level which would be beyond the reach of counter-proposals from debt-financed takeover companies like Kohlberg Kravis Roberts, the so-called leveraged buy-out merchants. It was a turning point: Ogilvy realised that WPP would be virtually unbeatable and it was time to negotiate. The mud-slinging, which involved encouraging clients and competitors to speak out against the takeover, stopped, and Roman and his board got down to serious talks. Ogilvy flew in from France to meet the 'odious little jerk', to be greeted with a renewal of the offer Sorrell had made in his original letter: that Ogilvy himself become chairman of the enlarged group.

On May 16, terms were announced for an agreed takeover at $54 a share, valuing the Ogilvy group at $864 million. WPP had pulled off an extraordinary coup. At no point had it formally made a hostile takeover, which could have dragged it into the American courts and led to many months of litigation over Ogilvy's 'poison pill'. This was a legal device that Ogilvy shared with many American companies making hostile takeover extremely difficult. Yet, Sorrell had, against the wishes of its management (at least initially), carried off one of the great companies of Madison Avenue. The takeover price meant that inevitably WPP would suffer some temporary reduction in the earnings per share that is might have made had it not gone ahead with the bid. But

Sorrell had once again captured one of the commanding heights of Madison Avenue for Britain.

Ogilvy was, in the words of Bruce Wasserstein, a 'trophy' company, of which there were perhaps only three or four in the advertising world. With JWT and Ogilvy under his belt, Sorrell now owned two of them. Equally important, it brought the combined billings of his group up to $13.5 billion worldwide, leaving WPP within an inch of overhauling Saatchi as the world's leading advertising group. Sorrell's response was to say that he was more interested in being the best than the biggest, but his victory must still have hurt his old employers. The City meanwhile quickly calculated that WPP's profits would rise to £70–75 million 1989 and rise again to £110–115 million the following year. Once the takeover was completed, the long work of integration would have to begin. There were bound to be some client losses, but, if Sorrell could manage the transition effectively, as he had done at JWT, then WPP might end up perfectly positioned for the global advertising battles of the 1990s

Sorrell's progress had been aided by a following wind. 'It is very important to be in an industry that is young,' he says. 'It is much harder to make US Steel work in a static market than in an industry growing at 10–15 per cent a year. It is not that difficult to tweak an extra bit of performance and achieve compound earnings growth of 20 per cent when your basic market is showing 10–15 per cent growth. To achieve rapid growth it is also important to be in an industry where there are no barriers to your entry. Marketing is really very similar to show business or the record industry. You are only as good as your last advertisement. To get on it's not simply a case of waiting to fill dead men's shoes.'

Sorrell is a great admirer of the Thatcher regime and the economic revolution of the last decade. Without the Thatcher achievements of low inflation and economic growth, City funding for his expansion plans would have been difficult, if not impossible, to obtain.

He does not claim any particular secret, although fear of failure is a strong driving force. 'It is a matter of hard work rather than any tremendous brilliance. You have to be able to work as long as is necessary and show commitment,' he says. The man who pulled off Wall Street's riskiest takeover raid is paradoxically a master of understatement, an unusual attribute in the advertising industry. While the gossip columns are full of the exploits of his competitors, Sorrell studiously keeps his personal life as private as possible. Beyond work and looking after his family, he lists only skiing and cricket as activities. He appears totally committed to the physical and emotional well-being of his wife and children and broke off from his takeover battle for JWT on two occasions: one to play in the fathers' cricket match at the school of his middle son, Robert, and the other to see his elder son Mark at his parent–teacher meeting. Says one adviser, 'Martin tries to get back each weekend to see his family wherever he is.'

Money is a motivator and financial success has brought its rewards. He has lived since 1972 in substantial house, shared with his wife, Sandy, in one of London's smartest residential roads close to Kenwood and Hampstead Heath, although how much time he has to enjoy the trappings of wealth is another question. Each weekday morning he sets off at between 7.10 and 7.15 in a chauffeur-driven Ford Scorpio for his office in Farm Street, behind JWT's London offices in Berkeley Square. At that time of the day the journey takes little more than 20 minutes and Sorrell is at his desk well before 9, or deep in conversation with one of his staff or advisers over breakfast at the Savoy or the Connaught. Twelve hours later he can still be found at Farm Street working on an aquisition or surveying the financial performance of his company. He is not afraid to sell his own products. One City man recalls how Sorrell had lunch with a businessman. 'By the time tea was served a brochure had landed on his guest's desk offering WPP's services to create a new corporate logo. He has a hands-on approach which he learnt from Gulliver: never miss the chance to make a couple of quid.'

Sorrell argues that the accumulation of wealth is if anything secondary to the main goal of creating a big business. 'Money is a measure of how successful you are, like your share price,' he says. 'Both are barometers rather than ends in themselves. After all, one can only wear one suit at a time and live in one house. What I care about is building something. There is nothing more satisfying than thinking about WPP in April 1985 and looking at it now – one wants to build something that people admire and respect. I suppose it's nice to do the impossible.'

He aims to push forward WPP's growth using its market capitalisation and leverage to acquire businesses with their own institutional culture and attempt to improve them. WPP itself will remain a purely a financial brand rather than being used to promote any service or product. Investors and bankers will be its only 'customers', while its only competitors will be other marketing services holding companies. The 1987 annual report said very little in words about WPP itself, although it was all there in the figures. Instead, the stress was on the institutional strengths of the businesses that the company had bought, even down to the reprinting of quotes from *The Thompson Red Book on Advertising*, written by the great J. Walter himself in 1899. The cover had no arty corporate logo, and just three items appeared on the back: the page number for the shares on the Stock Exchange's Topic information screen, and the symbols used for the share in the Reuters and Nasdaq electronic information systems.

WPP, Sorrell hopes, will convey a number of things: strategic and financial ambitions, the ability to carry out successful mergers and acquisitions, and exploit the benefits of cross-referral within different parts of the group, and the maintenance of good relationships with professional and private shareholders. 'When people hear the letters WPP I want them to reach for their Quotron machines and buy the stock,' he says. 'But it will only be a successful financial brand if financial success is achieved through professional excellence. The failure of JWT to achieve both was why we could take it over.'

Name: *Michael Green*
Title: *Chairman of Carlton Communications*
Born: *1947, London*
Education: *Haberdashers' Aske's School*
Qualifications: *4 'O' levels*
First Job: *Compositor with David, Osler and Frank*
Family: *Married Janet Wolfson in 1972; they have two daughters*
Joined Carlton: *In 1968 when, aged 20, he bought the loss-making Direct Mail Centre*
Made First Million: *Through the growth of Tangent Industries as a private company*
Most Exciting Moment: *The day he was told by Midland Bank that he was no longer required to guarantee personally his company's overdraft*
Awards/Honours: *Chairman of the Open College, director of Hambros Advanced Technology Trust, founder of the Tangent Charitable Trust, 1988 Guardian Young Businessman of the Year*
Hobbies: *Bridge, poker, snooker, skiing and watching television*
Drives: *Rolls-Royce Corniche convertible, Bentley Turbo, Range Rover, Mini*
Personal Stake: *£50 million*
Latest Salary: *£197,000*
Latest Company Statistics: *1987–8 sales: £217 million; profits: £49 million*

Chapter VII

Michael Green
CARLTON COMMUNICATIONS

*'At quite a young age I knew exactly
what I wanted to do: to build a
business that would exploit the most
significant development of our
age – communications.'*

It was a hot Manhattan morning in June 1988. Michael Green, the 40-year-old chairman of Carlton Communications, Britain's leading television and video company, entered the magnificent General Motors building near Central Park. His destination was the 59th floor, the sumptuous headquarters of the mighty Revlon cosmetics company. Since November 1985, the offices, decorated with ornate grandeur by Revlon's founder, Charles Revson, had had a new occupant. It was Ronald Perelman, a short, cigar-toting financier who had conquered a citadel of modern American capitalism in one of Wall Street's most bitterly fought takeover battles, and now Revson's corporate palace had become his.

Green had come to negotiate the purchase of Technicolor, the world's leading film processing and video duplication company. Perelman, the classic takeover artiste of the 1980s' Wall Street bid boom, had bought the business for $125 million in 1981, but seven years later he was ready to sell – at a price. Green, an equally classic manifestation of the so-called 'Thatcher bull market' in Britain, wanted to buy.

To participants in the negotiations they must have made a remarkable pair. Both are arch negotiators, both are financially astute, both are chain smokers. They share the same faith,

Judaism. But as characters they could not be further apart. Perelman is a humourless, impatient businessman from Philadelphia who appears to revel in his reputation for rudeness. Shunned as a child, he is now one of Manhattan's most notorious social climbers. Green, by contrast, is a well-connected Londoner, born of wealthy parents, who combines frenetic workaholism and nervous energy with irrepressible enthusiasm, charm and humour.

The June meeting was simply an information exchange. But after a day's talking, Green returned to his suite in the Carlisle Hotel on Madison Avenue convinced he could accomplish the most important transaction of his business career. Three months later, after tortuous negotiations, he bought the company for $780 million. Suddenly, a parvenu company, which had only been quoted on the stock market since 1983, was the proud owner of a world-class brand name that was synonymous with the silver screen.

Technicolor was yet one more international American brand name like Smith & Wesson, Brookes Brothers, Hilton International and J. Walter Thompson that had been captured by British businessmen in the 1980s. It was to be a cash flow dynamo at the heart of Green's wide-ranging blend of television and video services and manufacturing businesses. Its institutional strength, built up over many years, would be a fitting balance to the younger entrepreneurial aggression of the existing Carlton group.

By the summer of 1989, Carlton's market value was getting close to £2 billion and Green had added the £500m UEI video equipment and engineering business to his list of corporate scalps. The group had taken its place in the *Financial Times* Stock Exchange 100 index of Britain's leading companies; and, valued at far more than the entire quoted independent television broadcasting sector, Carlton was perfectly placed to take advantage of the deregulation of television broadcasting and the explosive growth of video, cable and satellite TV.

Green himself has emerged in the last decade as one of Britain's most talented and influential young businessmen. When he brought his company to the stock market in 1983 it was making profits of £1.5 million and was valued at £10 million. Six years later its near £2 billion valuation was based on the expectation that profits in 1989 would show a rise from £49 million to £115 million and that the 1990 total would reach £180 million. But Green is more than just a business builder: he has changed the attitude of the City to entertainment by introducing financial disciplines into a sector notorious for poor profits. What Saatchi did for advertising, Green has done for video and television, an achievement recognised by the Thatcher government. When civil servants began working on the idea of an Open College as a junior radio transmitted version of the Open University, they asked Green to be the first chairman. And when Lord Young as trade and industry secretary looked to industry for ideas on the liberalisation of television broadcasting it was to Green he turned.

Before the emergence of Carlton, the television sector had been one of the most lowly rated sectors of the stock market, despite the glamour of the world of entertainment. Though not as poorly perceived as tobacco companies or banks, the network stations were not seen as good homes for City cash. Their short franchise periods gave them the characteristics of a short leasehold tenancy. They were forced to pay out high dividends to maintain interest, with marketability in the shares often restricted by the existence of major commercial shareholders and often a complex structure of voting and non-voting shares. In City terms they only hit the headlines when they ran into trouble, like Lord Grade's Associated Communications Corporation.

They were also badly run. They may have been in Lord Thomson's words 'a licence to print money', but much of the money did not come to the shareholders. Their monopoly control of local television advertising gave power not to their owners but to trade unions, which used a panoply of restrictive practices to milk their employers of virtually all their profits. In 1985, despite its advertising monopoly, Thames TV actually managed to lose money on its mainstream business, and only recorded a profit through overseas sales of programmes.

Green may mix well with the creative 'media folk' of film and television but mentally he is a world away from the industry's tinsel glamour, and his company has revolutionised the sector by introducing effective financial controls and incentives. 'Television and video is exciting and sexy and historically volatile,' says Green. 'What we have done is to say to City: here is a company that is bringing accounting procedures to the industry. Here is a company that cares about cash flow and return on capital employed. We talk to City investors in their own language – the top page of our management accounts is the source and application of funds statement, the cash flow in other words; the profit and loss account only comes later. Few people in the world of television are able to do that.' One banker says, 'Michael is first class. He is very thorough in the way he analyses businesses. He spends a lot of time looking at things and listens to other people's advice and is really rather conservative. But he is not afraid of his own shadow and is prepared to take sensible risks.'

Green, whose boyish looks belie a brilliant business mind, learnt financial disciplines at an early age. Born two years after his brother David (who today, besides being a Carlton director, runs the interior design business Colefax and Fowler), he was the child of wealthy middle-class Jews. His father, Cyril, floated a company called Tern Consulate on the stock market before retiring in his mid-fifties to live in Spain. His mother Irene is a child psychologist. Between the two of them they were determined to educate their son about the proper value of money rather than let him become a spendthrift like so many children of wealthy parents. Green recalls, 'My parents gave me a bank account at an early age. Each year they would give me a set amount of money – it was not very much – and I was told that was all I was getting. I could spend it in a week but it had to last me a year. From that I learned about budgeting and I always did manage to keep some money in the bank and I never asked for more.' One close friend says, 'Michael could read a balance sheet when he was 12.'

At the age of 13, after passing his common entrance exams, he was sent to Haberdashers' Aske's, the London public school. His parents were confident their son was destined for academic achievement and a place at university. But it did not quite turn out that way. After just one year of 'A' levels the young Green decided to drop out and go into business. 'At quite a young age I knew exactly what I wanted to do: to build a business that would exploit the most significant development of our age – communications,' Green recalls. 'Many of my contemporaries were much brighter than I was but they did not know what they wanted to do.' One businessman who has known him for many years says, 'Green is singularly ambitious and determined and has been since the age of 16.'

At 17 he joined a printing company called David, Osler and Frank in Euston and started work as a compositor. In a year he had mastered all the stages of the printing process and, because the company was a small one, he had got practical experience all the way from selling through to production. 'I liked printing because it was creative,' he says. 'You started with a blank sheet of paper and at the end of a process you had a finished product.' David, Osler and Frank had been doing a certain amount of direct mail like leaflets and letters, and Green decided that his first venture out into the world of business on his own would be in direct mail.

In 1968, at just 20, he found his quarry in the shape of a loss-making business called The Direct Mail Centre, in Tooley Street on the south bank of the Thames opposite the Billingsgate fish market. The company, which had been founded in 1906, was owned at the time by one Thomas Bartholemew, an elderly man who wanted to sell. It was the first of many highly successful acquisitions, although at the time it was a struggle. Green was given no seedcorn capital by his parents and had to trudge around the banks desperately trying to raise a loan for his venture.

But even at 20 Green was an astute negotiator, a characteristic the banks no doubt recognised. Advised by Stuart Lipton, who later emerged as one of the richest and most creative property men in Britain, he secured the company at well below the market value of its building in Tooley Street and within a few weeks had sold the property on at a big profit. Suddenly he found himself sitting on what must have seemed a huge fortune for a teenager and he was showered with advice from his family and financial advisers to liquidate the business and pocket his profits.

But liquidation was the last thing on Green's mind. He wanted to turn The Direct Mail Centre into a viable business. Rather than complete a cynical asset strip, he moved the company into new premises in Crimscott Street, to the south of Bermondsey, investing in more modern and sophisticated equipment. 'I had what I wanted,' he recalls. 'At 20 I was the youngest person in the company and yet I had 150 staff working for me. I had found my vehicle and it had a cash flow, a history and a management structure – that was important.'

He still had a tidy sum left over from the Tooley Street disposal, but a large amount was lost when the postal workers came out shortly afterwards on a three-month strike, bringing the direct mail industry to a halt. Green stuck with it, restoring the company to profits. Renamed Tangent Industries, it remains his private holding company, owning not just some of his Carlton shares, but also some choice London properties.

Green's experiences at The Direct Mail Centre taught him how to earn the respect of staff. 'I never went into the pub and pretended to be one of the lads. But I did understand the process. I knew how to work the machines.' He also learnt how to deal with organised labour. The company, with just 150 staff, had no fewer than three unions, the NGA, SOGAT and the old NATSOPA. It was a veritable baptism of fire in the murky world of printing industry industrial relations. Green was willing to acknowledge the benefits of organised labour – rather than negotiate with an amorphous mass of people, he need only talk to the mother or father of the chapel. But he also saw how destructive unions could be, and in his later business life he was to exploit to his own benefit the weakness imposed on competitors by over-powerful trade unions. Indeed, much of the later growth of Carlton was the product of appalling trade union practices within the established television companies, practices that prevented the introduction of efficient new technology and flexible working patterns for many years. They left a vacuum into which he was only too happy to leap.

In 1970, Green made his first diversification move into photographic studios by purchasing a company called Carlton. At the time he was dating Janet Wolfson, the eldest daughter of Lord Wolfson, and what began as a social relationship with the Wolfson family soon turned into a commercial one. Much of his early work came from producing the mail order catalogues of Wolfson's retailing combine, Great Universal Stores. For the young Green there can have been no better tutor than Wolfson. 'Just by listening to the Wolfson family conservations one learned a lot more about companies and the problems they face,' he recalls. 'Leonard Wolfson is a very able and brilliant man. I did not talk much about my company but I learned the virtues of sound financing and cash flow. The balance sheet of GUS must be the strongest of Britain's top 100 companies and is indicative of the way Lord Wolfson thinks.' A friend comments, 'Michael has never missed an opportunity to learn from people who have made it.'

The shift from photography to video was a natural move. In the late seventies Sears Roebuck had experimented with putting mail order catalogues on video disc, and it looked as if a whole new market was starting to open up on the back of technological change. Green's own photographers were keen on the new medium and so he bought Transvideo, a small video business that became the core of Carlton Television, the group's facilities division. As the company grew, so did Green's confidence in his abilities and his chances of making an impression on his elders. Friends describe how, even as a relatively young and minor businessman, he would walk straight up to the most important person in any social gathering and introduce himself: 'Hello, I'm Michael Green.'

By late 1982 Green was confident he had assembled a video and photographic business that could float on the stock market. The printing and property interests were stripped out to be retained as private businesses, and Green set about looking for a shell company in which to inject what was to be called Carlton Communications. 'I decided on a reverse takeover [a City term for a transaction where a company is bought but where its management ends up in control] rather than taking the company public in its own right as it was a good deal less expensive,' he says. Another influence was the fact that Saatchi & Saatchi, whose joint founder, Charles Saatchi, has been both close friend and business mentor, had itself reversed into another public company on its stock market debut in 1975. His financial adviser was Stuart Young, then senior partner at the accountancy firm, Hacker Young, and later Chairman of the BBC before his death in 1986. Their first target was a small Welsh printing company called David S. Smith, which specialised in printing cigarette cartons. N.M. Rothschild was appointed to advise Smith, but the negotiations broke down over price. Young advised Green to pull out.

The second attempt was more promising. In late 1982 Green found a small publishing company called FSL Publications. It specialised in publishing investment newsletters like the *Fleet Street Letter* (hence FSL), the *Penny Share Guide* and the *New Issue Share Guide*. It was a business that was growing on the back of the Thatcher bull market and the expansion of wider share ownership. At the time of Green's approach it was sitting on £1 million of cash. Besides its balance sheet, its assets included Nigel Wray, its chairman, then 34 years old. Wray, himself an ex-printer turned fund manager, had bought the business for £6,000 in the mid-1970s and had steadily built it up, proving himself a canny spotter of talent and enterprise. 'Nigel liked Carlton and understood us,' Green recalls, 'and I liked him. We were both about the same age and had similar ambitions, although his publishing business was not of great interest to us and we sold it when we could.'

Carlton, once merged with FSL, immediately became a glamour stock, trading on more than 30 times annual earnings. Green and his older brother, David, who was a co-director, took their FSL shares at 115p, in a deal that gave them 50.1 per cent of the enlarged group, which they promptly renamed Carlton Communications. When the shares began trading again after shareholders had voted on the proposals, they soared to around 200p and from then on never looked back.

It was easy to see why the City found Carlton such an appealing business. The video industry was showing great growth rates, yet no industrialist had attempted to rationalise the sector to gain from the benefits of size. Video services was a cottage industry peopled by former film directors, producers and technicians. Many had technical expertise but few had any genuine business talent of the type that could transform a small company into a major enterprise. Video tape had been around for a long time, but it was only in the late 1970s that a time code was put onto the tape, a move that transformed the production of television and video items. Instead of messing around with bits of film in a cutting room, a video editor could edit with great ease on an electronic video edit suite. Similarly the ability to create special effects was transformed. On film the creation of special effects is a time-consuming, labour-intensive and expensive process. But a generation of computerised video products designed by companies like Quantel (which was to become a part of Carlton after its takeover of the UEI group) and Ampex of the United States, had deskilled the art of producing special effects, reduced their cost and widened their use.

Yet the established users of video – the network television companies and the BBC – did not make effective use of the new technology. Just as the Fleet Street print unions held up the introduction of modern equipment in newspapers, so did the unions in the television industry. Like other attempts at Luddism, the unions' resistance to change merely helped small companies such as Carlton, which were less exposed to union muscle, to get off the ground. It also ultimately reduced the number of jobs available within traditional network television. Says Green, 'We started to do a lot of work for the TV stations, who appeared happy to give us business because they did not have the equipment. Even today we tend to spend far more on hardware than the television companies.'

Carlton's work starts at the moment creative TV ideas move from the drawing board and does not end until the image created arrives in people's homes. It is the kind of work that has helped to build the reputation for creativity and imagination that British television has gained around the world.

Each day teams of producers and technicians are at work transforming the raw ideas of London's adland into effective and sometimes award-winning TV commercials. One such was a Hamlet cigar commercial conceived by Collett Dickenson Pearce immediately after the stock market crash in October 1987. The Hamlet ads usually show someone enjoying a Hamlet cigar while all goes wrong around him, and the CDP copywriters conceived the idea of showing the viewers a City share dealer's computer screen, with a line on it indicating the *Financial Times* 30 share index plunging wildly downwards. The line then bottoms out and the viewer can see that it is burning like a cigar. Finally it gives off a puff of smoke and the ad ends with the catchphrase that features in all the campaign ads: 'Hamlet. The mild cigar.'

Work on the ad began one afternoon at 4 o'clock when CDP told Carlton's Moving Picture Company subsidiary that it had just 20 hours to make the commercial. The director of the ad, Bernard Lodge, assembled a team of computer programmers, video editors and producers and began to create the ad on a Paintbox computer graphics machine. Working through the night the team built up the various critical details of the ad, like the burning tip of the index line and the smoke, before adding the sound track the following afternoon.

At each stage the high-technology equipment made by Carlton's Californian subsidiary, Abekas, was used to preserve perfect picture quality regardless of the number of layers of video combined during the editing and addition of special effects. Finally, in the evening, the ad was delivered to the television network (which includes Central Television, the company where Carlton has a 20 per cent holding) ready for transmission during ITN's News at Ten – bang after an item about the plunging stock market. The work won a 'gold arrow' at the 1988 British Television Advertising Awards, the Oscars of the ad industry, and a silver at the competing Designers and Arts Directors awards.

'At Carlton we have concentrated on staying in a field that our managers understand and coming at it from as many angles as we can from prop hire through to television production,' says Green. By the middle of 1989 his company was eight times larger by stock market value than Thames Television, the biggest broadcaster, and it made four times more profits.

The process by which Green has built up his business has been similar in style to Saatchi & Saatchi. From Charles and Maurice he quickly learnt the importance of selective public relations among key City opinion formers, and the necessity of expert merchant banking and stockbroking advice. While the Saatchis used County NatWest as their bank and Phillips & Drew as their broker, Green used Hambros and L. Messel (which became part of Shearson Lehman after Big Bang). In PR, the two companies both used Brian Basham of Broad Street, one of the City's top consultants. Like the Saatchis, Green tended to buy private companies, usually on a deferred payments basis linked closely to profits performance. In this way he tied in and motivated the key professionals within his group and taught them the financial disciplines that made Carlton such a successful company. He was often tempted by the idea of making a quantum leap but, at least before the Technicolor deal, his acquisitions tended to be relatively small deals. In this way he was able to limit the number of shares issued while doing for the television services industry what the Saatchis were able to do in advertising.

While Carlton enjoyed breakneck growth after its flotation, it remained without debts and with large amounts of cash in the bank. It was only the prospect of gaining control of Technicolor that persuaded Green he could afford to have debt in his balance sheet, and his stock market followers predicted that the £117 million of borrowings taken on as part of the takeover would be repaid by 1990 out of cash flow. Says Green, 'I'm incredibly conservative. Many of my contemporaries believe that if you are on a good rating you should do deals if they lead to an improvement in earnings per share over the next 12 months. But I am not a member of the "less of more" school. In my mind the only real way to build a business is to stick with the business that you and your managers know.'

Green is a believer in motivation and incentive. 'It is important to have a stake in your business and that it be a meaningful stake,' he says. 'I remember the first deal I did when it took our holding below 50 per cent. It caused me a lot of anguish at the time – it took a leap of imagination to understand that I finally did not have voting control of the company. I suppose that makes me more of an owner-occupier than a professional manager.' In 1988, he paid himself a salary of £197,000, a relatively modest sum for his position at the helm of a billion-pound company, but had managed to hold on to a share stake that was valued in the spring of 1989 at over £50 million.

By that time he was starting to be compared with the young Arnold Weinstock, one of his great heroes, and people were openly speculating that he might be a future managing director for Weinstock's creation, General Electric Company. GEC may have in recent years become an unfashionable company with its profits growth coming to a virtual halt, but Green has tremendous admiration for its management style. 'I respect GEC because it is a genuinely creative business that is well run in many of its areas. Lord Weinstock has a remarkable record in some very tough areas. He is totally sound and is not fooled by some of the creative accounting procedures of other firms.'

Green wants to create a similar durability within his own company. Even before the Carlton flotation, his private company, Tangent Industries, prided itself on the presentation of its accounts. They were drawn up as if Tangent were a public company and were even distributed to the City and the financial press. During the reverse takeover of FSL, the accountants, Coopers & Lybrand, were amazed by the sophistication of the company's management accounting systems, which were well ahead of what was required for the business as it was then constituted.

Another role model is Derek Birkin, the tough-talking chief executive of the RTZ mining conglomerate. No business could be further away from television services than mining and Birkin's original businesss, cement, but the former head of Tunnel Cement has become a sort of father figure to Green. They first met in the departure lounge of San Francisco airport while waiting for a plane back to Britain. Green had just agreed the takeover of the Californian-based Abekas television equipment maker and wanted to show the deal to someone. While Green saw himself as the owner-occupier of his business, Birkin was the professional manager. He also had a gritty Northern directness that Green found most stimulating. Today Birkin attends some Carlton board meetings in an unofficial capacity and provides Green with background strategic advice on all his big deals. 'What is nice about Derbzek is that he has no axe to grind within the company and it is important to be able to turn to someone without any particular interest. Over the years he has been most helpful in a purely advisory role.'

The influence of Charles Saatchi is clear both in business and outside it. His company is regularly compared to the Saatchi group, even though Carlton had comfortably outgrown Saatchi in terms of market value and profits by the summer of 1989. The competitive drive that both men have shown in building their companies is equally in evidence in their weekend and evening games of snooker, chess, poker and bridge. Along with Gerald Ratner, the second-generation jeweller who has transformed his family's business into the country's leading jewellery group, they compete for their own private snooker trophy, the GRASA Cup, whose name is derived from the first two letters in each of their surnames.

After the 1983 flotation, Green moved quickly to engineer the takeover of Moving Picture Company, a Soho business at the heart of television production. Bought for £13 million in July 1983, Moving Picture counted among its customers the BBC, Granada, CBS, LWT and the leading ad agencies like Saatchi and J. Walter Thompson, and its purchase took Carlton from the sidelines of television and turned it into the leading independent video facilities house in Europe. But Green did not rest with Moving Picture. Eight months later he scooped up Video Time, a business specialising in transferring video items from one national format to another, and transferring film and slides onto video. Shortly afterwards Carlton also added Superhire, a company that hired out props to makers of television programmes and films.

The best example of a Green takeover, a deal that has worked so well for the company and its shareholders, was its December 1984 purchase of Abekas. Green had been told by the engineers within his small British manufacturing arm, IVC Carlton, about a young Californian business staffed by some very bright engineers who had worked for the giant of the industry, Ampex. On their own they had come up with some good products, of which the most important was the A42, a machine that enabled TV producers to store slides electronically on video discs and then call them up electronically. The company, which was owned 50 per cent by its founders and 50 per cent by some venture capitalists, was just breaking into profits when Green started to look at it.

He made his first approach in September 1984, while touring the International Broadcast Convention, the most important British show in television electronics. At his side was June de Moller, his corporate lawyer. On the Abekas stand were two of the founders, Phil Bennett, a Briton, and Junaid Sheikh, a Pakistani. Green simply suggested they all have a coffee and began telling them about his company and his desire to sell products internationally. Would it not make sense, he suggested, for the two companies to work together? Perhaps they might even merge their interests.

For the moment the Abekas men just listened, but Green later invited them to London to visit his offices – then in a spartan building in City Road, just north of the City of London – and Moving Picture Company in Soho. Gently wooing them he outlined the possibility of doing an 'earn-out' deal. Abekas at the time had only modest profits so on conventional earnings valuations was not worth very much. But what if they allowed themselves to be bought on a formula related to their profits over the next few years? If they hit their targets they would be extremely wealthy, while Carlton would be able to pay them out of their own cash flow.

Two weeks later Green and de Moller went to California to continue the negotiations. These eventually crystallised in a deal in which the owners of Abekas would get $12.8 million up front; $9 million would go to the venture capital backers; the rest of the payment, up to an additional $17.2 million, would be based on profits growth over the next five years. Green later recalled, 'For all of us it was a great deal. They had cash in the bank and did not need to sell. They were, after all, in profit 18 months after being set up. But the chemistry was right and they could see how, inside Carlton, they could maximise their opportunities.' And so it turned out. Each year Abekas met its targets, pushing its profits up at a compound rate of over 30 per cent a year, and its founders eventually got their full $17 million. Carlton meanwhile made a significant expansion into the world of electronic television equipment and locked in the key staff, paying a multiple of below three times earnings for the privilege. Says Green, 'It is the stuff of a Harvard Business School case study.'

Abekas showed the importance of trust and reputation in taking over companies where the people are the main assets rather than bricks and mortar. 'If you think I am going to do things to reduce your profits and hence your "earn-out" you should not do the deal with me,' he told the Abekas founders over dinner one Californian evening. 'If you think I am a crook or a bit fast you should not do the deal as we will own 100 per cent of the stock and we will control your business.' His business motto was simple: do not get a reputation for 'screwing' people or you will not be able to do the next transaction.

One merchant banker who has worked with a number of acquisition-driven growth companies says, 'Michael is very good at motivating people. He is a perfectionist who likes things to be right and everyone who works with him has to be on their tippy toes doing their best. Carlton has worked because he has great genuine charm and has been able to convince people of his vision. Most of his deals have been successful private companies whose founders have shown themselves willing to work within a larger organisation.'

Above all Green is an opportunist, ready to seize the initiative by moving quickly into growth markets like video duplication. He took his first step into high-volume duplication six months before the Technicolor deal. Carlton had bought Modern Video, a private Philadelphia company, for a maximum $83 million, the actual amount paid being tied closely to the company's profit performance over five years. Modern had all the right technology: it was able to record a full-length feature film in 80 seconds, and was rapidly taking market share from the older-established companies that made their money out of operating huge plants full of simple 'slave' videos rather than usinbzg the latest high-speed technology.

Green liked the market: he had seen how the price of pre-recorded videos had dropped steadily to the point where outright sale was starting to be a replacement for rental. The switch was fuelling a sharp rise in the duplication market, and those that were quick enough to seize the opportunity would make a lot of money. Green quickly came to see how swift he was going to have to be, particularly if he wanted to buy the sort of institutional branded company that would make him a world player. Others had also spotted the opportunity and were willing to pay a lot for a foothold: within days of the Modern deal, another British company, Rank Organisation, announced it was paying $120 million to take over the joint venture duplicating business owned by Bell & Howell, Columbia and Paramount.

Technicolor was therefore the obvious next purchase: it was a far more attractive company than the Bell/Columbia/Paramount venture, particularly if Green could gradually graft

Modern's high-speed technology onto its firm contracts with giants of the video world like CBS/Fox, Warner Brothers, Walt Disney and Lorimar. In late May he asked Felix Rohatyn, the head of mergers and acquisitions at Lazard Freres in New York, to approach Perelman to see if he might be willing to sell. The company had not been put on the market but Green felt Perelman was not emotionally attached to it and might be willing to sell if he could come up with the right price.

Green was determined not to pay too high a price for Technicolor, and in typical Carlton style it was the subject of the most detailed investigation possible. Perelman was not at all keen to part with information: Carlton was already a competitor and he feared it might attempt to poach Technicolor's clients if the deal fell through. But gradually his organisation disgorged the figures, while Green and his managing director, Bob Phillis, the former head of Central Television, toured each plant. A two-inch thick acquisition review from Coopers & Lybrand showed it to be a sensible Carlton purchase with steady and forecastable earnings and cash flows rather than the volatile and speculative profits associated with much of the entertainment industry.

The purchase was funded with a £364 million rights issue. The autumn of 1988 was not the best time to be raising equity from City investors. The day Carlton announced the deal, its shares tumbled 14 per cent and it looked to some as if Green, after five years at the helm of a public company, had made his first false move. Despite the logic of his commercial arguments, the influential 'Lex' column in the *Financial Times* concluded, 'the City was only semi-convinced, worried about the effect on margins from savage price-cutting in videos, and a little sad to see Carlton moving away from some of its more glamorous, faster growing television services into a highly competitive, mass volume business.'

But two months later, those same traders who had anxiously marked down Green's shares in September had pushed them back, and the rights issue, completed within days of the anniversary of the October 1987 crash, was taken up by the vast majority of Carlton's shareholders. They had begun to see how explosive the growth of video duplication could be and how safe and strong the cash flow generated by it. Green's City backers had also come to recognise that through Technicolor he had institutionalised the business and had placed it on a far firmer footing than it had been previously.

By the summer of 1989, the big pension funds and insurance companies had lost their confidence in so many of the high-growth 'people' businesses which had come to them for expansion funds during the Thatcher bull market. Green's great friend and guru, Charles Saatchi, had seen his profits collapse and his share price tumble, and in June his firm signalled a humiliating retreat from its global strategy by putting a 'for sale' sign up outside its management consultancy division. Days before the Saatchi retreat, the Department of Trade and Industry showed how deep was the scandal at the Blue Arrow employment agency combine, when it appointed inspectors to investigate the circumstances surrounding a controversial £25 million loan to Peter de Savary, the maverick property developer. Only Martin Sorrell of the WPP advertising group and Green himself were able to turn to the City for cash.

In May, Sorrell took advantage of his popularity when he launched a bid for the Ogilvy ad agency, while Green came back for his second big slug of City finance in less than a year when he launched a £526 million takeover of UEI, an engineering and electronics group that specialised in video and TV equipment. Just as he had used Techicolor to turn Carlton into the world's leading duplication company, so he used the UEI takeover to pole-vault Carlton into a position as a world-class manufacturer of video equipment. UEI's Quantel subsidiary had some of the best devices used in special effects and the manipulation of visual images, but it also gave Carlton as a whole a depth of product that would allow it to become a supplier of complete television studios rather than being a simple purveyor of individual items of equipment. The combined research and development resources would put Carlton in a position to challenge the American industry leaders, Ampex and Grass Valley.

After the takeover Carlton was able to boast a market value of approaching £2 billion, a figure in excess of mature and established electronics businesses like Ferranti and BICC.

Green has had his upsets. Inside the business, he lost the services of Mick Luckwell, the founder of Moving Picture Company, after a personality clash. His elder brother, David, also gradually drifted away to concentrate on his own business interests although he remained as a Carlton director. Hardest to stomach was his thwarted attempt to take over Thames Television. Thames's two main shareholders, Thorn EMI and BET, had been happy to sell out and had quickly accepted Green's £80 million offer to buy the business, made in October 1985. Green also felt he had been given an informal green light by the executives of the Independent Broadcasting Authority to proceed with the takeover. Then disaster struck: when the IBA came to rule officially on the transaction it decided that Thames could not be sold. A franchise, the IBA ruled, could only change ownership in the middle of a franchise period if it was in financial trouble. It was a bitter pill to swallow.

Carlton also led the abortive 1986 bid by DBS UK, a consortium backed by Columbia Pictures, Saatchi, LWT and Dixons, among others, to operate a satellite television franchise. The rival bid from British Satellite Broadcasting, a consortium that included Pearson, Granada, Virgin and Amstrad, won the day with the IBA. Green was left to pursue other avenues into satellite broadcasting. Although he was already handling the transmission of Rupert Murdoch's Sky Television, which was at the time fed into cable television systems around Europe, it was hardly compensation. Eventually he did make his break into the TV network when he bought a 20 per cent stake in Central Television from Cyril Stein's Ladbroke Group in March 1987, but he was well aware that he would have to wait for a change in the regulatory framework before being able to bid for the whole company.

In 1987, the *Sunday Times Magazine* attempted to predict which of the nation's young talent would emerge as the most prominent people in the 1990s. The pages were filled with politicians, actors, musicians and writers, but the magazine also selected a few businessmen, including Michael Green. Two years later some of those picked had already shown themselves to have feet of clay, but Green had more than justified his inclusion. In the summer of 1989 he was at the helm of a company which was uniquely positioned to take advantage of the rapidly expanding world of television produced by the twin effects of technological change and government deregulation. Once the Technicolor and UEI deals had been completed his next logical move was the full takeover of a television station.

One option was to negotiate a full merger with Central, where the springboard of the 20 per cent stake and a seat on the board for his own managing director, Bob Phillis, could facilitate a get together. Before joining Carlton in early 1987, Phillis had been managing director of Central. Soon after taking its 20 per cent stake, Carlton had bought Central's independent production subsidiary, Zenith, as part of its strategy of adding production to facilities and equipment. As a result, Carlton became Britain's largest independent film and television maker. Its film work included *Wish You Were Here*, the film based on the early life of Cynthia Payne, and John Huston's last work, *The Dead*, while its television programmes included Paul Simon's *Graceland – The African Concert* and *Inspector Morse*.

A merger with Central was not inevitable, however, and Green was working on a number of other ideas as television broadcasters from around the country debated the merits of the government's 1988 White Paper on the future of broadcasting. It was intended to introduce a new and far more liberal regulatory framework in the 1990s. Green was viewed as a potential candidate to operate the national fifth channel proposed in the White Paper, and someone who might get more heavily involved in satellite television at some stage despite his 1986 rebuff at the hands of the IBA.

Satellite and cable were forecast to produce a sharp rise in television programme production and Carlton, as the leader among the independents, was well positioned to gain. When the Astra satellite was launched into orbit, it was intended to broadcast sixteen new channels, of which nine were targeted at Britain, while the BSB satellite was due to have five channels.

For Carlton, the prospects in mid-1989 looked enormous. Green's Hanover Square office, with its white-washed walls and contemporary art dominated by a giant Richard Avedon photograph of a uranium miner and pictures from the Technicolor archive, had become a Mecca for all those interested in the future of British broadcasting. Green can be found here, often padding around in stockinged feet, chain smoking as he negotiates with industrialists and investment bankers, putting together the deals that have built his company. He appears to have almost boundless nervous energy, but claims no special talents, insisting that the professional and technological strength of the company lies, not with the board of directors, but in the talented and motivated people who staff the operating companies. 'My skill', he says, 'is in picking people, motivating them, and making decisions.'

Name: *Tony Millar*

Title: *Chairman of Albert Fisher*

Born: *1941, Kent*

Education: *Haileybury; Imperial Service College*

Qualifications: *8 'O' levels, 2 'A' levels, chartered accountant*

First Job: *Articled clerk for Champness Corderoy Beesley*

Family: *Married Judy Jester in 1964, they have two daughters*

Joined Albert Fisher: *In 1982 after buying a substantial stake*

Made First Million: *In 1983 through the rise in Fisher shares*

Most Exciting Moment: *When Albert Fisher took its first steps overseas through acquisitions in America*

Awards/Honours: *None*

Hobbies: *Horse racing and bridge*

Drives: *Mercedes*

Personal Stake: *£6 million*

Latest Salary: *£227,000*

Latest Company Statistics: *1987–8 – sales: £536 million; profits: £33.4 million*

Chapter VIII

Tony Millar

ALBERT FISHER

'Life is about building relationships
with people, and if you can limit the
number of business enemies you have
to the fingers on one hand then you
have achieved a lot.'

In mid-December the peasants of Vicuna and Copiapo in northern Chile start to pick the grape harvest. Loaded on to lorries, the bunches of grapes are taken from the hot and arid vineyards to nearby packhouses to be made ready for transport. The first priority is to cool the grapes, taking the heat of the field out as quickly as possible. Once they are at the right temperature, 6–7 degrees, they are graded according to colour and size, and packed in boxes. Five days later, having been flown out of the country and distributed in refrigerated lorries to supermarkets, they can be sitting in a fruit bowl ready for eating.

In the 1960s there was no such thing as a grape from Chile: the Vicuna and Copiapo regions were virtual deserts. Grapes were hardly available in the industrialised countries of Europe and North America outside a short harvest season. Today the fresh seedless Chilean grape is a Christmas delicacy cherished as much in Los Angeles as in New York, in London as in Paris. It is also part of a global sourcing network aimed at providing the industrialised west with increasingly exotic fresh produce all through the year. For the Chilean grape read the Californian strawberry, the Israeli avocado or the New Zealand kiwi fruit. Twenty years ago apples, oranges and bananas were the sum of fruits that were available all the year round to the average British

137

family. Strawberries and even pears were luxuries to be enjoyed for just a few short weeks. Today they can find extraordinary fruits like kumquats and star fruit regularly on display on their supermarket shelves.

For those businessmen who can organise an efficient international distribution network, this revolution in eating habits provides great potential for profit. One such is Tony Millar, who took over Albert Fisher, a tiny northern food wholesaler, in 1982 and within seven years had transformed it into one of Britain's major food groups selling 400 different varieties of fresh produce. It was a Fisher subsidiary that encouraged the Chileans to grow their grapes seedless to enhance their attraction to customers in America and Europe, and it was Fisher that introduced the representatives from the big British food chains like Marks & Spencer, J. Sainsbury and Tesco to Chile to show them the benefits of sourcing their products as far away as South America.

By June 1988, when Millar assembled the top managers of Albert Fisher for their annual dinner dance at Chateau Impney in Worcestershire, he could be confident about his achievement. Chateau Impney, a Victorian mansion built in the French style by an industrialist for his mistress, was a fitting place to celebrate the year's efforts. Between some welcoming words to his colleagues from overseas and a few risqué jokes, Millar reflected on the group's progress and saluted the sixteen companies that had that year joined in the Fisher 'partnership in management and in the strategy for the future'. Sales were running at £575 million, of which two-thirds were in Europe with the rest in the US, and brokers were forecasting that profits for the year about to end would top £30 million. It was an evening when the normally chain smoking Millar could afford to relax and reflect on his progress in turning Fisher into one of Britain's leading companies. On display was his ability to combine warmth and charm with a competitive thirst to extract maximum performance from himself and his staff, an intense eye for detail with a broad strategic vision.

In the event, profits emerged at £33.4 million and analysts were soon forecasting a further rise to £43 million in 1988–9, with Fisher continuing to benefit from rising living standards and the trends towards healthy eating. Each time a private family, restaurant or hotel shifts from tinned or processed food to fresh or chilled produce, Fisher gains. What had begun as a tiny seven-depot wholesaler to northern high street greengrocers with a market value of £500,000, had by 1989 become a group with a market value approaching £400 million. Its shares had multiplied in value sixty times in six years, and the growth engine showed no signs of running out of steam, the only limit being the appetite among City investors for the company's stock.

Humble greengrocery, a highly fragmented industry, was being profitably rationalised under the leadership of Fisher and the other international food groups like Asil Nadir's Polly Peck. Says Millar, 'Everything I've done I have surprised myself. Each time I have found that I have not yet reached the limit of my abilities – that is exciting and a lot of fun.' A friend remarks, 'The only thing that could kill Tony is boredom. He is happiest when life is exciting. He is clearly hyperactive, a driven man who will use every hour of the day, not just for work but also on leisure.' Millar is a keen bridge player, but his great love is horse racing. He owns horses, and has a great knowledge of the world of racing.

The achievement of partnership – between staff and employer, the company and its suppliers and customers, the management and the shareholders – is at the heart of the Millar business philosophy. In early 1989 no fewer than 1,500 of Albert Fisher's 5,000-odd staff held share options and the figure would have been higher but for limitations imposed by pension fund and insurance company investors on how many shares can be offered to staff through options. But partnership goes a long way beyond monetary inducements like options. It is the cement that holds together a company that prides itself on its decentralised management style.

Each time Millar goes into acquisition negotiations potential vendors of businesses are asked if they believe in his corporate strategy and how they can contribute to maintaining and improving it. They are effectively asked if they want to join a club. 'We are piecing together a series of relationships where people want to join the partnership, and each new acquisition is intended to add to the strength of our strategy,' he says. 'To show them how keenly we are interested in partnership we give them a list of telephone numbers of the existing members of our group so they can ring them up at random and find out how it really works.'

Once inside Fisher, senior executives become part of the Fisher family, presided over by Millar and his wife, Judy. 'Tony wants all his people to work together and enjoy working together,' says an adviser. 'One can make money and have fun as well. He brings

Judy into the business – she is part of the partnership deal. Stylish and smooth, she is a great ambassadress and knows just what to do.' In return the workaholic Millar expects total commitment from both staff and advisers. 'He uses people well but he is very tough and demands one hell of a lot from people,' comments a consultant. 'If I am not back to him 10 minutes after a phone call he wants to know why.'

Tony Millar was born in October 1941, the first son of Des Millar, a Beckenham retail chemist, and his wife, Jo. After a spell at Beaumont House, a small Hertfordshire prep school, he was sent to Haileybury and Imperial Service College where he excelled at sport, being a keen rugby wing three-quarter and swimmer. His strong competitive drive was plain at an early age.

There was no particular business culture in the family, although Millar's maternal grandfather had both made and lost a lot of money trading in canned food, and he initially wanted to study to be a vet because he liked animals. Fortunately for the shareholders of Albert Fisher, Millar made no progress. 'I went for an interview at Glasgow University and I remember sitting in front of about twenty people who asked me whether my father or my grandfather had been a vet,' he recalls. 'I said there was no family connection. "Well, Mr Millar, you are hardly qualified to become a vet in that case," was the reply, putting a firm end to my ambitions.'

The young Millar did not receive much career guidance and was left without any avenues to pursue after the Glasgow rejection. His only course was to follow his father's advice and spend two weeks researching careers at the local library after which he was expected by his parents to produce a plan. Becoming articled to train as a chartered accountant seemed the only prospect in which he was interested and for which he had the right qualifications, so in October 1959 he began work at Champness Corderoy Beesley, a partnership in St Swithins Lane in the heart of the City of London. Champness had some big clients like Reed Paper, but Millar wanted to escape the confines of an accountancy practice and break into industry. Within six months of qualifying he left to join Viyella International, the textile combine under the legendary leadership of Joe Hyman. 'I wanted to be a decision maker,' he says. 'I am a doer rather than a reactor.'

It was an exciting time. Hyman was in the process of building up Viyella as a multi-fibre, multi-process, vertically integrated textile combine through a vigorous programme of acquisitions, often funded by selling off unwanted property assets inherited from the takeovers. Millar's initial job was to be an assistant to the management accountant, working at Viyella's head office in Saville Row, the home of the British textile industry. His first task was to prepare in pencil on a large sheet of paper all the critical ratios of the subsidiaries within the group, including their profits, stocks, debtors, creditors, current cash position and cash projections. 'One had to write it in very small handwriting,' he recalls, 'but Joe did always like everything on one sheet of paper.'

Millar made good progress. He was promoted to assistant to the treasurer but quickly saw the flaws within Hyman's creation. 'Joe had a good commercial plan but he could not handle relationships with people and a lot of people suffered from his actions. The textile sector needed rationalising but not enough regard was paid to the consequences on people's lives,' he says. 'In the sixties the balance between the employer and the employee was different and the employer dominated. Today good employers create partnership.'

The climax for Millar came when Hyman, in response to hand-writing analysis to which he subjected all his staff, offered the young accountant the chance to be his personal assistant. 'I was invited to a board meeting by Joe and asked if I wanted to be his personal assistant. He had assembled his colleagues around the half-moon board table, and when I arrived he asked me to take a seat in front of them. Of course there was no chair to sit on and I had to find a chair. I lasted just 23 hours and 31 minutes – the next day I was told by one of his aides that Joe had changed his mind,' he says.

In 1964, he married Judy Jester. After three years the couple decided that Millar would have to move more quickly up the pay scale to support the lifestyle they wanted, and that would probably involve a move outside Viyella. The right opportunity came up when he was offered a top management position within the Kenyan branch of United Transport Overseas. For the young accountant it was invaluable experience. 'I came back a more flexible person than when I went,' he recalls. 'Working in Africa can be very hard work.'

The couple returned to Britain in January 1970, and Millar became United Transport's assistant financial controller, working at the company's Berkeley Square headquarters. United Transport employed a completely different style of management from the autocratic Joe Hyman at Viyella. It was concerned about the feelings of its people and only came to decisions after consensus had been achieved. But it had its faults. 'Joe was right in having short lines of communications and in making decisions quickly,' says Millar. 'At United Transport people could get frustrated. I for one did not like the long decision-making process, which seemed to result in a lack of flair and entrepreneurialism and I became frustrated with the system.'

It was, he reckoned, time to move into a more entrepreneurial business. 'After United Transport I made up my mind that I wanted to do things in terms of business philosophy,' he explains. 'I wanted to apply what I had learned. I had seen the pluses and minuses and I had worked out that there were a number of simple philosophies that if applied to a business would be successful. I always wanted to make a million, rather like the schoolboy dream of wanting to be a train driver. But it was more than that. I wanted to create a subtle balance between the strong leadership I had seen at Viyella and the partnership at United Transport. One should never fudge decisions, but one should try to find ways round the historic conflict between employers and unions.'

His first escape route was into a private property development business, called Fairfield, run by a childhood friend, Grant Wilkinson. He had always promised Millar that if he managed to build up a reasonable-sized business he would invite him in as finance director. But the timing could not have been worse, and the job did not last long. The property market had been soaring but looked as if it was close to boiling over, and Millar took fright when he delved into the company's financial structure. Fairfield had big investment commitments yet its funding was short term. If the banks decided to call in their loans – and they could do so at very short notice – then the company might be insolvent.

He told Wilkinson to look for a big brother, either a financial institution or a corporate buyer, who would give the company long-term finance. Negotiations were progressing smoothly with a number of companies when a bombshell struck in the form of Anthony Barber's Development Gains Tax, introduced in December 1973. It was one of the key factors behind the stock market collapse. Millar recalls, 'The effect on the property market was crucifying. Values crashed over night and all dealings came to a halt. Eventually we managed to sell out to MEPC on January 6 but at a price of well under half of the received offer that we had a few weeks previously from Law Land.'

From Fairfield Millar went into consultancy and was offered the job of managing director of a tiny laundry company called Provincial Laundries in July 1977. At the time, the company was making small losses from its two laundries in Manchester and Newcastle. But it was in essence a clean 'shell', the stock market term for a company with a quotation but very little else. It was therefore ripe for transformation through the growth strategy on which Millar was dying to embark, putting into practice all that he had learned at Viyella and United Transport. When he arrived it was valued at below £280,000 and the shares stood at 7p. Millar bought £5,000 with his savings.

It looked like a solid base from which to start at last building his own group, but all was not well. Millar discovered that one of his major shareholders was a secretive Swiss company that was sitting on a 29 per cent stake cloaked behind an anonymous nominee name. The presence of a major shareholder who might be *persona non grata* among City institutions could be a handicap if Millar was to begin raising funds for expansion, so he had first to remove the Swiss representatives from the board and then persuade them to sell out. The boardroom coup worked well but when the stake came up for sale rather than being placed out with institutions it went to Michael Ashcroft, another talented young businessman. At the time Ashcroft was building up what was then known as Hawley Goodall, and had been interested in taking control of Provincial ahead of Millar's arrival with the intention of bolting industrial services on to his base in tent making.

For three years the two men enjoyed a good working relationship. Ashcroft had been impressed by the work that Millar had put in to turning round the two original laundries and was prepared to allow him to run the business as chief executive while Ashcroft himself was non-executive chairman, throwing in ideas on strategy. Says Millar, 'I met Michael on Good Friday 1978 and within three-quarters of an hour we had come to an agreement. What we both wanted to do was compatible and our overall plan would work better in combination. I decided that he could be fun to work with. He has an incredibly creative mind.'

With Ashcroft on board as a major shareholder, Provincial went on the acquisition trail, picking up a number of businesses in laundries, office cleaning, painting and contracting. After a loss in 1977, the company returned to profit and the pre-tax total eventually reached more than £1 million. Millar borrowed money to add to his shareholding in rights issues, and by May 1981, when Hawley made an agreed takeover bid for Provincial, he had a decent-sized stake worth £150,000 and the title of deputy chairman of the enlarged group. Inside Hawley he played an important role in the negotiations for the highly successful purchase of Electro-Protective, the American security company, but he knew from the early days that he wanted to move on. 'When I was in the US doing the Electro-Protective deal I had time to think. I now had a capital base and wanted to do my own thing.'

His experiences with Ashcroft had taught him a lot. 'Michael has one of the most agile minds I have ever come across,' he says. 'He always has a whole range of potential solutions to potential problems. He brought out of me a lot of skill and talent. Working at Provincial and Hawley taught one the ability to get up and go. It is better to think things through but you have to make decisions and you must make mistakes – the critical thing is not to make the same mistake twice.'

The break from Hawley in September 1981 was a difficult decision. Millar was turning his back on a £40,000-a-year salary and he also had to deal with his chairman. Ashcroft does not like losing top staff. But Millar was determined to make his break and build a major company out of the £150,000 he raised by selling his Hawley shares. 'Tony had seen a great number of managements and wanted to prove that he could draw on his experiences to do something for himself,' says an adviser. 'He was clear about his own capabilities. The Electro-Protective deal stands to this day as one of Hawley's best transactions and showed that Tony could deal. Now he wanted to build his own team.'

The search for a suitable 'shell' company took six months. At first he made his criteria pretty wide. He was interested in all quoted companies with a market value of under £1 million so that his £150,000 would enable him to buy a reasonable stake. Working in the drawing room of his secretary, who had left Hawley with him, he weeded out those businesses that were highly borrowed or making major losses. He had no intention of spending the first year or 18 months of his tenure sorting out big problems.

Albert Fisher, then a small food distributor controlled by Frank Hawtin, the entrepreneur, and run by his grandson, Jonathan, was suggested by the Hon. Mervyn Greenway, younger brother of Lord Greenway and a stockbroker with Capel-Cure Myers.

'Mervyn thought that if I got together with Frank Hawtin I could persuade him to sell me the stake,' he recalls. 'Jonathan had not done much with the business so I went up to Blackpool and went round the company's seven depots and was able to agree a deal in which I and some friends took Hawtin's 29.9 per cent holding at an effective price of between 1p and 2p. My friends soon wanted to sell so I was able within a few weeks to top my original stake up from 14.4 per cent to over 21 per cent.'

Millar chose the food sector for a number of reasons. For a start, he would not be competing with Hawley and Michael Ashcroft. But food had its own attractions and looked the kind of sector in which a big company could be built without huge capital demands. Although the food industry as a whole is static (the population of the industrialised countries is stable while the third world struggles to feed itself), the fresh food field is growing strongly, particularly in the United States which tends to set the trends for the rest of the western world.

Historically the food wholesalers had been highly fragmented for good reason – most of their customers, the high street grocers, were small businesses. But the growth of the supermarkets and their rapid penetration of fresh food was transforming the shape of the market. At the same time ownership of the hotel and catering industry was also concentrating in fewer and fewer hands and the national chains were increasingly looking for distributors who would be able to satisfy their needs on a national basis. Says Millar, 'The Mama and Papa style of organisation was no longer valid and we wanted to position ourselves to grow in a market that was changing naturally. The multiple supermarkets were looking for more sophisticated distribution, while in food service those companies shifting from a single unit to a multi-unit chain were looking for their distributors to do the same thing.'

The arrival of Millar in the Fisher boardroom sent the shares soaring. Within a few months they had gone up more than ten times, and Fisher became a 'go-go' stock among City *cognoscenti*. 'Oranges and lemons can add up to big business – not to mention apples, pears and grapes,' wrote the *Mail on Sunday* a year after Millar's arrival, 'which helps to explain why the Albert Fisher Group, from relative obscurity in Manchester, has become a star of the London Stock Exchange.'

However, Millar knew he had to get the basic business trading profitably if he was going to have any credibility with the professional investors who would back him with the cash to grow. If anything he was worried by the soaring share price after his arrival. He feared expectations would be disappointed and did his best to take some of the froth out, making sure people knew just how difficult was the task he was setting himself. Fisher itself had been in a declining market, servicing the high street grocer with fresh food at a time when the share of the fresh food market satisfied by supermarkets had grown from virtually nothing to 25–30 per cent. But the company did have established contracts, connections and relationships and it was on the back of these that Millar built profits up to around £150,000.

From that base Millar began to expand. Stage one was a £385,000 rights issue to provide the company with a war chest. Stage two was to introduce employee incentive schemes, including a share option scheme that was unique in that it penetrated below the senior and middle management into the rank and file of the company. That first scheme made 30 per cent of the company's 100-odd staff option holders, including people like the salesmen and lorry drivers. Millar would have liked to go much further but for the constraints on share options imposed by the city institutions. He comments, 'The current 10 per cent limit irrespective of one's philosophy is highly illogical. There should be a graduated scale of limits linked to the percentage of people involved in the scheme. Obviously a share option scheme that just includes directors is very different from what we do. I would like all our employees to hold options because every employee in the business has a significant contribution to make to that business.'

He then set about looking for the first purchase. Just as the Saatchi brothers had done in their early days, he fired off around 250 letters to possible sellers of private companies that might fit in with the Fisher growth plan of expanding the company into the supply of supermarket chains and institutional food users like hotels and restaurants. Often the replies were scathing: many of his would-be candidates would take one look at his tiny company and write back that they could do a lot better without him. In the end one of his staff suggested he get in contact with David Pearce, a respected food industry figure and the principal shareholder in Wentworth Import & Export, an international importer and distributor of fresh produce sourcing its product principally in South America and selling it mainly in Britain and Europe. Their initial meeting was over dinner and began with some competitive sparring. Pearce was quick to point out that Wentworth was at the time a bigger business than Fisher. But he also saw the potential of being part of a group with greater resources and the prospects of participating in a profitable rationalisation of his sector.

The deal, announced in March 1983, was a model for future Fisher acquisitions. At the time Wentworth was making profits of £116,000 on sales of £4 million. Millar offered a maximum price of £1.05 million of which £800,000 was paid up front in a mixture of cash and shares, with the balance paid on a formula related to profits for the subsequent 14 months. These so-called 'earn-out' deals had been an important part of Millar's growth strategy at Provincial and he saw them as a central plank in the Fisher partnership. 'The upfront cash payment gives security for an individual,' he says, 'while the deferred element either in cash or shares creates a mutuality of financial interest which is vital in negotiations over problem solving in the post-acquisition period – and there are always problems to be solved. Beyond that we insist people hold on to their shares for at least two years.' On top of shares, Millar also introduced profit sharing linked to the achievement of organic growth rates of 20 per cent a year, the sort of target that would be demanded by shareholders.

Once he had formed his partnership with key staff in the original Fisher company and with Pearce and his team at Wentworth, Millar put in place the first planks of his partnership with the City. In the first year private investors that had made money out of his stewardship of Provincial formed the bulk of the new shareholders in Fisher. In particular, clients of Paul Boyland, a stockbroker with the small firm of Hitchens Harrison, were heavy buyers. Says Millar, 'They gave me an amazing level of support.'

But as the company grew he wanted to improve the quality of the shareholders by bringing in big institutions. Millar's early moves included the replacement of Henry Cooke Lumsden, the Manchester broker he had inherited at Fisher, with Laurie Milbank, a City firm. Later he upgraded again, appointing Rowe & Pitman, the firm that became part of the S.G. Warburg investment banking combine. Hill Samuel was appointed as merchant bank in September 1982, while Schroder Wagg was brought on board three years later. The first big institutional backers invested in October 1983 when the company launched a £950,000 issue of convertible preference shares to fund its purchase of the Henry Long transport, warehousing and distribution subsidiary of Ocean Transport & Trading. Two institutions, Equity Capital for Industry and 3i (the venture capital firm owned by the clearing banks), took the entire issue, a move that earned them vast returns in the years to come. Tony Lorenz, head of ECI, was so impressed with Millar's achievement that he began to use the Albert Fisher story as a casebook study of the rewards to be gained from investing in small, but growing, companies.

Millar is not a natural extrovert. But he worked hard on his presentation skills, taking training to help him cope with big audiences. Some have been surprised by his attention to detail and willingness to spend hours crafting the words of an annual meeting speech or press release. Comments one adviser, 'I remember when an advertisement was being put together on his five-year record. He actually came out of a board meeting to measure the bars on the chart to check they were accurate. His concern for detail is almost frightening, but he also thinks carefully about the larger picture.'

With some big backers on board and profits heading towards £1 million, Millar decided it was time to raise the tempo of the expansion programme by starting the search for his first purchase in the United States. 'We saw fresh produce as an international business,' he says. 'We believed we should establish an international sourcing network and get as close to the grower as we possibly could. If we were able to establish the network we would be able to offer our customers continuity of supply in fresh produce.' Eating habits were changing, with the changes coming first in the United States. According to US government figures, eating of fruit rose nearly 12 per cent between 1970 and 1980 and was continuing to rise gradually. In vegetables the increase had been 13 per cent. Healthy eating was really taking hold. At the same time the percentage of food eaten outside the home in restaurants and hotels was rising – from 23 per cent in 1970 to 29 per cent in 1982. 'In the US as in the UK we could see a growing and fragmented market where the historic reason for the fragmentation – the fragmentation of the customer base – was disappearing,' he says. 'We could therefore see the prospects of enhanced profits from both rationalisation and cost saving and market growth.'

The target areas were California and Florida, the two states that grow 70 per cent of the fresh produce in the US. 'The plan was to get into distribution in these two states to get as close to the growers and food sources as we could,' says Millar. 'As we grew, we would have good strong relationships secured. It is a building block approach.' Obtaining a base in California would fit in well with Wentworth because the company's South American apples, pears and grapes suppliers were also big suppliers to the US outside the Californian growing season. Bolting the two together gave the group strong sourcing connections in both hemispheres, enhancing its ability to supply all the year round and giving it greater buying power. Instantly it could bid for a whole crop rather than just a part. The Americans would buy the bigger fruits while the Europeans, who prefer smaller fruits, would take the rest.

Back at his Windsor head office Millar worked hard at creating a management structure capable of supporting his growth ambitions. In David Pearce he found a man of great commitment, who from his base in Wentworth was able eventually to take charge of the group's entire UK and European fresh produce operations. Richard Portergill, who bought a company called Stokes Bomford into the group, headed the packaged food operations. Stephen Barker, an old colleague from Provincial, was recruited in March 1984, initially as finance director but later elevated to the title of chief executive. Four years later, Barker moved on to do his own thing, but not before playing a vital role in the growth of the company.

Fisher's partnership strategy was based on passing responsibility as far down the organisation as possible. People were given as much autonomy as possible in the achievement of results. But executives still had to be accountable for their actions. The counterweight to decentralisation had to be rigorous financial control at the centre based on the availability through computer networks of daily cash positions plus a whole host of weekly, monthly and quarterly statistics. 'You have to have your finger on the pulse if you are going to give your operating officers the autonomy to get on and run their businesses,' says Millar. 'You also need a creative centre to get the various parts of the group to share their best ideas and contacts on purchasing, customers and suppliers. The advantages of creating a network are in this way increased.'

In the American south-east, the key executive to emerge was Paul Tavilla. Millar had made his first move into Florida with the purchase of Carnival – a company specialising in distributing fresh fruit and vegetables to hotels, restaurants and other private and public sector institutions – for up to $7 million in September 1984. Carnival performed well but it began to suffer from competition from a company called Tavilla. Millar decided therefore that it would be sensible for him to meet its chairman, and very early on in their talks it became clear that the two companies had similar plans to develop a strong and deep distribution network within the state as quickly as they could. It was the natural basis for a partnership.

Together, Millar and Tavilla could create a network capable of dominating the state's fresh produce distribution industry – and by 1988 it was clear the strategy had worked, with Albert Fisher controlling 20 per cent of the fresh produce food service market through its subsidiaries, while the nearest competitor had just 1 per cent. Says Millar, 'Such a network would be virtually impossible to duplicate. It would be hideously expensive to buy and we already have all the key businesses linked into our partnership.'

Assembling the network has not been without its problems. But all acquisition targets are rigorously researched by the group's accountant, Ernst & Whinney, and acquisitions have been turned down if they have been found to have been using kickbacks to win business. Says Millar, 'It is golden rule number one – no kickbacks.'

By the end of 1988 Millar had bought no fewer than fifteen companies, committing his company to pay a maximum of $140 million including profits-related payments to build up Fisher's American business. Outside Florida he established a strong position in California and in New England, wooing the sellers of businesses with his promise of management autonomy combined with the strengths of a group that could achieve economies of scale and thus gain customers in what remained a fragmented industry. In 1986 the company bought a New England business called Ziff, which distributed paper products – from paper and plastic cups through to decorations and cleaning supplies – as part of its strategy of broadening its product range beyond food while servicing the same customer base. Other deals followed as a significant United States business was put together.

In May 1985 the *Sunday Express* wrote, 'If the City were to award medals for achievement, there is little doubt that 43-year-old Tony Millar would run away with the gold. For he has, in the three short years since he moved in on the ailing Albert Fisher fruit and vegetable distribution group, pulled off so many deals that most people have had trouble keeping up.' Five months later the *Financial Times* was equally positive: 'The Albert Fisher deal is simple: you give me the money and I will give you soaring earnings per share. The group's strategy is to achieve rapid earnings growth through acquiring companies with strong management in places which extend it geographically or into related product areas. It seems to be paying off.' By the end of 1988 Millar had achieved a compound growth in earnings per share of 66 per cent during his six years at the helm and dividend growth per share of 68 per cent, giving him one of the finest medium-term records in the London stock market.

Having turned Fisher into a genuinely Anglo-American food group, his next aim was to look towards Europe. Some tentative discussions were held between Millar and Asil Nadir, then a victim of considerable City scepticism, about the possible injection of Polly Peck's food interests into Fisher in return for a significant shareholding. But the discussions did not develop beyond an initial skirmish. City reaction to a deal would not have been good. Millar was concerned about the City reaction to the deal. It might have hit his share price and destroyed the high rating that he had worked so hard to create and that was vital to his continued success.

Instead he opted for a more piecemeal approach, targeting the Low Countries as the base from which to build a major business in Europe ahead of the removal of trade barriers and the creation of a single market within the European Community in 1992. Holland was the hub of the European distribution network for fresh food. Much of the produce was imported from other continents into Rotterdam and then re-exported to other countries. The first deal came in July 1987, when Fisher bought Reingold, a Rotterdam food importer; over the next year and a half the company made another four purchases, ending up as the largest fruit handler in the Netherlands and occupant of a third of the Rotterdam fruit pier. Once again Millar was able to obtain his dominant position because the £20 billion European food distribution market was highly fragmented. It was if anything more attractive as a region than Britain because the retailing channels were less concentrated and therefore were more open to change.

At the start of 1989 Fisher was in a good position to maintain its growth. Despite years of acquisitions its ability to place shares with City institutions had enabled it to come through the October 19 crash with cash in the bank and in the year following Black Monday it was able to make ten acquisitions. In expanding a business rapidly through acquisition there was always the chance that one particular purchase could run into trading difficulties and Millar was determined not to compound a trading problem with a stretched balance sheet. Thanks to his good City communications, his investors remained loyal despite a flurry of share issues, of which the biggest was an £82 million rights issue in May 1987. 'It is a steady process of talking to people and educating them,' he comments, 'and we have never said anything that we have not delivered.' Much of the skill comes in keeping the flow of shares onto the market at below the level of demand, in order to create a feeling of scarcity. Says Millar, 'We want to see our arms being wrenched out of their sockets before we increase the supply of shares on to the market because access to City funds is the real controller of our rate of growth.'

Millar concentrated on buying independent private businesses from their founders because these companies have the most to gain from the strong financial controls and reporting systems of a public company. The marriage values of the deal then become quickly apparent in enhanced sales and profits. 'We only do agreed deals and we have far more to offer a private company than a public company,' he says. 'It may be a slower process of development but it has been far more solid because everything is built up more gradually and people relationships are formed.'

However, public company acquisitions were not out of the question. In November 1986 Millar bought three of the old Distillers companies from Guinness in a £38 million deal – Stratford-upon-Avon Canners, a supplier of catering-sized cans of fruit and vegetables, MCC Foods, a maker of ingredients used by caterers and bakers, and Frank Idiens, a supplier of frozen vegetables and fruit pulp. Their subsequent performance demonstrated that Millar's approach has an application not just to private companies, bought on a deferred performance-related payments basis, but also poorly performing subsidiaries of public companies. Remarks Millar, 'The three companies were lacking in motivation. We took the lid off and let the managers have their heads. They were frustrated, but now they are able to exploit the opportunities that exist.'

There was no reason why Albert Fisher, as it entered 1989, should not make a major public company acquisition if it could win agreement and retain its rating in the City. Millar has an ambition of taking his company into the *Financial Times* Stock Exchange index of Britain's top 100 companies within five years, and a big public company deal is one sure way of getting there. If he does make a big takeover it will not be hostile but neither will it be in any sense a cosy merger – the Fisher culture will have to dominate. 'In my naive original thinking I wanted to be a millionaire, but when you reach that target you realise how unimportant it is,' he says. 'After a while it is never a real motivating force. The real force is the desire to create something corporately. Life is about building relationships with people and if you can limit that number of business enemies you have to the fingers on one hand then you have achieved a lot.'

MEN OF
PROPERTY

Name: *John Beckwith*

Title: *Chairman of London & Edinburgh Trust*

Born: *1947, Chelsea, London*

Education: *Gadebridge Park Prep School, Hemel Hempstead; Harrow School; articled with accountants Arthur Andersen*

Qualifications: *9 'O' levels, 3 'A' levels. Accountancy qualifications FCA ATII*

First Job: *1965, running father's prep school. 1966, trainee accountant at Berisford Lye, Chartered Accountants, in Kent*

Family: *Married Heather Robbins in 1975; they have two sons and a daughter*

First Business Venture: *1969. 41 St John's Avenue, Putney*

First Company: *1971, Second London Wall*

Formation of LET: *In 1975. Company changed from Second London Wall to London & Edinburgh Trust after profitable project in Edinburgh*

Made First Million: *In 1973*

Awards: *Various civic and architectural awards*

Most Exciting Moment: *Company flotation*

Hobbies: *Tennis, skiing, running, male chauvinism!*

Drives: *Porsche 928S, Range Rover*

Latest Salary: *£357,000*

Personal Stake: *10.3 per cent plus 3.4 per cent family trust worth £32 million*

Latest Company Statistics: *1988 – profits: £50.4 million; assets per share: 136p*

Name: *Peter Beckwith*

Title: *Deputy Chairman of London & Edinburgh Trust*

Born: *1945, Barsilly, India*

Education: *Merchant Taylors', Sandy Lodge; Harrow School; Cambridge University*

Qualifications: *9 'O' levels, 3 'A' levels. BA Hons Cantab. Solicitor of the Supreme Court*

First Job: *1967, articled clerk to Herbert Smith & Co. (Solicitors)*

Family: *Married Paula Gay Bateman in 1969; they have two daughters*

First Business Venture: *1972, joined John Beckwith at Second London Wall*

Formation of LET: *In 1975. Company re-formed as London & Edinburgh Trust after profitable project in Edinburgh*

Made First Million: *In 1983, when LET floated on stock market*

Awards/Honours: *Personal: various sports awards. Corporate: 1986, Civic Design Award, European Steel Award for Ropemaker Place, London EC2*

Most Exciting Moment: *Becoming chairman of the Spitalfields Development Group in 1987*

Hobbies: *Travel, golf, tennis, running, reading*

Drives: *Mercedes 500 SL*

Latest Salary: *£350,000*

Personal Stake: *10.3 per cent family trust, jointly held, worth £32 million*

Latest Company Statistics: *1988 – profits: £50.4 million; assets per share: 136p*

Chapter IX

John and Peter Beckwith
LONDON & EDINBURGH TRUST

*'I want to run a huge company
making huge amounts of money'
(John Beckwith)*

The Beckwith brothers are tall, handsome and rich. They stride elegantly through life with the confident ease of those who have made it.

They appear to have been born with a silver spoon firmly between their lips. An early childhood spent in India and Egypt was followed by the rigours of Harrow, one of the top public schools in Britain. When they left with their full quota of academic and sporting successes, John trained as an accountant while Peter became a lawyer.

They soon grew restless with their chosen professions, where they could see little immediate prospect of serious money making, and while still in their early twenties they formed the beginnings of London & Edinburgh Trust, one of the most successful property development companies of the 1980s.

John broke away first and Peter joined him two years later, just before the 1974 property crash. A decade afterwards, when the company was launched on the stock market in 1983, John and Peter Beckwith, then in their mid-thirties, instantly became worth over £5 million each. The rapid growth of the company meant that by mid-1989 they each had shares worth over £32 million.

By the mid-1980s, LET was regarded as one of the top five property developers in London. Leading retailers such as Sainsbury's and Sir Terence Conran's Storehouse group sought out the Beckwiths to form joint ventures to redevelop properties that were either surplus to requirements or needed modernising. The deal with Storehouse in the spring of 1989, involving £120 million of properties, was the biggest joint venture between a retailer and a property developer at the time.

The company's major office projects so far include Ropemaker Place in the City of London, which was let as the headquarters of the mighty American securities house Merrill Lynch; the transformation of the old Billingsgate fish market on the river Thames; and a spectacular office block in Paris. The company's most ambitious project is the plan to develop London's Spitalfields vegetable market into a 1 million square foot office and shopping complex. The scheme entails moving the original market, which has required an Act of Parliament and involved drawn out talks with scores of local and special interest groups. LET is also transforming the Bull Ring in Birmingham, famous for its ugliness, into a new shopping centre to be called The Galleries.

Peter Beckwith has been particularly caught up in the Spitalfields scheme and clearly relishes creating something new and elegant out of dereliction. 'Each generation should be allowed to create their own style of architecture, otherwise you get nothing but pastiche,' he says, hitting out at those who cling to the past. 'Modern architecture should be capable of living alongside the old.'

He is well aware that, as a breed, property developers are responsible for the building of the offices and shopping centres people use every day. The boom of the 1980s has put much of the rebuilding of Britain that is going on all around the country into their hands, and, in the case of LET, they believe they have responded to the social as well as the commercial challenge.

When London & Edinburgh Trust floated on the stock market in 1983 it was hailed as the most significant new property company for more than a decade. Although the company was capitalised at a little over £25 million when it made its debut, it already had large stylish projects under way. LET acquired a reputation for quality buildings at an early stage in the company's fortunes. The Beckwiths claim they would never develop a building they would not occupy, or houses or flats in which they would not live.

In the early 1980s, when niche retailing was still in its infancy and Alan Sugar was dreaming of cut-price word-processors, John and Peter Beckwith were well advanced in creating a new type of property company. The innovation was partly to do with the greater emphasis on good-quality architecture and partly with new, faster ways of putting up buildings. But it was also in the method of financing.

They, with a handful of others such as Trevor Osborne of Speyhawk, Godfrey Bradman of Rosehaugh and Stuart Lipton of Stanhope Properties, led the way for a new post-crash breed of property men, who built up their companies, not in the traditional manner by buying office blocks and living off the rent, but by developing imaginative new buildings and selling them, often to the institutions who had put up the money. The risk every developer takes – that tenants would not be found when the building was completed, or that the hoped-for rent might not materialise – was therefore largely taken by the pension funds and insurance companies with strong cash flow who could afford to play the long game. The only problem was that they took most of the profit as well.

As the decade progressed and the clutch of 'merchant developers' who arrived around the same time prospered, they found the banks increasingly willing to lend money for development. LET led the way in persuading the banks to put up 'non recourse loans', which related only to the specific project in hand, and not to the entire company. That way, if the project failed, it would not bring down the company. As bank lending grew, it enabled the companies to put up a larger proportion of the development costs themselves, taking more of a risk but also more of the profits.

The eighties were the first time that property companies like LET, Speyhawk and Rosehaugh became judged and valued in the stock market on their profits and future profit potential rather than on the value of their assets. In mid-1989 LET was capitalised at around £260 million on the stock market and profits had soared from £1 million in 1982 to over £50 million in 1988.

The Beckwiths live up to the reputation of archetypal property developers. They drive fast cars, live in big houses in fashionable areas and send their children to the right schools. They are staunchly Conservative and devoted to Margaret Thatcher. They give the impression of being typical products of the upper middle class – and automatic recipients of wealth and success. It is a carefully polished image.

According to Peter Beckwith, they were inspired in the early years of building the company by a desire to show that they could be just as successful, if not more so, than those who *had* been privileged by birth. At Harrow, they had been very much in the lower financial and social echelons, along with the doctors' and lawyers' sons. Their father had been a Professor of Economics at Stanford University, California, before he joined the army during the Second World War. After the war he stayed in India and, urged on by his wife, he sent the brothers to school in England on an army salary. 'I never wanted to have to struggle to educate my children the way my father did,' says Peter.

Agnes Duncan, their mother, had a powerful personality and high aspirations for her sons. 'She was the one who had the bright idea of sending us to Harrow,' says Peter. Although she was just 5'3" tall, both boys were in awe of her. She came from a well-off Scottish family with a tartan to be proud of. In true Scottish tradition she was keen for her children to get the very best education.

Despite their relative poverty to many Harrovians, they had a comfortable childhood. Their father was posted to India during the war and the family enjoyed the easy lifestyle of the last days of the Raj. Peter Beckwith, the elder of the two, was born near Delhi in 1945, while John's birth took place two years later in Chelsea.

Before the war, Agnes had been a sister at the Great Ormond Street Hospital, now one of the Beckwith's favourite charities. During the war she served as a nurse on the Burma front and rose to become a Major by 1945, a higher rank than her husband, who was a Captain at the time.

Both brothers remember their early childhood with great affection. They spent their early years in India, and then moved to Egypt, Cyprus and Germany. It was the sort of life most small boys dream about. At one of their many parties in India, an elephant made an unexpected appearance and dug a huge hole in the garden. Egypt too was fun. 'In Egypt life was easy,' says John. 'There were lots of servants. We spent our time swimming and enjoying ourselves.'

The two brothers, whose different temperaments were already apparent, got on much as boys do. In short, they fought a lot but united against any outside enemy. 'There was the time when Peter pushed me into the Great Bitter Lake, in Egypt, but it is so salty I floated anyway,' laughs John. The bond between them is a deep one. 'As we spent all our time together as kids of course we fought, but we have always supported each other if the going got tough,' says Peter.

Despite the ease of life, their parents believed in discipline. Their mother's strength of character owed much to her traditional Scottish Presbyterian family background, and their father was also half Scottish. 'We were brought up pretty strictly,' says Peter, 'and taught to believe in the right things of life like the family, and putting back something into society.'

Both are conscious that their parents made considerable sacrifices to send them to one of the best public schools in Britain. As far as the boys were concerned their penalty for this privilege was only seeing their parents once or twice a year. They were sent to prep school at the age of 9 and went on to Harrow at 13. When their father was based in Hong Kong, the journey took 36 hours on a Comet – not much fun, even for young boys. Peter used to watch his fellow Harrovians getting ready to go off skiing at Christmas and Easter and vowed that one day that would be him. He and Peter are today avid skiers. 'I wanted "fuck-you" money,' says Peter firmly.

But they both adored the school. The emphasis at Harrow on competitive sport suited both Beckwiths. 'I loved school, it was terrific for anyone who enjoyed sport,' says John, who played most sports for the school and was prominent in the athletics team, running the 100 yards for the school.

They also believe that Harrow was a great education for getting on with a broad cross-section of people. In the pecking order they were pretty far down the league. Their fellow pupils were princes and sons of great industrial families like the Players and Wills children. Mike d'Abo, the future pop star, was also there.

John's will to succeed and a certain degree of nerve emerged on one occasion when he wasn't selected for a particular sports team. He walked several miles to the master's house and demanded to know the reason. He was 14. 'I believe in reaching up and trying to touch the cloud', he says.

Because of their excellence and enthusiasm for sport, they made their mark on the school. John, the younger and the more abrasive of the two, admits to having been 'a bit of a bully'. Perhaps it was to compensate for having a successful elder brother in the school. Peter became Captain of the Harrow football team in his final year.

Both boys were expecting to go to university. Then tragedy struck. Their father died of cancer. He had been ill in the Far

East, but he had apparently recovered and bought a prep school in England. But, a few months later his condition became worse and he died. It was not long after John had taken his 'O' levels, and at 17 years old, he left Harrow to run the prep school. He taught maths and took over the administration. Finally it was decided to sell it. Although John glosses over it now, it was clearly a traumatic experience for someone of that age and forced him to grow up very quickly.

After the death of their father, both men opted for the security that the professions offered. Peter was already articled with a law firm, and John decided that accountancy might come in more useful than going to university. He started with a small firm of accountants in Kent, but finished his training at Arthur Andersen, one of the biggest and best-respected firms in the City. However, their entrepreneurial spirit soon emerged.

In his early twenties John was the archetypal young man about town, driving a Porsche and living in Chelsea. There were lots of girlfriends, but in the end he married Heather, who was a nurse like his mother, and of whom he is reputed to be almost as much in awe. John was already climbing the personal property ladder. 'I had moved three times by the time I was 22,' he says. 'I saw clients doing up houses and selling them for a good profit and I thought it was a lot more interesting than auditing other people's old records.'

An elderly spinster aunt lent them £2,000 apiece to get them started. John, who was operating mainly on his own at this stage, wasted no time in buying a property. The first venture was in 1969 when he bought 41 St John's Avenue, Putney. It was the tail-end of a lease and he doubled his money in a few months.

National Westminster also lent them some money and the next project was buying five flats with two sitting tenants. Luck lent a hand again. Within weeks one of the tenants had been offered a permanent job in the North of England and another had died. The flats were refurbished and sold at a profit of £45,000, a tidy sum of money in 1970. Several flat refurbishments in the Putney and Richmond areas followed. To begin with, it seemed just an interesting way of supplementing their meagre professional incomes. But the business began to take over.

John was conducting all his business affairs from his office in Arthur Andersen where Ian Hay Davidson, later to become head of Lloyd's of London, was then senior partner. One day John's name was tannoyed 25 times with urgent calls, and Hay

Davidson summoned him to tell him he had to choose between accountancy and his private business affairs. He chose to launch his own business.

In 1971, he started his first company called Second London Wall, which eventually became London & Edinburgh Trust. The Beckwiths were fortunate to meet Arthur Bergbaum, an old property hand, in 1972, at a crucial stage in the development of the company. He formed a joint company with them called Lyndean in 1973. The first project was a 70,000 square foot industrial estate at Greenwich. Bergbaum had been a high-flyer during the boom times of the 1960s and a contemporary of the great property men of that era, like Harold Samuel and Charles Clore. He had become chief executive of a major London property group called City Wall when he was only 32 years old and had astutely sold it to Rank, the leisure conglomerate, although he remained chairman. Some observers of the property scene say he rescued the Beckwiths after the property crash of 1974–5, although they deny that they needed rescuing. But he certainly helped them through their transition from small-time refurbishers of houses into serious commercial developers.

Peter Beckwith joined John at Second London Wall in 1972. He is the linguist of the two brothers, speaking fluent French and German, which he studied up to 'A' level and kept up through his extensive travelling. As an academic himself, their father was naturally keen for both sons to go to university. Peter applied to read modern languages and was offered a place at a respectable red brick university. 'But being an 18-year-old snob I didn't want to go.' Soon after, he was offered a place at Cambridge to read law, which he jumped at. 'A door opens and you either spring through it or you don't,' he says.

It turned out to be a useful degree course, but it is his fluency in languages that has helped the company expand in Europe, where so many businessmen feel alienated and uncertain because of the language difficulties. LET, along with Gerald Ronson's Heron International has spearheaded the drive of British property companies into Europe. LET has projects in France, Germany, Holland, Spain and Portugal.

Peter Beckwith's inventiveness came out early. He joined the law firm Herbert Smith after graduating, the same year that his father died, but he stayed only months. 'I wanted to get married but I was only getting paid £8 a week.' Instead he found a small one-man firm in Kent who would pay him £17.50 a week.

He married Paula Bateman, whom he had spotted walking her dachshund outside his house. One day he plucked up courage and asked her to a party. They have been together ever since.

After qualifying as a solicitor, Peter returned to the City of London and joined the well-established law practice of Norton Rose Botterell & Roche, where he spent three years on the international banking side, something that has proved extremely useful later at LET.

However, international banking, he discovered, is not as glamorous as it sounds. 'I spent a lot of time in exotic places like Peru, but mostly in dingy hotel rooms drafting documents,' he comments. It may have been tedious, but it gave him valuable practice at meeting timetables and working under pressure.

Peter had been giving advice and encouragement to John at Second London Wall while he was still at Norton Rose. But as the company got bigger, it was evident that he was going to have to join full time, and in 1972 he resigned from the law firm. For the first two years the business flourished. It was towards the end of a long bull market in both property and stocks and shares. Business had been so good for so long that nobody saw the disaster coming. A whole host of under-capitalised banks had sprung up, lending huge amounts to the property sector, which eagerly took on as much debt as it could get.

Then towards the end of 1974, the government sounded the alarm by hoisting interest rates up by several points in a few weeks and the property market came to a dead stop. 'Overnight it was impossible to sell anything,' they remember.

The crash caught the Beckwiths by surprise as much as anyone else. They had five houses in Kew in the middle of construction, the first new houses to be built on Kew Green for 100 years. The builder went bust, and the bank that had lent them the money for the development also went into liquidation. But somehow the Beckwiths managed to hang on to them. 'Nothing was selling, so we moved our families into one each,' says John.

The picture that Christmas of 1975 was bleak, but, always the optimist, John decided to go skiing as usual. The FT index was hitting its low of 146. It was not a good holiday. 'I broke my ankle the first morning and when I was tucked up in the hospital I began getting these really heavy threatening phone calls from creditors.' Things were so bad he had to sell his Porsche and a few other expendable assets besides, but they managed to keep the company afloat, if moribund.

They had £5 million borrowed against assets of only £3 million. That meant that they were effectively bankrupt. Their only hope was to convince the banks that they would be able to pay the money back eventually. They approached the two big banks involved, which were National Westminster and the Bank of Scotland. 'We said, "Either we can put the company into liquidation, in which case you will never get your money back, or you can support us and buy out the other creditors",' recalls Peter. These 'other creditors' were the less stable secondary banks that were themselves in financial crisis, like 20th Century Banking and First National Finance. Their youth, energy and optimism won through and they manoeuvred into a position where they had just the two creditors.

For the next year or so their ingenuity was to be tested to the full. 'We did just about anything to say alive,' says Peter. There is the story of the two containers of boots, destined for the Nigerian army, which always makes the Beckwiths grin when they tell it. They had got into the import–export business in a small way. They had bought 45,000 pairs of boots from the Brazilians and sold them to the Nigerian army. When they went to inspect one of the containers there were only left-footed boots inside. They didn't dare look in the other container. 'To this day we don't know if large numbers of the Nigerian army were hobbling around in left-footed boots.' A number of unlikely businesses went through their hands at that time – including a couple of furniture companies and a sausage factory in Cornwall selling sausages to the Royal Navy – all of which kept them solvent.

The 1974 crash taught them not to be greedy and gave them confidence in their ability to survive when older and supposedly wiser heads were going under. Coming at the beginning of their business careers, the crash taught them a number of invaluable lessons.

First, they decided that never again would they borrow from less than impeccable sources. If it hadn't been for NatWest and the Bank of Scotland, the lesser banks would have foreclosed and they would have been forced into liquidation. Secondly, from then on they resolved always to use the best professional advisers. They had seen the wisdom of having everything watertight. Thirdly, they had learned the value of quality. Prior to the crash they had used 'funny little workmen' and whoever they could find to do it cheapest. They discovered that good-quality developments stand a much better chance of selling when things are bad and there are fewer problems afterwards. 'We were lucky,' says Peter. 'We had only been in business for two years so that it was extremely uncomfortable but not disastrous.'

They still believed that their destiny was in property and towards the end of 1975 they managed to get a 45,000 square foot office development off the ground in Leith docks, just outside Edinburgh. They bought the project from British & Commonwealth, who was sick to death of it. But somehow they persuaded the Property Services Agency to take a 60-year lease at reasonable rents and, more importantly, persuaded Scottish Mutual to lend them the money at 10 per cent when base rate was 17 per cent. It was the deal that put them back on the road again. They repaid all the debts on their residential developments, and that, says Peter, was at a time when some of their friends were having to skip the country. As a tribute to their backers in Edinburgh, they renamed the company London & Edinburgh Trust.

From then on, they adopted a tougher, more professional philosophy. They withdrew from residential developments and decided to go for substantial commercial projects. To limit their risk they would pre-fund (i.e. get the money up front) and pre-let, so there was no worry about getting a tenant once the buildings were completed. By early 1976 they were back in serious business. The first big scheme was the redevelopment of the old Manbre & Garton sugar refinery in Hammersmith, funded by Barclays Bank Pension Fund.

The crash taught the Beckwiths to be risk averse. 'My philosophy is to put things in boxes', says John. The company's policy of borrowing money for projects from banks on a 'non-recourse' basis, a practice commonplace on Wall Street, caused a considerable stir in the City. Since then, many property developers have followed the Beckwith's trail.

The redevelopment of the old Billingsgate fish market was the first non-recourse syndicated bank loan ever done in the London market, and was put together by County NatWest, the investment banking arm of National Westminster. Godfrey Bradman of Rosehaugh Stanhope then went on to use County for the funding of Broadgate, the massive office complex being built next to Liverpool Street station in London.

At the time (late 1984), the pre-letting of the 185,000 square foot Billingsgate building to Samuel Montagu (the merchant banking arm of the Midland Bank) was the largest single pre-let ever seen.

Their escape from bankruptcy after the crash also taught the Beckwiths the value of having top people on your side. Both brothers have a deep affection and regard for Bruce Patullo and Sir Thomas Risk at the Bank of Scotland. Lord (Jimmy) Remnant of Touche Remnant is another favourite. 'They are people who will give you a decision in 24 hours,' says John admiringly. Between 1977 and 1980, LET successfully undertook a number of medium-sized projects with the help of still nervous institutions, whom they persuaded to back them with a mixture of charm, energy and bullying.

Then, in 1980, with the Conservatives in power, they increased the pressure. Having learned the merits of joint enterprise through Arthur Bergbaum, they set up two joint companies: one with Balfour Beatty, the building and construction arm of BICC, called London & Metropolitan Estates, and Macwall, formed with another builder, Tarmac. The rationale was that now LET could handle much bigger projects without having either to recruit a large contracting staff or to worry about outside contractors the whole time. London & Metropolitan was eventually so successful that they floated it off, two years after their own debut on the stock market.

LET made its first foray into retail development with Princess Square in Bracknell, a major shopping development; it built the 200 bedroom Ramada Hotel in Reading and redeveloped Fleming House, a stylish office building on Reckitt & Colman's Cherry Blossom site at Chiswick.

By 1982, the company was moving so fast that the brothers needed to talk seriously about making the company public. As their aspirations grew, they found they were now tendering for plum sites in competition with the really big property players like British Land and MEPC. The property establishment did not like it much, but grudgingly conceded them a place in their ranks.

In 1982, against fierce competition, they won the biggest site of their careers so far, when they bought the site of the old Billingsgate fish market in partnership with S. & W. Berisford. It was one of the biggest schemes ever undertaken at the time, although it has since been dwarfed by mega projects like Broadgate at Liverpool Street and their own plans for Spitalfields. Billingsgate was to provide 185,000 square feet of new offices in a twin tower block.

It is now an eye-catching building – light and airy with fountains galore and wall-climber lifts – occupied by Samuel

Montagu, who have dubbed the building affectionately the blue fridge. The old market hall was also designed to provide another 80,000 square feet of space, some office and some retail, which was let to Citicorp.

It was at that time that they – and indeed most property developers – began to pay real attention to good architecture. A new mood was abroad in London, a feeling that property men should not be allowed to repeat the mistakes of the 1960s, when vast rectangular slabs of concrete were thrown up for minimum cost. Centrepoint, in London's Tottenham Court Road, was one of the better examples. Design was becoming the buzz-word in many areas, and property was in the forefront. Prince Charles did much to bring the subject to the public's attention, often to the intense irritation of the professionals.

Peter believes that it was the architectural designs of Covell Matthews Wheatley that won them the Billingsgate project. But he and John can get quite impatient with the wider debate. 'Architecture is very personal and I do not believe that one person or one body can be the arbiter of public taste,' says Peter.

Billingsgate also concentrated their minds about going public. They realised that they had been helped by having a public company, S. & W. Berisford, alongside as a partner. Public companies, they had to concede, had credibility, had status, had clout. There was also the question of their personal wealth. They were making a good living out of the business, but launching the company on the stock market would make them seriously rich. The Beckwiths have never been shy about their enjoyment of money. 'It means I can build my own tennis court, go skiing in comfort and educate my children,' says Peter.

The actual flotation was something of a disaster. They had been advised by de Zoete & Bevan, the stockbroker, to launch the company through a 'tender issue', whereby would-be investors choose a price they will offer for shares above a stated minimum price. The bank then looks at all the offers, and decides on a 'striking' price. All those offering above that price get shares, while those below do not. Unfortunately the government was selling a tranche of Cable and Wireless, the international telecom-munications group, via a tender offer. Although the LET issue was taken up, the demand was far lower than had been expected and investors offered little more than the minimum price of 150p. 'It should have been a straight offer for sale and the striking price should have been lower,' says one observer.

Although they have not used the shares in the company to take over other property companies, the ability to issue paper has fuelled LET's growth. There was a £14 million rights issue in 1985 and at the end of that year they bought properties in St James Street in London for £12 million, paid for by shares. In November 1986 they raised £100 million, through buying an investment trust for paper and then liquidating the trust for cash.

Since the flotation the board has grown, and there are now six full-time directors and three non-executives. John is chairman and Peter deputy chairman and they have shown a rare ability to build a team of high-calibre people around them.

The joint companies have prospered, and LET has also launched a couple of Business Expansion Schemes, one of them a racquets club with John Gunn, the Chairman of British & Commonwealth. Gunn, who served on the LET board for several years, was also involved in the reshaping of the financial services group, Kellock. LET bought a large stake in Kellock, renamed it Rutland Trust, and brought in Michael Langdon, a former partner from the accountancy firm of Price Waterhouse, to run it. They retain a stake in the company and Langdon is a non-executive director of LET. They also took a small stake in Control Securities, a hotel and property group run by Nazmu Virani, one of the most successful Ugandan Asians operating in Britain.

Like John, Peter Beckwith arrives most mornings at their smart, functional Knightsbridge offices around 8 a.m. and leaves at around the same time in the evening. Their dedication is fuelled by the knowledge that they own a substantial slice of their own business. Even so, being worth over £30 million each doesn't mean they live off meagre salaries. The 1988 accounts showed John earning £357,000 and Peter £350,000. They are both firm believers in the theory that if more of industry was owned by the management there would be many better-run companies.

Despite their racy lifestyle, both brothers are disciplined to the point of fanaticism. To this day they don't eat between meals; in fact biscuits are banned from the LET office in Knightsbridge. As part of their policy of putting back something into society, they have put £2.5 million into a trust for the local community, as part of the Spitalfields scheme.

They are enthusiastic, obsessive sportsmen who like to combine their love of sport with raising money for charity. In 1988 both

Beckwiths, John's wife Heather and seven other LET directors ran in the London Marathon as part of a team of 26, raising a total of £450,000 for Great Ormond Street Hospital.

They have always been highly competitive with each other, regarding it as healthy. Apart from the Great Bitter Lake incident, Peter pulled other little stunts on his young brother such as feeding him poison berries when he was 5 and ringing doorbells and then running off, leaving John to face the music.

Outsiders often wonder how they run the company without falling out. The key to their working relationship is that they have different talents. 'Peter's always been good with languages and people but not very good at figures. Maths was always my strong point,' says John. At first John used to do all the deals, leaving the administration to Peter. These days, Peter likes to be actively involved, although they tend to divide the projects between them. The intensely complex negotiations with the various local authorities and the City of London planners for the Spitalfields market scheme have been left almost entirely to Peter. According to business colleagues, he is by far the more patient of the two.

Peter is more honest than John about the relationship between them. 'We are like chalk and cheese,' he says simply. They have their own circles of friends and different interests (apart from a joint passion for tennis and skiing). Peter enjoys reading books, while John likes golf, which Peter loathes.

It is a relationship of tension. 'They talk to each other about most things,' says Stuart McDonald, who joined the company as finance director in 1985 and is now a joint managing director. 'But every now and again one of them gets possessive about an idea . . . Peter tends to be softer when it comes to financial deals, whereas John will always try and get the last penny out of it. But Peter is much better with people.'

According to fellow directors, John is the strategist and philosopher of the two, while Peter enjoys chasing a project. They share tremendous physical stamina. Peter thinks nothing of lunching in Frankfurt, dining in Paris and flying back to London the same night. Although Peter does not enjoy the financial nitty-gritty as much as John, he relishes creating a new scheme and works tirelessly with planners and architects.

They are, however, outspoken with each other. Having been brought up to believe that sulking was the worst crime of all, they say what they think. If it happens to be at a board meeting, well that is tough. The rows have been known to frighten other board members. But once the air is cleared they both claim they forget about it.

Their relationship with the City has also been stormy on occasion. LET, like most new companies, went through a phase when it could do no wrong in the City's eyes. Analysts could see a string of developments that would yield growing profits for years to come, assuming that tenants were in easy supply. Then came the stock market crash in October 1987 and the shares were hammered more than most. One reason was that as a trader–developer, selling all their properties rather than building up an investment portfolio of buildings, they had a relatively small asset backing. The other was a concern that they were diluting their property content with other activities. Institutional investors and stockbrokers' analysts like to know into which category a company falls. LET was a property company and should not, they felt, be messing around with sports and financial services. The Beckwiths are unrepentant and feel that their success in property should allow them to build a wider-based group. John Beckwith, in particular, has begun to feel that pure property is slightly restrictive. 'John has about 900 ideas a day,' says McDonald, who with the rest of the board attempts to sift the good from the mad.

Despite a continuing buoyant property market, the LET share price had not recovered by mid 1989. The situation has been aggravated by what analysts see as the Beckwiths' arrogant and almost hostile attitude to the City. John Beckwith argues that all the projects are soundly funded, usually with fixed-rate money, so although higher interest rates are not exactly welcome, they are far from being in the kind of situation faced by the property world in 1975.

That is true enough, and the company has a core following of City analysts who have a high regard for their abilities. The reason for the low rating of the shares has more to do with underlying 'sentiment' (a measure of confidence) than a cool assessment of the facts. 'The problem is that LET was a bull market stock,' said one analyst. It is also quite a big company and, as in other cases, to travel hopefully was more enjoyable than arriving.

The size of the company means that the hectic growth in profits and assets of the last few years is bound to slow. But the Beckwiths have shown their ability to thrive in an increasingly tough environment.

The British property industry has become intensely competitive over the past four years. The planning authorities relaxed and developers were given a freer hand to reshape Britain's cities. The number of property companies mushroomed as entrepreneurs scrambled aboard the bandwagon. In the City of London itself there have been schemes up for tender of a size no one would have contemplated five years ago. When the Beckwiths were tendering for Billingsgate in 1982, any project of over 100,000 square feet was regarded as large. Now it has to be over 500,000 square feet to be newsworthy. During 1988, the commencement of the vast Canary Wharf scheme, which should provide around 8 million square feet of offices in Docklands, dwarfed anything yet seen. The only company brave enough to take it on was a private Canadian firm, Olympia and York.

LET's most ambitious project to date is the planned redevelopment of the Spitalfields site, and it has brought the Beckwiths into conflict with other companies in the sector, most notably Godfrey Bradman's Rosehaugh. They won the battle for Spitalfields against Bradman. At the time it caused a lot of ill feeling in both companies and is symptomatic of the fierce competition in the industry.

Whatever the personality clashes, and John Beckwith is famous for his lack of tact, LET's track record speaks for itself. The aim now is to grow into a large, dynamic conglomerate with interests in many areas and countries. 'I want to run a huge company making huge amounts of money,' he says only half-jokingly.

LET has operations throughout Europe, in the United States and early in 1987 formed a joint venture company in Hong Kong. The Beckwiths managed to woo Andrew Denman, the chief operating officer of Hongkong Land, away to run the Hong Kong company.

The prospect of a formally unified Europe in 1992 offers new possibilities in an area where LET is ahead of the game. These countries now need new, efficient buildings if they are to compete with the rest of the world. 'We got stuck into Europe two to three years ago,' says Peter. Peter Beckwith believes that, apart from the Dutch, British property companies are the most progressive and best organised in Europe. 'The antiquity of the buildings in Germany is staggering,' he says. There is also plenty of scope left for them in Britain, particularly if the government decides to tackle the problem of the decaying infrastructure and hand some of the road and bridge building to the private sector.

The Beckwiths have not enjoyed the City's loss of confidence in their company, but they are convinced it is temporary and will continue to expand in the way they believe makes sense. Leisure and financial services are natural bedfellows and there is every reason why those sectors should grow as a proportion of the overall business. The high interest rates of 1989 put a damper on the whole property sector; but the Beckwiths are long-term strategists.

John Beckwith has his heart set on becoming a Lord Hanson of the 1990s, although he intends to build the company organically, through nurturing young companies and continuing the proven formula of joint venture, rather than through buying other companies. 'Whenever I look at a potential acquisition, I always find it is too expensive,' he says smiling. 'We are starting small businesses all the time – and some of them will grow into big businesses.'

MAKING
THINGS

Name: Alan Sugar

Title: Chairman and Chief Executive of Amstrad plc

Born: 1947, Hackney, London

Education: Local state schools

Qualifications: 8 'O' levels, 2 'A' levels

First Job: 1965, trainee statistician, Ministry of Education

First Business Venture: 1968, set up Amstrad with £100 to supply TV aerials to retailers

Family: Married Ann Simons in 1968; they have two sons and a daughter

Made First Million: In 1980, when Amstrad floated on the stock market making Sugar worth over £2 million

Amstrad Produced First Home Computer: 1984, launched the CPC464 selling at £299

Produced First Word-Processor: 1985, launched the PCW8256

Awards: 1984, Guardian Young Businessman of the Year; 1988, awarded Doctor of Science by the City University; 1987, Amstrad named as Britain's most profitable company by Management Today; 1988, named as Britain's most efficient company by the Sunday Times

Most Exciting Moment: When Amstrad floated on the stock market

Hobbies: Tennis, watching TV

Latest Salary: 1988 – £130,000

Personal Stake: 43.9 per cent, worth £180 million

Latest Company Statistics: Year to June 1988 – sales: £620 million; profits: £160 million

Chapter X

Alan Sugar
AMSTRAD

*'Pan Am takes good care of you,
Marks & Spencer love you, Securicor
cares. At Amstrad, we want your
money.'*

Alan Sugar, the founder and chairman of Amstrad, the company that brought personal computers to the masses and self-doubt to IBM, is a simple man. He thinks of a product, gets the people to make it for a knockdown price, finds the punters to buy it and away he goes. It is an approach that has given him the largest market share in word-processors and home computers in Britain and a company at one time worth over £1 billion. Although you would never guess it to look at him, he owns nearly half of it, which made him the fifteenth richest man in Britain in March 1989.

There have been two keys to Sugar's success. The first is that he hit new 'price points' in a product, making it so cheap that the market multiplied dramatically. The prime example of this was the Amstrad word-processor. But because his purchasing was so astute, the profit margins were still wider than those of the competition. The second is that he understood that the public likes simplicity. From the early Tower music centre, he packaged his products into complete units using one plug. There is no shopping around for extras after the initial purchase.

'Alan Sugar doesn't suffer fools at all,' wrote the *Investors Chronicle*. The *Evening Standard* called him the 'Brentwood Bruiser', while much is made of his furrowed brow, which is put down to the 'result of a perpetual frown'. His brusque manner, particularly with City analysts, customers who don't pay on time and journalists who get it wrong, is as legendary as his marketing genius.

The problem originated at the beginning of his City career, when the company was launched on the stock market in 1980 by Kleinwort Benson, the merchant bank. Sugar failed to convey his potential right from the start. 'He was very diffident, almost in awe of the City. He was selling derivative products and he seemed to have no winning formula – he just wasn't very impressive,' remembers one journalist.

Over the last couple of years he has shown just the slightest signs of mellowing. But for most his startling career he has been described as abrasive, aggressive, down to earth, and blunt – all polite ways of saying he can be bloody rude.

All those column inches devoted to his personality have tended to detract from his brilliance and outstanding achievements. Perhaps because he recognised this, 1988 became a year of 'glasnost', one of granting interviews to the Financial Times, which rewarded him by dubbing him 'the wizard of British industry for most of the 1980's', and talking to the City University Business School, where he received one of the warmest receptions ever. He also appeared on the Wogan show and on a mercifully brief series of television ads exhorting British firms to embrace business in Europe. He has even become interested in charity, setting up the Alan Sugar Foundation, which gives money to a number of charities including the Great Ormond Street Hospital to which he has given £25,000. Amstrad also sponsored the annual pro-celebrity tennis night for muscular dystrophy at the Albert Hall in June 1989, where Sugar played Richard Branson. Industry associates do not seem to feel he is, as yet, throwing the Sugar millions around, but it is indicative of his broadening horizons.

It could be that posterity is beginning to feature in his life. 'Alan went through a phase where he was almost ambivalent about the future, but in the last two years he has become obsessed with the need to become more and more successful,' says one of his customers.

To be cynical, it could also be that 1988 proved to be the toughest year for Amstrad since the company floated in 1980. A shortage of 'memory' microchips, production delays of the new personal computer, delivery problems on the audio side and a sticky start to distribution in West Germany all conspired against Sugar. For the first time ever he had to announce a downturn in profits, which fell from £90.1 million to £75.3 million in the half-year to 31 December 1988. Analysts were predicting a dramatic fall in profits for the year to June 1989, from £160 million in 1987–8. City concern was such that in the year to August 1989, Sugar saw the worth of his company more than halve. His personal stake tumbled in value by £400 million. Talking about the tougher times, a new, almost humble Alan Sugar emerged. 'We made some bad mistakes. I don't really know why so many things went wrong at the one time,' he said, although he promised the group would be firing on all cylinders in the new year. It seems unlikely that the company that emerged two years running as Britain's most efficient company in the *Sunday Times*/P–E Inbucon Business Index of 250 quoted companies will falter for long.

Born in 1947, Sugar has passed 40 and shows signs of wanting to create a dynasty. One of his sons is working in the business, while another son works at Dixons, Amstrad's biggest customer.

Anyone meeting Sugar in the street would be amazed to be told he was worth nearly £200 million. Sugar does not look rich. Plain shirts with white collars are worn with the top button undone and the tie pulled loose. Medium height and stocky he looks like Joe Bloggs with a beard. His shoes are slip-on with a crocodile insert and toggles. Aesthetics are clearly not something to which he gives a lot of thought.

Sugar has resolutely refused to move his operations to central London, preferring to stay in Brentwood in Essex, an ugly strip of a town with a surprising number of florists, just 40 minutes from Liverpool Street, British Rail permitting. However, he has had the unprepossessing 1950s headquarters building refurbished and, for the first time in twenty years, he now has a large office to himself.

In the carpeted entrance visitors are asked to 'sign in' on an Amstrad personal computer. For those who fail this initiative test, a conventional signing-in book lurks behind the desk. One wonders if he checks up on who manages it.

True to all the reports, Sugar's manner is deliberately terse. Small talk is not on the agenda and his body language says, 'Don't ask me bloody silly questions.' Once asked however, the questions get a straightforward and surprisingly articulate reply.

Sugar likes to get on with what he is good at – running the business – and he makes it clear that most other things are an irritation.

Yet he clearly relishes having created a big public company and what he himself refers to as 'the marketing success story of the century'. 'Have you ever woken up in the morning and thought "done it"?' asked a television interviewer in 1986. 'I suppose it was when we floated on the stock market in 1980,' replied Sugar. Since then, he feels his greatest achievement was when Amstrad joined the *Financial Times* Stock Exchange 100 index of Britain's largest companies. Sadly, for him, the problems in the first half of 1989 caused the company to dropout of the 'Footsie', as it is called in the City.

Sugar, more than any of the other people in this book, values personal wealth and the security and control over his destiny that it gives him. Owning 43.9 per cent of the company not only makes him worth nearly £200 million pounds, it also means no one can take it away from him.

'In the early days I needed money and security,' he admits. When the company was floated he became worth £2 million overnight, but even that didn't seem a great deal to Sugar. Part of his distaste for making acquisitions for shares is that it would dilute his holding. 'I want Amstrad to become a very big company from organic growth,' he says.

He is not much interested in prestige or socialising, although he did accept an invitation from the Queen to visit Buckingham Palace. 'I thought they must have something wrong with their telly,' he joked at the London City Business School. Even Sugar could not refuse the lure of royalty. 'It was an offer I couldn't refuse.' Mainly, though, he likes to stay at home with his family in the evening and watch 'rubbish TV' or play tennis.

He claims to have balance in his life, working from 8.30 in the morning to 7 at night and hardly ever at weekends. People who know him well, however, report that he has little interest in anything outside the business.

The myth of Alan Sugar's rags to riches story has become distorted in the telling. The popular version is that he was a poor East End lad who left school at 16 with hardly any qualifications and sold car aerials off the back of a van in a street market. One day he discovered how to make half-price word-processors and conquered the world.

The truth is that, although a late developer, Sugar was very bright at school, particularly in the sciences, which explains his grasp of electronics and technology. After scraping through the 11+ the second time round, Sugar went to one of the first comprehensive schools in Britain, Brookhouse School in Hackney. He was placed in the accelerated stream, so that when he left at the age of 17 he had eight 'O' levels and two 'A' levels in physics and chemistry to his credit.

His selling aptitude had also emerged in the playground. According to Sugar's parents, the headmaster declared that he could sell anything from a matchstick to a motor car.

Sugar had a tough, poor but fairly typical working-class Jewish upbringing in Hackney, in East London. His father, Nathan, was a tailor in a clothing factory and his mother brought up the four children, of which Sugar was the youngest. He has two sisters and a brother.

By the time he was 16 he was earning more from working in his spare time than his father. 'It wasn't saying a lot, considering how much he was paid,' says Sugar with a hint of bitterness. The money came from 'skivvying in a greengrocers' doing jobs like boiling beetroot. On Sundays he took photographs of family gatherings and as a sideline bought 100-yard reels of surplus 35mm film and sold them to friends. The idea sprang from his interest in photography and, he says, like the job in the greengrocers, was just for pocket money. It seems he had worked out that money was the means of escape from a harsh environment as well as a way of feeling secure.

When he left Brookhouse School he took a job as a trainee statistician in the Ministry of Education. It was not a propitious start for one of Britain's best-known entrepreneurs and he lasted precisely three months. 'There were no professionals in the family and people around me seemed to think the Ministry of Education would be secure and would use my qualifications. But really I was just a clerk.'

After that he went to a private company called Richard Thomas and Baldwin, now part of British Steel. It was much the same story there, except that some of the older men took a liking to him and encouraged him to get out, possibly into sales. 'They didn't want me to be stuck in the same sort of rut that they were,' he says. He was already displaying the incredible restless energy which has characterised his career. Never do one job if you can do two or three, seemed to be his motto.

His next stop was a sales job with a company called Robuck Electrical, which sold tape-recorders. Finally he wound up as a salesman for a firm of electrical wholesalers, selling, among other things, television aerials. But before long, the young Sugar realised he could do what the company was doing himself and make a lot more money. 'I didn't feel I was being rewarded very well.' Having made the contacts with the retailers, he broke loose, bought a van for £80 and a pile of aerials and began selling them to his former customers. Contrary to the story that has appeared several times in print, he did not sell them in street markets; in fact, with his kind of personality, he probably wouldn't have lasted five minutes. Essentially Amstrad was set up with £100.

People have trouble understanding how Sugar got from selling aerials to running one of the most successful and controversial companies in the country in twenty years. At the London City Business School he told it dead-pan. 'We sold the first lot of aerials and then we went back for some more. There was a rust problem so we bought an automatic greasing machine. Then we went back for some more aerials. Then we mounted them in a plastic pack and went back for some more.' There was a pause. 'And then my uncle died and left me £20 million.' The audience duly cracked up.

The truth is more interesting. Sugar called his company Amstrad – short for Alan Michael Sugar Trading – short and to the point. By the time he got married he was buying and selling turntable accessories and the business was thriving. 'He spent a lot of time selling tertiary products,' says a competitor sourly. The year before it came to the market, the company made £1.4 million before tax, a substantial sum for a private company.

But it was not until the flotation in 1980 that the dramatic growth started. Until 1989 the company almost doubled profits every year, a phenomenal record by any standards. Almost unbelievably, in view of how Amstrad is regarded today, the company did not produce a personal computer until 1984.

Amstrad's extraordinary rate of growth has not, in the main, been fuelled by acquisitions like most of the other companies in this book. On the whole, Amstrad's growth has come quite simply from spotting gaps in traditional markets, and going for it hell for leather, undercutting any competition by miles. 'Alan is a visionary,' says Stanley Kalms of Dixons. The acquisitions that Sugar has made have been logical add-ons. And there has been the occasional master stroke like buying out the genius of Sir Clive

Sinclair. In April 1986 he bought the Sinclair brand name and the intellectual property rights of Sinclair Research plus stocks for just £16 million. It was a unique link between a brilliant inventor and a mass producer.

In 1980, Sugar was very much an unknown quantity and he did not go out of his way to win friends. There were few in the City who rated his abilities very highly, or who had an inkling about the potential of this gruff East Ender.

Looking back, the return on sales (the profits divided into the sales) should have given a clue that here was no financial dummy. In 1980, profits before tax were £1.4 million on sales of £8.8 million, a ratio of 16 per cent, which is well above the average for a company in manufacturing where the average is under 10 per cent. By 1987, helped by the increased financial clout with both suppliers and customers, that ratio had improved to 26 per cent. Sugar is not a manufacturer in the strictest sense. He is an assembler, a packager of parts bought from different parts of the globe, including, increasingly, the United Kingdom.

His early experience in the electrical industry had already shown him there were gaps in the market. At the time, the microchip was in its infancy and the Barber boom of the 1960s was still in full swing. He realised that electrical consumer durables were going to be an explosive market and he aimed to be part of it. One of his early ventures was to manufacture and sell tinted plastic turntable covers for hi-fis. From there he went into the mainstream hi-fi market.

He soon discovered that if you wanted to keep your prices lower than the competition it was difficult to manufacture in the United Kingdom, particularly if you were a small company. He also noticed that all the parts came from Japan. 'We would order components from Plessey and when they arrived it was clear they came from Japan. So it seemed sensible to go to Japan direct,' says Sugar.

The Far East was beginning to emerge as a powerful manufacturing force, but with much lower labour costs. He was still in his early twenties when he made his first visit to Japan. At that time the Japanese were in the process of taking on the Swiss in the watch market and beginning to worry Western car manufacturers.

The Japanese were almost as amazed by Sugar as he was by them. When he came through passport control and introduced himself to the waiting Japanese executive, it was assumed that his father was right behind. They could not believe that someone so young was running a company. He was impressed, especially with the relentless Japanese efficiency, and has remained so. But he also recognises their faults. 'They are just like machines, like ants. There is no innovation, flair or flexibility in the way they work. But as long as a mass market awaits they will provide the best product to meet it,' he says.

Sugar's early visits to Japan taught him about reliability of delivery and attention to detail. 'When the Japanese talk about the colour white they send you a colour card with 25 shades of white on it and ask you to choose,' he says.

Sugar realised that the way to undercut the competition was to have the goods made in the Far East and import them into Britain. He negotiated hard bargains with his Far Eastern suppliers right from the start. As haggling is part of the Eastern culture, they respected this boy from London who insisted on beating them down to rock-bottom prices.

For his first word-processor he found a Japanese supplier with 3 inch discs, instead of the more usual 5 inch, willing to sell at a keen price. The discs have become part of the Amstrad package for the PCW8256 models.

Amstrad is now renowned for its teams of buyers who scour the Far East and the rest of the world for the lowest-price product and the best deals. The sophisticated electronic components come from Japan, the rest of the package from places like Hong Kong, Korea and Taiwan.

Karen Russel, one of Amstrad's young design coordinators, told the *Reader's Digest*: 'We are very price-oriented here. We never accept the first price, rarely the second. We hold out for the very bottom. That's Amstrad's way of thinking.'

Sugar also understood that what the non-technical consumer wanted was a simple package with everything in it. When he started making hi-fis, all hi-fis then on sale came in several bits – turntable, tape player and speakers. He brought out the first British music centres, an idea copied from the Japanese, but then Sugar has never claimed to be a pioneer in technology. His expertise is marketing. 'We are known for identifying niche markets and expanding them into mass markets,' he says with some pride.

The Tower hi-fi was an early example. The all-in-one tuner, tape deck and turntable was his first outstanding success. And he, more than anyone, understands how to capitalise on his successes. With the packinging of several electronic functions in one product he knew he was onto a winner. 'At the time that kind of product was out of the price range of most ordinary people, so I produced something they could afford.'

He began to apply to the formula to a wide range of electronic consumer durables. In-car stereo systems, clock radios and twin-deck cassette players followed. All of these products undercut the competition's prices by miles. In an increasingly materialistic and status symbol conscious Britain, what people cared about was owning the latest consumer durable, not who made it.

When Amstrad came to the stock market, sponsored by the stockbroker Greenwell (which has since ceased to exist), the main source of revenue was hi-fi products. In 1984, against all the odds, he made the decision that was to turn the computer world upside down. He launched himself wholeheartedly at the home computer market.

At the time everyone thought he was mad. The market for home computers was extremely fragile, with a number of companies struggling to stay afloat. All the systems on the market used the householder's existing television screen and comprised complex trailing wires and at least two plugs.

Sugar reckoned that if you packaged an independent terminal screen, keyboard and disc drive at a low enough price, the public would come flocking.

They did. The first model, called the CPC464, sold at just £299, less than half the nearest rival. The public couldn't wait to give him their money, and within a year Amstrad had sold over 200,000 of them through chains like Dixons and Comet. The next step was to add a word-processing function and a printer. Hey presto, there was a word-processing, which dramatically increased the size of the market. In September 1985, under a year from its conception, the PCW8256 was launched. Nicknamed Joyce after his then secretary, Joyce Kayley, it was a huge success, and sold at £399, a quarter of the price of the nearest competition. The word-processing programme was written by Chris Hall, who had his own company. Called Locoscript it had some early problems, which have since been refined and improved. Although it was far from user friendly, the price won the day, delighting both Sugar and his retailers.

'I have never seen a product walk out of the shop like this one,' said Stanley Kalms, the chairman of Dixons at the time of its launch. Kalms is one of Amstrad's biggest customers and has also become a friend over the years. As both are tough bargainers and work on short fuses the relationship has been squally, but Kalms has great regard for Sugar. 'I think he has extra-special genius. He thinks a problem through and he listens. He is always seeking to expand himself in business.'

Personal popularity is something Sugar can live without. In the early years of Amstrad, he was often compared to a barrow boy – something he is not at all unhappy about. 'Marketing is just like a stall in Petticoat Lane market,' he told *International Management* in 1987. 'The sales pitch, though very rural and loud, is no different from what some high-cost advertising agency might apply.'

He is master of the brusque reply. More importantly, he is the entirely self-made man. He can afford to be arrogant. After all, he has built up Amstrad from scratch, and has revolutionised the lives of millions of writers, journalists and small businessmen along the way. From nowhere he won over 40 per cent of the UK market for home computers, much of that at the expense of the American world leader IBM, which has taken to trying to produce machines that Amstrad can't 'clone'. Although IBM is still leading the field in personal computers used in commercial environments, it has virtually withdrawn from the home computer market in the United Kingdom.

Talking to Sugar, it is evident that at one level he is still trying to prove himself. 'No shareholder could ever turn round and say I've sold him down the river,' he said defensively in 1988, a remark that echoed strangely in 1989 after the dive in the share price.

Some of his insecurity may stem from his stormy relationship with the City and the business press. Sugar has had several run-ins with the press, particularly the computer press, which may well have been fed stories bby his competitors. The most notable example was when the first IBM compatible personal computer was launched at the end of 1986. The story got around that the machine overheated because, unlike other machines of its kind, it did not have a fan. A story in the *Sunday Times* said that ICI was rumoured to be rejecting the machine because of the overheating worries, and there was a long and potentially damaging press campaign which coincided with him selling 5 million shares. The combination sent the share price into free fall.

Sugar still maintains firmly that the machine did not need a fan, but the 'dirty tricks brigade' had done too much damage. 'So we said, they want a fan, we will give them a fan. And if they want pink spots, we will give them those also.'

Fast-growing companies in untried product areas tend to be viewed with suspicion by the young men and women who make their living in the City as stockbrokers' analysts and their customers, the fund managers. Because of their quite obvious lack of faith in his ability to keep doubling his profits year after year, Sugar decided for a while simply not to communicate with them. As a result he continually produced profits way over what they had forecast; they were made to look foolish and took revenge by putting out yet another circular saying that this kind of performance was unsustainable. Any industry gossip that a new product was not performing or was faulty was seized on and usually passed on to the press.

For most of Amstrad's life as a public company, Sugar failed to generate goodwill among the investment community and the press. On the one hand, he viewed them as inconsequential parasites, but on the other he was infuriated by their lack of understanding. Two years ago that began to change, mainly due to his bringing in some professional public relations advisers.

The analysts now visit Brentwood when the results come out, and Sugar has been persuaded to go to some lengths to explain the company. As the results kept coming through with profit rise after profit rise, the analysts learned to respect him. When he did finally disappoint, City followers were reasonably kind. And he became more open than ever before. He has even managed to establish a good relationship with the financial press, notably David Thomas on the *Financial Times*.

One justifiable worry City investors had about Amstrad was what would happen if Sugar ever walked under a bus. Sugar is undeniably the driving force at Amstrad. He is fond of saying that it is the company that he wants to be well known – as well known as Coca-Cola or Sony – rather than him personally. Sugar stresses that he has built a strong team around him and a definable corporate culture. But, like an orchestra without a conductor, without him the company would quickly lose direction. Nevertheless, observers agree that the philosophy of the company is crucial to its success. When the company made its stock market debut there was already a tangible corporate spirit. 'In our company, we attract people that either catch on very quickly, or they last two minutes,' Sugar is fond of saying.

People are expected to take risks and make swift decisions. 'When an executive joins Amstrad, they see their colleagues using innovative ways and methods to achieve their tasks, not conforming to the standards that are written down in the books,' says Sugar. He openly preaches a gospel of cutting corners, taking a few risks and persuading the rest of the team to come along. The rule is that there are no hard and fast rules.

Take credit control. Sugar reckons that if Amstrad had stuck to conventional credit control criteria the turnover would be half what it is today. 'You have to look at the customer, assess him and behave accordingly,' he says. For example, a small Spanish company called Indescomp approached him a few years back saying they wanted to distribute Amstrad products in Spain. They were wildly enthusiastic but they were under-funded. Although at Sugar's insistence they paid for the first consignment up front, they quickly ran out of money. They went back and told him exactly that. Sugar was so impressed by their honesty and keenness that he decided to give them a lot more credit than would normally be deemed prudent. 'It was this candour and a feeling that you can't learn from books that sparked off something in my mind to back these boys,' he says. Today those men are running Amstrad's highly successful Spanish subsidiary, now called Amstrad Espana, which has well over 50 per cent of the Spanish word-processor market.

Sugar does not like the term entrepreneur, but he can live with it. 'It is a lot better than what Stanley Kalms calls me, not to mention Uncle Clive,' he told the City University Business School. In the main body of his speech he pinpointed four essential qualities for an entrepreneur running his own business. He should:

1. Lead like a captain steering the ship;
2. Identify potential opportunities in both products and markets;
3. Identify the danger signs and how to avoid them;
4. Overcome obstacles, set-backs and hold-ups.

It all sounds refreshingly simple, but like most simple things it is gruelling to put into practice. And it does not include Sugar's own visionary genius and his natural sense of timing. Sugar's own regard for his managers is not always upheld outside the company. 'They are like him in manner; they think it is smart to be rude, but they lack his ability,' said one business associate.

Sugar is, to put it mildly, strong on the work ethic and he has scant regard for anyone who isn't. 'There are those who are happy to be non-achievers all their lives, who get buried in big corporations. Then there are others who are I suppose like me who never expect anything for nothing. That is the type we at Amstrad attract. I suppose they are called Alan Sugar clones.' In mid-1988 there were seven 'Sugar clones' each doing the work of around five people according to Sugar.

'If a competitor of similar size could see how we operate on a narrow skeleton of decision makers, they would be amazed,' says Sugar. He is convinced that the main problem in British industry is that nobody makes decisions.

Amstrad executives are in sole charge of their divisions, which may be tough on them, but it helps with the decision-making. The only way decisions seem to be made at Amstrad is fast. This company is not one for memos. 'Memos would slow us down,' says Sugar. Instead messages get shouted across the floor. Other things that would slow him down are talking too long and hard before making a decision. 'We are doers,' says Malcolm Miller, Amstrad's sales and marketing director. 'If you have a good idea, every day you waste talking about it is a day's lost profit.'

Product manager Anthony Sethill, aged 28, could not believe it when shortly after joining the company he came up with the idea for a new product. 'Before I could turn round, Alan came to see me, asked me a bit more about it and said, "Great, let's go for it." '

People like Sethill find tremendous excitement in working for Sugar – despite the unglamorous surroundings at the Brentwood offices. 'There's a real sense of excitement around the place and it's exhilarating to be part of it,' he says.

Amstrad managers obviously like it as they stick around. Jim Rice, who is group operations director, has been with the company for eleven years. 'We are all driven by the need to be successful,' he agrees.

What if one of the managers doesn't come up to scratch? Sugar looks puzzled. 'It's not a question of them not coming up to scratch,' he says. 'If things are not going well we know quickly and address the problem.' Amstrad executives tend to be home grown and get spotted early on. He has two women directors, not because he has any strong feminist feelings, but simply because if they can do the job better than anyone else they get it. Callen So is a stunningly attractive Chinese woman who became the sales and marketing director for the Far East at the age of 27. She joined Amstrad as a secretary at 19. 'She is mustard. I'd match her against any businessman in the world,bz' Sugar told the *Financial Times*. She has now joined Sugar full time in Brentwood, masterminding the sourcing world-wide and working on production.

Sugar believes wholeheartedly in hands-on management. At Brentwood he prowls around the offices, asking questions, checking on progress. For a long time he conducted operations from a battered armchair in the middle of an open-plan office, simply shouting at the other managers. These days, he sits in relative splendour with a Topic screen in front of him to keep abreast of what is going on in the City. But he is still very much seen and heard around the building.

The Brentwood offices may not seem appropriate for an international billion-pound giant. But they keep the company's feet on the ground, not to mention those of his executives. In 1988, when the group celebrated a 67 per cent rise in profits, the group still only directly employed 1,000 people, including those in the growing number of overseas subsidiaries.

One of Sugar's alleged obsessions is efficiency. 'I can't stand inefficiency in anything,' he has been known to say. His customers, however, reckon he is no better than average, with the normal amounts of bits and pieces failing to arrive with the main machine. But he certainly tries hard. He has always had the tightest management controls and is all too aware of the problems that sheer size can bring. He is determined to avoid bureaucracy if Amstrad is not to become 'like all the rest of those companies'. In his 1988 chairman's statement in the annual report he stated: 'A major part of our success is our management philosophy which dictates that we have a small team of flexible decision makers with none of the bureaucracy to be found in some companies with half our turnover.' He points out that the management team did not increase in proportion with the sales volume and profits.

However, he is well aware that the company has to change as it grows. At the City University talk he said: 'We recognise that as we grow we need to put in place more layers of management, control systems and a lot of other paraphernalia. The problem is that the whole machine can lose its speed and direction. We are addressing that.' At the end of the day, though, he feels it all comes down to management attitude, 'We have a small management team that can see the wood for the trees.'

Sugar is not worried about running out of growth potential. 'If we were as big in every major country as we are in Britain, we would be three times the size of General Motors.' But he does acknowledge that things are different in different countries. 'We have to learn to mould our culture to overseas markets. In the United Kingdom, £2 million will give you a decent size national advertising campaign. In the US, £2 million spent in one state won't even make you blink.'

On the other hand, he won't be drawn into fancy advertisements, wherever the company goes. He is not interested in his ads winning awards; he is interested in them selling products. 'We tell them about the product, tell them how much it is and where to buy it.'

Sugar set up his Hong Kong company as far back as 1981 and that was followed by a French subsidiary in 1982. Growth was going so fast in the United Kingdom that it wasn't until 1986 that companies were set up in Spain and Italy. The latest foray into Germany, where Amstrad set up in its own right at the beginning of 1988, was something of a disaster. Initially Sugar had sold product through a German group, which, when dropped as distributor, dumped its surplus stock on the market, undercutting Amstrad. The problem, however, was of a temporary nature and, as the biggest consumer market in Europe, Germany is clearly the most exciting. Although he believes that a continuing flow of new products will fuel further growth in Britain, he is looking outward. The United States so far has been tough going, something that partly accounts for Sugar's extreme distaste for Americans. 'I've had a bellyful of Americans. The only thing one learns from them is how to be a bullshitter supremo,' he says.

Amstrad's first foray into America is a lesson for any British company. 'We sold our products to the mighty Sears Roebuck – where the left hand does not know what the right hand is doing.' Sears bought the marketing rights, bought several thousand word-processors and forgot about them. Amstrad's big marketing launch in the United States just never happened. Since then he has launched the personal computer with a small but energetic company which he hopes will learn the Amstrad culture. So far, though, it has been uninspiring. 'We are plodding away there and learning about the country,' he says.

One of Amstrad's most controversial ventures has been making a satellite dish for the masses in a joint venture with Rupert Murdoch, the Australian publishing tycoon who revolutionised newspaper production in the UK. Murdoch is making the programmes for Sky Television and Sugar is producing the dishes that receive them for under £200. Unfortunately, production problems meant that very few were available at the time of the Sky launch in early 1989.

Sugar and Murdoch have much in common. Both are controversial figures who have shaken up their own industries, both put profit before most other things, both take huge risks, both have recently hit rough water and both personally own around half of their companies.

Various factors, like the curbing of consumer spending and the downturn in 1989 profits, are conspiring to make Sugar look outwards. His problem is how to move an already large and successful company forward. He has already encountered some of the pitfalls of global expansion and recognises that one step at a time is fast enough. But while he may retreat from the United States for the moment, he is committed to Europe and well aware of the opportunities that a unified market in 1992 will present. To this end he is putting more of his production in Britain and on the Continent. His ambition is to make Amstrad as well known in Europe as Pepsi Cola.

Name: *Nigel Rudd*

Title: *Chairman of Williams Holdings*

Born: *1946, Derby*

Education: *Bemrose Grammar School*

Qualifications: *8 'O' levels, chartered accountant*

First Job: *Articled clerk at R.J. Weston & Co*

Family: *Married Lesley Hodgkinson in 1969; they have two boys and one girl*

Joined Williams: *In February 1982 following an agreed partial takeover bid*

Made First Million: *Through property dealing before joining Williams*

Most Exciting Moment: *Purchase of J. & H.B. Jackson*

Awards/Honours: *Director of East Midlands Electricity, trustee of Bishop of Derby's urban fund, governor of Derbyshire College of Further Education*

Hobbies: *Shooting, golf, squash, tennis*

Drives: *BMW 750*

Personal Stake: *£6 million*

Latest Salary: *£403,000*

Latest Company Statistics: *1988 – sales: £826 million; profits: £116 million*

Name: *Brian McGowan*

Title: *Chief Executive of Williams Holdings*

Born: *1944, Chiswick*

Education: *Isleworth Grammar School*

Qualifications: *7 'O' levels, chartered accountant*

First Job: *Articled clerk at Edward Moore & Sons*

Family: *Married Julia Brock in 1966; they have two boys*

Joined Williams: *In February 1982 following an agreed partial takeover bid*

Made First Million: *In 1985, as a result of the rising Williams share price*

Most Exciting Moment: *Purchase of J. & H.B. Jackson*

Awards/Honours: *None*

Hobbies: *Salmon and trout fishing*

Drives: *BMW 750*

Personal Stake: *£2 million*

Latest Salary: *£403,000*

Latest Company Statistics: *1988 – sales: £826 million; profits: £116 million*

Chapter XI

Nigel Rudd
and Brian McGowan

WILLIAMS HOLDINGS

'I felt I was really just a well-paid
dogsbody and I asked myself where
I was going to be in 10 years' time.'
(Nigel Rudd)

In February 1982 two young accountants called Nigel Rudd and Brian McGowan launched a takeover bid for a tiny Welsh engineering company called W. Williams & Sons. The company was losing money at the rate of £1 million a year and its bankers were within days of putting it into receivership. The bid valued the company at less than £900,000.

Six years later, Rudd, the man who many reckon could be the Lord Hanson of the 1990s, and McGowan took that same company into the *Financial Times* Stock Exchange Index of Britain's 100 largest companies. Its 1988 profits had risen to £116 million and were heading towards £160 million in 1989, its market value was over £1 billion and its share price had multiplied more than 30 times in the intervening period. What had been a family-controlled maintenance and refurbishment subcontractor for British Steel had been transformed as Williams Holdings into a powerful household products and engineering combine embracing brand names like Crown and Berger paints, Polycell and Rawlplug do-it-yourself products, Swish curtain tracks and Smallbone luxury kitchens. It had also become one of Britain's leading retailers of prestige cars, a world leader in aerospace fire detection and suppression devices and Europe's top manufacturer of 'micro' switches.

The story of Rudd and McGowan is an extraordinary tale of corporate growth by acquisition. It began with small purchases of bankrupt or semi-bankrupt companies, the detritus of the great industrial recession of the early 1980s. But within a few years Rudd and McGowan were negotiating with some of the largest companies in the world, like Hoechst, the West German chemicals giant, and Britain's Reed International.

It is also a story of how two young men from lower-middle-class backgrounds were pushed by their parents into accountancy because 'you never see a poor accountant', but used accountancy disciplines to vault themselves into a world well beyond the modest ambitions of their families. For Rudd and McGowan, accountancy became much more than just an entry ticket into the comforts of 'professional' salaried employment. It became a passport into some of the most powerful corporate boardrooms in the country. What began as a professional friendship built on shared concern about the state of industry in the late 1960s and 1970s developed into a partnership that has turned Williams into one of Britain's most respected companies. 'As entrepreneurs Rudd and McGowan are both extremely capable in their own right, but together they make a virtually unbeatable combination,' says one merchant banker. 'They are perfect foils for each other. Rudd is the ideas man. He will ask "What if we do such and such?" while McGowan is a shrewd judge of what is or is not possible.'

Williams was one of those classic family companies that had been savaged by the recession. Peak profits for the company, which was founded in 1957, totalled around £300,000. In the late 1970s, the Welsh Development Agency had propped it up by taking a substantial stake. It must have looked an unattractive vehicle from which to build a big business. But Rudd and McGowan in 1982 were in no position to be choosy. Their ambitions were limited by their financial resources. Both had been salaried employees for most or all of their working lives and had no inherited wealth.

Rudd was born in Derby on New Year's Eve 1946, the second son of a 50-year-old weights and measures inspector with Derbyshire County Council and his 41-year-old wife. He remembers an upbringing of genteel poverty. What little money his parents did have was spent on 'keeping up standards' in their home and on dressing Nigel and his older brother Graham. Rudd recalls a childhood of intense introspection. His father was too old to relate to him while his mother had no social life at all. 'My mother did not believe in baby sitters,' he recalls, 'and hardly ever went out until I was 14. I was painfully shy.'

Shyness held him back at school initially and he entered the first year of his grammar school in the bottom stream. But his natural intelligence soon started to show through and he quickly moved up through the streams and took his 'O' levels a year early at 15. His teachers reckoned he was Oxbridge material and he was also a talented sportsman, being selected to play tennis for Derbyshire. But Rudd's parents had little interest in their children's academic achievements and his father, on his retirement, took him out of school. He could no longer afford to support him.

His older brother Graham, who now runs another fast-growing public company called Thomas Robinson, had trained as an accountant and the Rudd parents decided an accountancy career would also be appropriate for their second son. 'I remember my mother telling me she had never seen a poor accountant, and there was a feeling in our family that we had to better ourselves through making money rather than through education or the arts.'

Rudd's father was a Freemason and it was through a friend at his Masonic lodge that Nigel was articled to the Derby firm of R.J. Weston & Co. in 1962, qualifying five years later as the youngest chartered accountant in the country. 'It was a tremendous training in the way businesses were run. As an auditor you could see management at the highest level at an early age, and also learn about businesses in the round. As an accountant you see all the departments and you have an effect on each department,' he recalls.

His training as an articled clerk showed him how badly British industry was run in the mid-sixties. 'I could not believe the waste and restrictive practices. I could not believe the state of the equipment and the lack of capital expenditure,' he recalls. 'No money was ever put back into the business. It was all paid out in dividends. The companies were certainly churning out product like there was no tomorrow but no investment was going in. It was too easy to sell bad product at the time and the whole thing was being milked. In effect dividends were being paid out of profits that were not really there.'

Rudd left Weston the day he qualified because he felt the initial salary of £1,000 a year was too low. 'I left for money, which was probably the wrong decision,' he says. 'What I really should have done was go down to London to get some real experience with a big firm of accountants.' His first job was as company secretary with Egan Contractors, an earth-moving and open-cast coal company run by two Irishmen. It was an early experience of crisis management. The company was taken over within a few months of his arrival by London & Northern, then a conglomerate run by Jock Mackenzie, for around £500,000. At the time L&N was viewed in the City as a fashionable or 'go-go' company. But Rudd did the negotiation in a state of complete disbelief that L&N was willing to pay so much for such a small business.

Once the deal had been completed, L&N investigated the company more thoroughly and discovered that Egan had won its business, mainly from the National Coal Board, through fraud. Both of the founders were sacked and one went to jail, leaving the young Rudd at just 23 running the business. The NCB cancelled all its contracts and Rudd was left to do what he could to save the company and restore it to health. His response was to take Egan into the trading of construction equipment, and thanks to the health of the construction industry he was soon making big profits. 'Mackenzie saw I was the only person in the field who had any idea of running businesses,' he recalls, 'and it became a real baptism of fire. I learned how to deal, how to buy and sell, the rudiments of negotiation and how to weigh up people in negotiations. For the next five years I became London & Northern's trouble-shooter, sorting out its construction companies in Ireland and various subsidiaries in the UK. They were awfully run.' He became known as 'the fireman'.

He first encountered McGowan, then a young L&N head office accountant with the title of Assistant Company Secretary, at the completion lunch at the Savoy Hotel after the group's purchase of Egan in early 1969. The two men hit it off almost immediately.

McGowan is also the product of a lower-middle-class upbringing. Born in 1944, he was the first son of an assistant company secretary of a small private company. As is often the case in a story of upward mobility, it was unfulfilled parental ambition that led him to train as a chartered accountant after leaving Isleworth Grammar School with seven 'O' levels. 'I ended up as a chartered accountant because my Dad had wanted to be one. He could not afford to get articles,' he recalls. The young McGowan became the first non-public school boy to become articled to the City firm of Edward Moore. One of his fellow articled clerks was Peter Goldie, who went on to become chief executive of John Gunn's British & Commonwealth Holdings.

But McGowan was not cut out to be an auditor. His ambitions lay in industry, and after five years he left to join Mackenzie's company. 'Moore's biggest client was London & Northern, and I had done a couple of investigations on London & Northern acquisitions and I jumped at the chance of working for him,' he recalls. The six years that followed were a dizzy period for Mackenzie and his company. In the City Mackenzie came to be looked on as a golden boy as he embarked on a flurry of bids and deals that pushed profits from £600,000 when McGowan first arrived to £10 million when he left in 1974. Mackenzie received his fair share of criticism in later years as the profits growth came to a halt, but McGowan's spell at the company proved an excellent apprenticeship for a would-be business builder.

'I learnt that you have to forget about the textbooks. You have to look at figures in an unconventional way. Company accounts are an art not a science and one has to go beyond the bald figures. Above all you have to be flexible in your thinking – and doing deals is not always a question of coming up with the highest price. I remember once we were buying a business from a widow in Scotland. Over a cup of tea I found out that she always had been given a new set of tyres for her car each year by the company. So we agreed to write the annual new set of tyres into the sale and purchase contract – it swung the deal.'

His company doctoring skills were learned from Mackenzie's right-hand man, Jim Barker, a one-armed and unqualified audit clerk who had risen thanks to his shrewd instincts to become London & Northern's managing director. 'Barker could work things out on the back of an envelope. Because he was not trained he had an unconventional way of doing things, but he always knew how much money a deal was going to make,' he says. 'It makes a sharp contrast with these guys in the City with all their computers. They always get things arithmetically right but often miss the point.'

The Mackenzie magic did not last, however. 'Jock had enormous personal charm. He was financially astute and knew what the City wanted. He could therefore get the best out of the Square Mile. Jim Barker meanwhile did the deals,' he says. 'Unfortunately neither of them knew how to run the businesses that they owned. Like so many would-be conglomerate builders of the early seventies they were good dealers but neither of them bothered to manage.'

From 1969 until McGowan's departure in 1974, he and Rudd formed a strong friendship built in part on a shared distaste for what they saw as appalling mismanagement within L&N. For hours and hours, often late into the night or during weekends spent together with their families, they would debate how to run companies properly. Says McGowan, 'We have to admit today that we were given responsibilities way beyond what was sensible. It was a boom period and we were in a boom company so we were given authority way beyond our abilities. But we could learn a lot.'

The number one lesson was that few people are good at both doing deals and running businesses. The dealer looks at the broad picture. If he worries too much about the details of day-to-day management, the deals do not get done. Both Rudd and McGowan agreed they did not have the talents to combine the two. If they were going to build a company, they would mastermind the strategic growth and leave the day-to-day management to the managers in each subsidiary.

The second lesson was to avoid at all costs leaving minority shareholdings in the subsidiary companies, because when problems emerged those minorities would restrict remedial change. Lesson three was to exclude operating managers from the main board, as they would fight for the interests of their businesses at the expense of the company as a whole. Lastly one should never overborrow. When L&N ran out of steam its debts stood at double shareholders' funds. Mackenzie was left boxed in: his rating had collapsed so he could not issue shares, but neither could he buy businesses for cash.

In 1974, at the age of 29, McGowan decided he would seek pastures new and took a job as acquisitions manager for P&O, the shipping and construction group. His boss at the time was Oliver Brooks, the one-legged finance director who later went on to become P&O's managing director. Unlike L&N, P&O was the real City establishment, and working at its City headquarters just off Leadenhall Street taught McGowan the importance of having close links with the financiers. 'I learned that respect in the City was all important,' he recalls. 'P&O was really establishment and I saw that the City was a club and it remains so today. The members may have changed but the rules are the same.'

But once again McGowan got itchy feet and the young accountant became one of the many talented people to leave Britain in the raging inflation of the mid-1970s. 'In 1976 I was 31 and was being paid £17,000 and a car. Inflation was running at 26–27 per cent and I decided I would need a £10,000 rise just to stand still. It was ridiculous: at 31 I felt I was at the peak of my earning ability. Things could only get worse.'

His chance to move overseas came through responding to an advertisement in the *Financial Times* asking for a finance director for China Engineers, a quoted subsidiary of the Sime Darby group based in Hong Kong. It was an exciting time: Hong Kong was booming, and McGowan worked his way up to become managing director of Sime Darby Hong Kong after the parent company bought out the outside shareholders in China Engineers. He was able to use his position in what was a broadly diversified conglomerate, spanning ship owning, motor distribution and food trading, to learn the skills of man management, controls and systems.

While McGowan was gaining broader management experience at Sime Darby, Rudd was becoming increasingly alienated at L&N. One of his last jobs was to sort out a troubled company called Bardolin, a housebuilder that had got into difficulties through poor land purchases. Rudd put the business back onto an even keel but decided he had had enough of L&N. 'I was 30. I felt I had a lot of experience running businesses at the highest level. L&N wanted me to move up to London from South Wales where I had been running Bardolin, but I did not want to. The business was either going to go bust or be taken over and the last place one wants to be when that happens is at the centre. I was spending no time at home but my career was going nowhere either. I felt I was really just a well-paid dogsbody and I asked myself where I was going to be in ten years' time.'

Out of his soul-searching came the decision to launch out on his own. He offered L&N £25,000 for one of Bardolin's small subsidiaries, C. Price & Sons, a loss-making contractor. It had a £150,000 overdraft secured on its development land, the major item in a balance sheet with about £150,000 of net assets. For the next 18 months Rudd and his partner, Roger Edwards, a builder who went on to become deputy chairman of Williams, worked 'night and day' to finish off the contracts, offering staff special bonuses to get the work done quickly. The land was gradually turned into cash and, after some astute property dealing, Rudd and Edwards found themselves sitting on a business worth £1 million. 'Property is a fast way to make money. You can double your money very easily because bankers will lend against it.

They will not lend you money against an idea, but land they can understand.'

However Rudd, whose bonhomie and modesty hide his creativity and flair, was bored. With C. Price tidied up, he spent three months during the summer of 1981 doing virtually nothing. Golf offered some outlet for his energies and his handicap fell from 24 to 12, but he realised he had to do something more challenging and exciting with his life. 'I remember the point at which I knew I had to do something. I was sitting with my second son, Edward, at 5 p.m. on a weekday afternoon watching Magic Roundabout,' he says. 'I recall getting up and saying "This can't go on". The long sabbatical had to come to an end.'

In the autumn of 1981 McGowan came back from Hong Kong to Britain for a holiday, and the two men had dinner on October 3, McGowan's birthday. He was satisfied with his job, but was well aware that as a Briton he would not reach the very pinnacle at the Malaysian-controlled Sime Darby. Julia, his wife, was tiring of expatriate life and was anxious to move back to Britain. McGowan recalls the conversation. 'I said why don't we do what we have always wanted to do: branch out on our own. We would make a good team. I told Nigel I did not want to work for someone else. I was stuck in Hong Kong for the moment so he would have to go out and find our vehicle.'

The 'vehicle' Rudd found was Williams. The family share-holding was for sale, with losses and bank borrowings threatening to overwhelm the company. At the end of October, the pair took their first tour round the company escorted by the managing director, Hewi Williams. It did not take long for it to dawn on them what a mess the business was in. Its core was a big aluminium die-casting plant at Caerphilly, which was both overmanned and desperately short of work. The company could be rescued from bankruptcy only if it was cut in half, but the Williams family did not have the stomach to carry out the necessary surgery, which would involve major job cuts among their old retainers. Barclays Bank was threatening to call in the receivers with £1.3 million of debt outstanding, so talks with the bank were every bit as important as talks with the family shareholders.

The family needs, it soon emerged, were simple: they wanted 25p a share, the same price as they had demanded when the company had been taken public two decades before. Inflation, it seemed, was irrelevant when it came to settling moral debts to friends who had backed them on flotation.

Putting together a strategy that would secure Rudd and McGowan's investment and appease the bank was another matter. Their first move was to draw up an action plan of the kind that Williams now uses on all of its acquisitions: a detailed description of what was required in the first week, the first month, and the first six months, concluding with a description of how the company should end up as an ongoing business, with all four stages backed up with financial analysis. The plan concluded that Williams needed another £1 million of loans on top of the overdraft and they had to persuade Barclays that it should, in effect, throw good money after what looked liked bad.

'We had to get the regional director to persuade London that it was worth a go. At the time a lot of companies were going bust and people were running league tables of receiverships, and plotting which bank was doing the worst,' says Rudd. 'Was the bank going to let another public company go bust? I told them we needed an answer within four days or we would walk away. We were not really offering them a banking proposition. In the end Barclays probably gave us the money for PR reasons.'

The bank squared, the stock exchange had to be persuaded to allow the duo, who were using Rudd's C. Price company as their bidding vehicle, to make a partial offer. In partial offers shareholders get the chance to sell only part rather than all of their investment to the bidding company, so they are normally frowned upon by the financial authorities. Yet the partial offer was critical to their progress. Williams was virtually bust, yet the pair had to offer 25p a share (against a 1981 low of just 10p), a price that most investors would have been only too pleased to accept. But Rudd and McGowan needed a stock market vehicle, and to prevent the stock exchange taking Williams' quotation away they had to stop the takeover being accepted 100 per cent. Had they been forced to make a full offer this would inevitably have happened, and they would have ended up with the entire company. Few City investors would have been willing to accept stock in a bankrupt Welsh engineering company run by two unknown and untested young accountants. The only way around was a partial offer.

The stock exchange was not very happy, but Williams' stockbroker, the Cardiff firm of Lyddon, made the Throgmorton Street officials well aware that the company was days away from receivership. A partial offer for 51 per cent of the shares would at least allow investors to take some money out. In addition,

Rudd and McGowan had the support of the Welsh Development Agency, whose officials were anxious to avoid yet another Welsh financial scandal – the WDA told the exchange it would help the duo by not accepting their bid. This enabled other shareholders to have greater access to cash than would have been the case if the state agency had decided to bolt for the exit.

McGowan knew the risks of what they were doing. 'I thought we could do better but I was desperate. I said I would fly back to Hong Kong to think about it and give Nigel my reply in 48 hours. But when I got back to my office I found a telex saying that the family were going to accept another bid. At that point, when I knew I could not get it, I wanted it. Three days later it emerged that the other party had gone away and we were back in with a chance, and I have often wondered whether Nigel had actually fabricated the telex to get me hooked.'

With McGowan on side, the pair needed a financial adviser willing to act in a bid for a virtually bankrupt company with a market value of under £1 million. It was not the kind of project that would interest a front-line merchant bank. In their desperation they turned to Oliver Brooks of P&O. At the time, P&O owned a small corporate lender called Twentieth Century Banking. It was hardly the most powerful name in the City, but its team of advisers did what was necessary. 'Without TCB we could have never got started,' says McGowan. 'They agreed that we would only pay them a fee if we succeeded.'

TCB demonstrated its skills nine months later when Williams made its first public company acquisition. At the time it had a market value of around £1.5 million and a balance sheet with debts worth three or four times the assets. The target was hardly impressive: a Derby-based castings and manufacturing company called Ley's Foundry & Engineering, which had fallen on hard times as a result of the decline in the British motor car industry. Losses of £4 million had been clocked up over two years but, once again, the family managers were unwilling to perform the radical surgery needed to get it back into profit. In that sense it was similar to Williams. But it had something Williams lacked: a balance sheet free of debt and full of assets like stocks and debtors which could be quickly turned into money. If the Williams pair could combine their entrepreneurial flair with the solidity of Ley's, they would have a real platform from which to expand.

First they had to find the cash, and it was to Twentieth Century Banking that they turned. Williams was hardly a bankable proposition but the P&O subsidiary was willing to put up the funds for the £3.5 million agreed takeover, although Rudd and McGowan had to give personal guarantees of £1 million each, huge sums given their modest resources. 'It certainly concentrated the mind,' McGowan recalls. 'But if we had not had P&O to lend us money on an unbankable deal I don't know where we would be today. Probably scraping around doing little deals desperately trying to get some sort of critical mass. As it was we gained control of an £11 million balance sheet.'

With Ley's the pair also gained control of an intangible asset that, though not quite as bankable as £11 million of stocks and debtors, was to prove equally important in their development: Roger Carr, one of the Derby company's senior sales executives. Carr was a bright grammar school boy who had begun his working career as a computer program analyst with Boots in his home town of Nottingham. He had then left to spend nine years with Honeywell, before deciding that the computer industry was too restricting and that he needed broader management experience.

Carr chose Ley's. It had been a Honeywell user and, though it needed change, he saw it as fundamentally sound. But then the recession struck, and Ley's, still stuck with values of a bygone age, failed to meet the challenges of a far more bracing business climate. Ian Ley would gather his directors round him at lunch, ceremoniously carve a joint in front of them, and get them to converse on pet subjects like cricket or space, but he refused to carry out the restructuring required to bring his company back to health. Ley's had been one of the dominant players in its sector and had used its position to pile up cash, but it could not adapt to changed circumstances. Carr produced a recovery plan designed to restore the company to viability at a cost of a large number of jobs, but the Ley's board would not implement it: the family decided they would have to sell because they could not bear to hack back what previous generations had built up.

It was left to the men from Williams to pick up and implement the Carr plan. Carr himself went on to become head of the Williams 'post-acquisition' team, whose task was to move in and sort out companies after they had been bought. Later his management skills earned him the job of Managing Director.

The post-acquisition team, or 'hit squad' as it became known in the financial press, was at the heart of the Williams strategy. At London & Northern, the pair had learned the importance of separating bids and deals from day-to-day operations. At Williams they decided it was equally necessary to separate post-acquisition work from operations, and after the Ley's deal they found they had the management resources to build up a team that could do the job. Carr and other ex-Ley's men like Chris Davies would be sent in to sort out any problem company within the groups of businesses that Williams started to buy, and the more companies Williams bought the more expert the team became at putting them to rights. They were first and foremost tough. 'Most of them were ex-foundrymen and if you can survive in foundries you have to be very good,' says McGowan. 'After that everything else is a doddle.' But they were not just demolition men – they had to leave behind them a business that could prosper and grow.

In the early eighties they had a big canvas on which to work: Rudd and McGowan would buy up companies full of old buildings and old machinery where morale was low. The hit squad would move in, sell everything from redundant equipment to the oil paintings on the chairman's wall, eliminate bad management and working practices and introduce the sort of elementary housekeeping so lacking in much of British industry at the time. Then came the positive moves, like getting all the offices painted and the factory cleaned up. Says McGowan, 'Suddenly the workers who probably were dreading the takeover of their company, start to like what they see. Generally we tend to get it all done in a fortnight and it has an electrifying effect on the workforce. Suddenly they are more receptive to new ideas. You effectively create a climate for radical change.'

A manager of one of the Williams' companies puts it another way. 'The changes they make are fairly basic. In fact many of them I had wanted to do myself but had not been able to get them past my colleagues. It is often very difficult to force through major and uncomfortable change when you are operationally in charge of a business. After all, you have to live with the consequences in terms of damaged egos. But the hit squad was able to walk in, hack out layers of management, cut back overheads and reduce costs generally. They would give people new responsibilities, set new budgets and then be off. AAfterwards, when people complained to me, I could put the blame on the "hit squad", but say that the goals had been set and now it was time to get on and achieve them.'

Each time a company was taken over, the hit squad went in; and each time the profits were enhanced. Rudd 'brought the entrepreneurial flair, the skill in targeting companies and the ability, second to none, to spot and pursue opportunities,' according to one colleague, while McGowan 'had the clarity of thought and total objectivity necessary in arranging the mechanics of funding the deals.' Neither had any operational ambitions. They did not want to run the businesses they took over, in the sense of making decisions on manufacturing, marketing or product development. Their task was to pick managers capable of doing that and then let them get on with their task, rewarding them handsomely if they succeeded. The responsibilities of the tiny head office were limited to maintaining financial controls and deciding the strategic direction of the company and putting it into force. 'Everybody has head room,' says a colleague. 'Once responsibilities are decided, individuals are left to get on with it and no one interferes.'

'I am not afraid to take time off,' says Rudd. 'Brian and I enjoy what we do, but we are not workaholics. If you take time off it gives the other people room to breathe. I do not like autocrats, who insist they have to make every single decision.' Says an adviser, 'They are good at planning the needs of the company and careful not to let the management capability fall behind the deal-making. They are first division and capable of going much further.'

Once the hit squad had finished its task, Rudd and McGowan would know that they had the management resources ready for another move forward, and one by one the deals came in. Garford-Lilley, a successful public company with an ageing management but a good portfolio of engineering, plastics and woodworking interests, was picked up for £5.4 million. Then came a specialist engineering business and a Mercedes dealership from Blackwood Hodge, and a number of smaller foundry and engineering companies.

By March 1985, Williams was back in profit as a group and the pair were ready for a quantum leap, making their first contested bid, a £24 million bid for J. & H.B. Jackson, a cash-rich plastics and forging group. After a brief campaign of opposition, Jackson surrendered to a revised offer of £30 million. Both men later described the takeover of J. & H.B. Jackson as the most exciting moment of their corporate careers at Williams. It was hardly the most dynamic company, but it transformed Williams' balance sheet because it was sitting on a pile of cash in the bank, gave it critical mass and took it into American markets for the first time.

With Jackson under the belt, Rudd and McGowan had to think how they could improve the quality of Williams' earnings as well as their quantity. It had started out as an engineering company and then been given the City tag of mini-conglomerate or 'minicon' and was ranked as one of the WETS, Williams, Evered, Tomkins and Suter – a new breed of growing industrial holding companies. But they began to work on ways of differentiating themselves as a durable and distinctive business. 'We had late-night discussions about how we wanted to get more into products with brand names rather than remain as engineering subcontractors, always at the mercy of our customers,' McGowan recalls. 'If you make castings for Bedford (as Ley's did) and it goes out of business then you are dead in the water even if you make the best castings in the world.'

The first move into brands came early on in the company's history when it bought two BMW dealerships in Hull and Doncaster from the receiver for £230,000. But for many months the car dealerships were an isolated adjunct to a business that was mainly in engineering, and the Williams pair only really started to build their branded products interests after the purchase of Rawlplug.

It was hardly the most glamorous name in the world. However, the company did have a good slice of the fixing material market for the construction and civil engineering industries and at least one of its domestic products can be found in most do-it-yourself tool kits around the country – and it was for sale. Its parent company, Burmah, was in the process of 'returning to core', getting out of peripheral interests to concentrate on its two businesses of branded lubricants and speciality chemicals. The pair originally saw it as a logical extension to their engineering businesses. But once it was on board they began to see what they could do with a branded product.

Says McGowan, 'In Rawlplug we found a good product within a sleepy company. It was a brand name you could stick on other products, and from the purchase of Rawlplug we began to think about getting into things with a brand name and where we could build up a dominant market position. If you have a brand name you are likely to be far more dominant than if you are a subcontractor. You can lead the market in pricing. Often the managers we take over simply do not see it. Indeed I have never ceased to be amazed at how weak-willed people can be over pricing.'

After Rawlplug, Williams failed in its February 1986 £140 million bid for McKechnie Brothers, a company twice its size but one with a broad spread of metal and plastic products, serving both consumer and industrial markets. Says one banker, 'As negotiators they understand what they want and know what something is worth. They are determined not to overpay and would rather walk away than get carried away.'

Williams succeeded three months later with a £79 million takeover of Duport. Best known in the City for its disastrous foray into steel-making in Llanelli, it had by 1986 been cleaned up and contained branded products like Swish, the curtain track, and Vi-Spring beds. Within a few months, other branded products like Larch-Lap garden fences, Compton concrete garages and Banbury greenhouses were added through the £53 million purchase of London & Midlands Industrials (LMI). Once in control, the Williams team set about selling excess properties, concentrating manufacturing on fewer sites, and pushing up prices in market sectors where the company had a dominant position.

As 1986 drew to a close, Rudd and McGowan could see from management accounts and their budgets that they were heading towards annual sales of around £200 million and profits of £20 million of more, not a bad achievement in less than five years. The City had liked what they had done. The share price had multiplied more than 20 times, and they were winning plaudits from the analysts. Neil Blackley, an analyst with James Capel, was an early follower but his comments are typical. 'Brian McGowan is one of the most logical thinkers I've met and Rudd supplies the flair. They make a strong team,' he said in the middle of 1986. 'They've restructured the group with Roger Carr's "hit squad". The price earnings multiple has doubled since we started following them. They have a "concept" rating now but that's probably a good thing as it helps with the acquisitions. Williams is highly beneficial for the economy.' After one particularly good set of results, the 'Lex' column in the *Financial Times* wrote, 'Williams Holdings has once again displayed why it is the City's favourite not-so-mini conglomerate. The exceptional growth it has achieved with the help of its highly rated paper may slow down but the spread and strength of the acquisitions should ensure there is no bubble to burst.'

However, it was also time for some hard thinking. Did they have the wherewithal to make a quantum leap out of the mini-conglomerate pack and into a position as one of Britain's biggest companies? LMI had given Williams a big move forward into the house and garden products market. But it also had a tail of poor-performing small engineering subsidiaries with no real prospects of growth. They were, in fact, very similar to the early businesses that had either been within the Williams company when Rudd and McGowan arrived or been bought along the way. All of them had been restructured to produce higher returns but they were not the stuff from which future Hansons or BTRs could be built, and by late 1986 they were proving a drag on the company, a drag that could inhibit its progress. Says McGowan, 'We needed to clear the decks. These businesses took up 50 per cent of our management time yet made only 5 per cent of our profits.'

Fortunately they found a buyer in the shape of Philip Ling, the former LMI managing director who had tried unsuccessfully to lead a management buy-in bid for the quoted Simon Engineering group in late 1986 and was now trying to build his own industrial holding company. Ling had an intimate knowledge of the LMI businesses. He was also prepared to take on some of the other more tired Williams businesses, and their debts, and on November 25 the disposal was announced. Under the terms of the deal, Haleworth, a private company backed by Ling but fronted by two LMI managers, paid just £2 million for 21 subsidiaries, but they also assumed £18 million of debts, which virtually eliminated Williams' borrowings.

It was the perfect deck-clearing exercise for a run of acquisitions that was to lift Williams' market value from under £300 million at the end of 1986 to over £1 billion two years later. The first move was an abortive one: a £570 million offer for the Norcros building products and printing group. The two companies would have made an excellent fit, but the Norcros management, headed by Terry Simpson, was determined to resist. Williams refused to raise its first offer and in the end it won just 48 per cent of the votes, 2 per cent shy of the all-important 50 per cent target. Simpson was later sacrificed in a boardroom putsch, as institutions that had remained loyal to the company during the bid pressed for changes. But defeat was still an uncomfortable experience for Williams. Says one adviser, 'They are extremely good at picking up the show and leading the team on to the next thing when things go wrong. They do not let people flounder around in disappointment. They just press on.'

Pressing on in 1987 meant entering the auction for Crown Paints and Polycell, two branded products businesses which had been put up for sale by their parent company, Reed International. A number of companies, including John Ashcroft's Coloroll, and an in-house management team took part in the bidding, but Rudd and McGowan were able to carry off their prize at a cost of £285 million. This was funded by a £285 million placing, the biggest cash-raising exercise Williams had undertaken.

Some felt they were paying too much for an acquisition that at a stroke made Williams Britain's second-largest paint company behind ICI's Dulux business. 'Lex' wrote, ' "Momentum" and other such intangibles have long been highly valued by image-conscious acquisitive companies. No doubt part of Williams Holdings full price . . . for Reed's paint and do-it-yourself division has been mentally tucked away as the price of a post-Norcros bounce back.'

But Rudd and McGowan had the last laugh when six months later they pulled off the purchase of the Berger paint subsidiary from Hoechst. It was a classic Williams deal: it transformed the economics of the first paint takeover and came to be seen as one of the most profitable big purchases after the stock market crash of October 1987.

It began four months before the crash when Rudd took a phone call at the desk of his comfortable Derby office from Brian Davies, Berger's managing director. Williams had just bought Crown Paints and Polycell. Now Davies was suggesting that Williams should buy Berger from its German parent, Hoechst, in a deal that would significantly strengthen its market position. 'I have Hoechst's permission to talk to you,' he told Rudd. 'We think we should get together.'

It was an ironic moment. Crown managers had long dreamed of buying Berger, and Rudd, on discovering their ambitions, had decided he would approach the German company. The Crown purchase had been a big leap forward for Williams. Its biggest purchase to date, it had given the company the most modern paint plant in Europe, a plant that had just received £27 million of capital investment. Yet the plant was working on just a single shift, with the result that its returns on capital employed were well below what they would have been if it had been worked more intensively. Berger offered the opportunity to work at closer to capacity: the Crown plant would simply take on the Berger production from its existing plants, which were far older and less efficient. Most of the extra volume would come straight through to the bottom line in sharply higher profits.

A few days later, Rudd and McGowan, were sitting down at the Heathrow Penta Hotel, close to Hoechst's British headquarters, for a preliminary chat with Davies. A week later Arno Baltzer, the head of Hoechst in Britain, joined the discussions and the matter was transferred into the hands of the merchant bankers.

Getting the money for the Berger deal was no easy task – in fact the timing could not have been worse. After tortuous negotiation the deal was due to be unveiled towards the end of October, but then came the crash. Within a few days more than a quarter of the value of British industry had vanished in an orgy of selling. After years of easy fund-raising, the market for equity capital dried up overnight. Williams and its advisers had to go back to the drawing board, renegotiate the terms and plead with its leading shareholders not to turn their backs on a good deal at a time when most fund managers were hitting the panic 'sell' button. And, despite the turmoil, Williams' investment in its City relationships paid off. Men like Mick Newmarch at the Prudential Corporation, Britain's leading investor, kept their faith with the company. Williams considered offering a security with a higher income like a convertible preference share, but Newmarch reassured them he was happy with Williams ordinary shares, and so did a number of other leading shareholders.

The result was that on December 7, just seven weeks after the crash, the company announced the Berger purchase for £133 million, financed by the issue of £100 million of new shares and the balance in cash. The City was stunned by the deal, which involved the first big equity fund-raising after Black Monday. The next morning the *Financial Times* commented, 'Yesterday's outburst of bid activity showed that there is life in the corporate finance game yet, but it also seemed to draw a significant line between the weak and the strong in the post-crash market . . .'

In the event, investors owning 92 per cent of the shares took up their new shares, a remarkable vote of confidence in the company's strategy in the post-crash environment, particularly when one considers that the Berger business had been bought for a price equal to 60 times its historic earnings. The confidence was justified: within a few months it was clear to even the most shell-shocked fund manager that Williams had pulled off a remarkable coup. All told, around £110 million had been raised from the sale of Berger's peripheral interests, including a major Australian subsidiary and a 20 per cent stake in A.G. Stanley, the FADS do-it-yourself chain.

Williams itself was left with Cuprinol, the wood stains and varnishes business, Robbilac, the dominant paint maker in Portugal, and £50–60 million of British paint sales under the Berger, Brolac and Magicote names, bought for a net cost of around £20 million. Berger's Bristol plant was closed with the loss of 200 jobs in April 1988, and production shifted to the Crown plants. Once the rationalisation was complete, more than £25 million of extra profits on a price/earnings ratio of well under one had been added to the Williams group. The numbers may not have been in the same league as Hanson, but the style and the panache with which Rudd, McGowan and Carr stripped the company down to its bare and profitable essentials made the deal one of truly Hansonian elegance.

City cynics had speculated that the Black Monday crash would put paid to the progress of acquisition-driven industrial holding companies. If the big pension funds and insurance companies were nervous about the economic outlook they would not put the cash up to fund the growth. However, Williams showed that, while it had been a creature of the great Thatcher bull market, it could prosper in a world where equity capital was in shorter supply. In February 1988 *Financial Weekly* described the company as 'One of the most impressive variations on the conglomerate theme around.'

With Berger sorted out, the acquisition drive continued. Williams' range of specialist engineering products was expanded in August by a bid for Newage Transmissions, a maker of gearboxes and transmissions used in rugged off-highway vehicles, marine gearboxes and manufacturing machinery. A few days later, it announced a £34 million bid for Smallbone, the manufacturer of luxury fitted kitchens and bedrooms, in a deal intended to take its range of consumer products for the home further upmarket.

But the biggest transaction of the year, and the biggest in the company's history, came in October when Rudd and McGowan unveiled a £331 million agreed takeover of Pilgrim House, an electrical and electronics group involved in instrumentation, controls and fire protection equipment. Pilgrim itself was in the midst of a £150 million purchase of the Kidde fire protection company, part of Hanson. Rudd and McGowan's aim was to build up the industrial and military products side of Williams and shift some of the emphasis of the group away from branded products that might be hit in a consumer downturn.

Within a few months they had sold off Pilgrim's peripheral activities, raising around £100 million, and were left with two core businesses. The first was the dominant world supplier of aerospace fire detection and suppression systems and the second was Europe's leading manufacturer of micro-switches. The two businesses added another £300 million to turnover, taking Williams well past an annual rate of £1 billion. With Pilgrim and Kidde under the belt, profits from Williams, with its workforce of over 20,000 (up from a low of 200 just after the original takeover in February 1982), were, according to City analysts, expected to top £160 million in 1989.

Yet despite the huge success of the company, both Rudd and McGowan remained cautious. In all the takeovers they made sure they did not pay too much, even if their conservatism deprived them of the glory of winning contested bids like the £570 million raid on Norcros. They did not want to be left with high borrowings and a low share price 'when the music stopped', as their old boss Jock Mackenzie had been in the early 1980s. Says McGowan, 'In the early days we had to make do with debts at astronomical levels of five times shareholders' funds, but the moment we could we got the borrowings down as low as possible. Ley's had lots of easily realisable assets in its balance sheet; J. & H.B. Jackson had lots of cash.'

In a number of the purchases from public companies, the Williams duo would ask the seller to load up the subsidiary in question with cash before purchase. This would involve Williams paying more, but the transactions were financed by shares, with the result that each purchase came with a little cash infusion on the side.

Like their heroes, Hanson and Sir Owen Green of BTR, Rudd and McGowan made sure they minimised the risks in any transaction before looking ahead to what prospects it might bring. Says Rudd, 'As we progressed, we kept at the back of our minds the idea that the bull market might stop and we never wanted to be in a position of being caught with our pants down.'

They do not want size for its own sake. Above all, they want Williams to be regarded as a well-run company. Despite the growth of the group, the head office staff numbers have been kept low at around 50, housed, up until the end of 1988, in rather modest quarters above one of the company's Jaguar dealerships in Derby. There Rudd and McGowan, who in 1988 paid themselves identical salaries of £403,000, plot their strategic moves.

Although they work hard, there seems enough room in their lives for outside activities. Rudd's non-Williams interests include his second public company, Raine Industries, which concentrates on housebuilding, construction and property development. He lives with his wife Lesley and his three children in a converted nineteenth-century Derbyshire stone stable block in the fashionable Duffield area of Derby, complete with indoor swimming pool and tennis court. In his spare time he enjoys golf, squash and shooting – indeed a shooting accident in late 1987 cost him the index finger of his right hand. 'Nigel is the cuddly one. He is an open, friendly person with whom I like to do business,' says one banker. 'He instils a lot of loyalty in his team and is completely without pomposity, showing no sign of believing his own PR, usually a good indicator of trouble. Brian is more serious when first encountered, but they both share a strong sense of fun and instinctively tell jokes against themselves and each other. They are almost like husband and wife.'

McGowan lives with his real wife Julia and their two children in an old country house two miles outside Uttoxeter. The building dates back to the sixteenth century, although the facade is early nineteenth century, and it is surrounded by fields where Julia indulges her passion for horses. While Rudd likes shooting, McGowan enjoys fishing for trout. Neither leads an extravagant lifestyle despite their Williams shares, which make them both millionaires a number of times over, and their families and homes are the main focus of their lives outside work.

But their relaxed style should not leave any doubts about the seriousness of their ambitions. 'I would like people to say that Williams is one of the ten best-managed businesses in the country,' says Rudd. 'If they thought it was genuinely true, it would give me a great deal of pleasure.'

Name: *John Ashcroft*
Title: *Chairman and Chief Executive of Coloroll*
Born: *1948, near Wigan, Lancashire*
Education: *Upholland Grammar School; London School of Economics*
Qualifications: *8 'O' levels, 4 'A' levels, B.Sc.(Econ.)*
First Job: *1970, management trainee at T.I. (formerly Tube Investments)*
Family: *Married Jenny King in 1972; they have two sons and a daughter*
Joined Coloroll: *In 1978, by invitation as Export Director*
Made First Million: *In 1985, when Coloroll floated on the stock market*
Most Exciting Moment: *Becoming Chairman of Coloroll*
Awards: *1987, Guardian Young Businessman of the Year; elected honorary Visiting Senior Fellow of the Manchester Business School; elected a Fellow of the Royal Society of Arts*
Hobbies: *Sheep breeding, reading, tennis, running and swimming*
Drives: *Jaguar, Range Rover*
Personal Stake: *Under 1 per cent, worth £1 million*
Latest Company Statistics: *1989–sales: £565 million; profits: £55.6 million*
Latest Salary: *1989 – £517,000*

Chapter XII

John Ashcroft
COLOROLL

*'To under-achieve is the
worst thing.'*

John Ashcroft, the creator of Coloroll, has in the 1980s done for Britain's favourite pastime, home decoration, what Sir Terence Conran's Habitat did for furniture in the 1970s. 'Before Ashcroft, wallpaper was wallpaper and DIY was DIY,' says one industry rival.

Since Ashcroft, wallpaper has become wallcovering and Coloroll's type of DIY is called home fashion. It is a phrase that embraces everything that decorates the home – from flying ducks on the wall to tufted carpets – and allows Ashcroft to expand into any area that falls into that category.

A relaxed, joky manner and sporty good looks counterpoint a driving ambition displayed with northern flamboyance. 'I always believed I would be running a public company by the time I was 35,' he says. He takes for granted his exceptional ability and drive. 'I don't know how or why but my aim has always been to do the task in hand to perfection and in a third of the normal time.'

Ashcroft was born and brought up in Upholland, an undistinguished village near Wigan in Lancashire. By the age of the 38 he was chairman and chief executive of Coloroll, one of the new breed of British manufacturing companies where design and marketing are as important as the process itself.

Coloroll is very much Ashcroft's creation and its success has been his success. He mixes in the highest business circles, takes tea with the Queen, lunches with Margaret Thatcher, and has the top advisers in the land working for him. He is a senior fellow at Manchester Business School and an increasingly influential voice on issues relating to the North West of England. When the BBC went in search of a bright young industrialist to take part in its 1989 budget coverage, it picked Ashcroft.

He also finds time for playing tennis, and breeding Charolais sheep (prize-winning naturally) on the family farm as a hobby.

Under Ashcroft's management, what was a sleepy family-run wallpaper company has become the biggest name in 'home fashion' – a term Ashcroft has promoted hard.

Coloroll's range of products, from mugs to crystal, duvets to curtains, carpets to wallpaper, has been put together with the distinctive Ashcroft style. It sells in varied markets. 'We put wallcoverings in the White House and carpets in Buckingham Palace,' he quips.

In early 1989 Coloroll could boast a market capitalisation of £400 million, a tenfold rise from the £40 million value put on it when the company floated on the stock market less than four years before. At that time, Coloroll (which Ashcroft expects to sell over £1 billion of products for the home in 1990) was merely a maker of pretty wallpaper.

Although Ashcroft is not a major Coloroll shareholder in the way that Michael Green is of Carlton, his personal fortunes reflect the success of the group. His modest 490,000 shares were worth just under £1 million in mid-1989, but he collected £517,000 salary in 1989, up from £162,000 in 1988. He also enjoys acclaim outside the company and, in 1987, won the Guardian Young Business Man of the Year. It was not for his retiring modesty.

Ashcroft flaunts his ambition and achievements on his immaculate sleeve. But his reputation for arrogance is tempered by his dry, occasionally self-deprecating, humour. And he does like to have fun.

At a Coloroll-hosted dinner in London in February 1989, he initiated an after-coffee game of making each of the four fellow entrepreneurs at the table tell a horror story about their company. He kicked off with a tale about visiting a subsidiary bought with the John Crowther takeover in 1988. He had found the company executives blissfully unaware that they were haemorrhaging money. Two days later it was closed.

John Ashcroft was born on Christmas Eve, 1948, the youngest of three children. He has a brother ten years his senior, and a sister five years older than him.

His father managed what had been the family drift mine, although his financial holding in the company was nominal. It was a hand-to-mouth, though reasonably comfortable, existence. 'We lived in an end of terrace house, and as a kid I always thought we were well off,' Ashcroft says.

But by the time he was at grammar school it was clear there were problems. After months of arguments between his father and fellow directors, the company headed into trouble. 'I always remember one director who drove an E type Jaguar and never seemed affected,' says Ashcroft. 'It gave me an innate distrust of a certain type of person.'

His father became seriously ill as a result, and just before Ashcroft's fourteenth birthday the company went into liquidation.

He still remembers that period vividly, but discounts the idea that it spurred his ambition. Even before this crisis, the young Ashcroft had been a high achiever. At junior school he passed the 11+ a year early but was too young to go to grammar school. When he passed it again a year later, his teachers advised him to go to a public school, but at the time the family funds were too low.

Instead he went off to Upholland Grammar School where he slotted easily into the 'accelerated' stream and had sailed through his 'A' levels in economics, French, history and general studies by the time he was 17.

He had already been accepted by the London School of Economics for the year after, but, rather than take a year off, he decided to stay on a year at school. He had a mass of non-scholastic interests, which he misguidedly thought would keep him entertained. He was house captain, played in the first teams for rugby and cricket, as well as performing the lead role in the school play. That year it was *Ring around the Moon*.

However, during that time, with no real work to do, he ran into trouble. 'The year sort of got blown away,' he remembers. After an impeccable school career he managed to get suspended twice and finally he was threatened with expulsion after a misunderstanding about drinking in the local pub after a school dance.

'The devil found work for idle hands', he says, admitting that once his immediate goals are achieved he quickly becomes bored. Like many teenagers in the 1960s he played in a pop group. The Ashcroft touch was that he asked the headmaster for a performance fee for 'The Brethren' to play at the school dance. This first try at financial negotiation was met with horror. He got the fee though.

Eventually he went off to the London School of Economics, which in the 1960s was famous for radical thinking. Full of anticipation about the delights of London, he found himself lodging in a house in Tooting where the high points of excitement were a string of obscene phone calls received by the landlady.

The initial culture shock of London university life was little short of traumatic. 'I didn't expect people at university to use four letter words,' he remembers. 'I didn't have any money; I didn't know London; I was totally green and politically naive.' He soon became embroiled in left-wing politics; it was a brief encounter. One heady night in 1968, the year of the student riots, Ashcroft was into his fifth pint of McEwans when in came the police. 'There is nothing like being thrust into the cold night air with a baton up your backside to make you reappraise the establishment', he laughs.

His student life had a few experiments in it, but he avoided the more destructive temptations. Even though the drug-taking 'hippie' movement was in its heyday between 1967 and 1970, he stayed clear of drugs. 'I had enough problems with cigarettes and alcohol,' he recalls. He also, like so many young men when they arrive in London, had hang-ups about women and how to meet them. Initially, work was bottom of the agenda, but he was spurred into action by being told in the middle of the first year that he didn't stand a chance of passing his Part 1 exams.

Against the recommendations of his old headmaster, who suggested law or accountancy, Ashcroft had chosen economics and was lucky enough to be taught by Bernard Donoughue, who later became heavily involved with the Wilson 'kitchen cabinet'. However, after a brief burst of academic activity he threw himself into extra-curricular pursuits rather than study.

In the second year he can't remember going to a lecture for six months. By the time he left he had been captain of the second eleven football team, captain of the second fifteen cricket team and president of the Athletics Union, successfully lobbying for a new gymnasium.

The lobbying experience proved useful when he became entangled in vast bureaucratic companies like the engineering conglomerate T.I. Group and Reed International.

He emerged with a disappointing B.Sc.(Econ.) lower second degree, indicating that his mind was already on other things. He had decided that the opportunities were in industry, and along with most of his fellow students he embarked on 'the milk round' of interviews with British companies.

British Leyland interviewed him three times, and after much deliberation offered him a job in the personnel department. But he finally took a management trainee slot with T.I. at £1,200 a year. It was then called Tube Investments and at the time was regarded as one of Britain's better-run companies. By modern standards, however, it was overmanned and bureaucratic. As one of 72 trainees, Ashcroft found his early time there intensely frustrating. 'We would spend one day a week going round the group, everything from Creda Cookers to the tube mills. It was useful to see so many industries but I just wanted to get into management before it was all sorted out. I remember thinking, "All I need is a desk and a telephone." '

It was then that the obsessional nature in his personality began to emerge. He identified strongly with historical workaholics and one of his early and somewhat curious role models was one Maria Chapdelaine, a character in a French novel he read while studying for his 'A' levels. The heroine had a goal of 'd'être tranquille' or being comfortable, a state which could only be achieved by working 16 hours a day.

Ashcroft began to crave achievement, and he found his progress painfully slow. After the initial training period, Ashcroft was sent to a T.I. Group subsidiary called Metal Sections (which later came to the stock market in its own right). He felt that any attempt at initiative was met with disapproval. At one stage he was asked to draft a press release to architects about a new product. He proudly presented what he felt was a snappy one-page release; his boss, a retired Colonel, simply redrafted it into two and a half pages of turgid prose. 'It was the sort of place where they issued safety caps for stiletto heels to protect the parquet flooring,' he says.

Living in a flat above a launderette in Edgbaston, life was far from fun. Jenny King was a schoolgirl sweetheart whom he started seeing again. An attractive brunette with a strong character, she provided some much-needed sympathy and support. To this day he says that she keeps his feet on the ground. By 1971 they were firmly back together and in October 1972 they were married at a Methodist church near Wigan. While his personal life was now on a stable footing, he found the lack of progress in his career deeply upsetting. He was way behind schedule in his game plan to be running a public company by the age of 35.

Luckily he ended up at T.I. working for a man called Tom Wood from St Helen's in Lancashire who took Ashcroft under his wing. 'He was a shelter figure for me,' Ashcroft says. When Wood decided to move to a smaller company, Ashcroft followed him with the proviso it would probably only be for a year.

For the first time in his career Ashcroft was in a company where what he did counted. 'If no one got the order, the machines didn't move,' he says. In 1974 he joined Crown Products, part of the mighty Reed International, as product manager in the international wallcoverings division. It was here that Ashcroft began to learn about the industry he would make his own.

The job took him to Europe, Australia, Japan and the Far East and included a short course at the London Business School. 'I did a competent job and I was acquiring a lot of experience,' he says. Part of that experience was learning how to get on with people, although Ashcroft had always been a good mixer. 'You have to get on with people if you play rugby,' he laughs. But there is part of him which is aloof and distrustful. In essence he is a loner, preferring to spend his weekends with his family and working on the sheep farm.

It was during the four years at Crown that he began to evolve the Ashcroft style and to work on management techniques pieced together from a series of new textbooks in the United States and his observations of business heroes like Lord Hanson, Sir James Goldsmith and Sir Owen Green. He still reads a lot, especially memoirs of legendary business figures like Akyo Morito, the head of Sony in Japan, and Lee Iacocca in the US.

He was continually experimenting, trying new ideas to make people notice what he was doing. It was the beginning of the now-famous Coloroll culture that has since filled pages of management magazines. Put crudely, he used gimmicks to attract attention to otherwise boring items. Whenever he wrote a report, he would head it with a little 'poem'.

The predilection for self-publicity has always been a feature of his career at Coloroll. A factory opening becomes a spectacular occasion when the British army's Red Devils parachute team, which the company sponsors, swoop in from the sky trailing coloured smoke accompanied by their theme music 'The Ride of the Valkyries' by Wagner.

He is probably the only company head to turn the humble coffee mug into a management tool. In 1986, shortly after Coloroll took over Staffordshire Potteries, which makes earthenware pottery, every manager in the business, and a number of investors and journalists, received a coffee mug bearing a smiling Ashcroft face and ten questions to which every Coloroll manager needs to know the answer. Around the rim are the words: 'Remember: This month is the most important month in the future of this company.' It is a lighthearted gesture with a serious message. 'Every time a Coloroll manager has a cup of coffee, he knows I will be thinking of him and asking those questions,' says Ashcroft.

Ashcroft has developed a recognisable style in marketing himself as well as the products in the company. No matter how august the function, Ashcroft and all the Coloroll managers wear a small lapel pin bearing the Coloroll logo.

During his four years working on international marketing at Crown he acquired a reputation for originality and biting humour. On secondment to one of the larger advertising agencies to spearhead the 'Pan European' promotion, Ashcroft created what he describes as a subtle French campaign. A colleague was involved in a series of German advertisements with the emphasis driven home with full Germanic force. When the director of the German campaign claimed that he didn't understand the French advertisements, Ashcroft responded: 'Well, Dieter, it's the difference between nuance and blitzkrieg.'

In 1978, Crown offered him the job of UK marketing director. For most aspiring 29 year olds this would have seemed like the pinnacle of success. But, although pleased, Ashcroft saw the danger of becoming too comfortable. He had just moved to a new house in a fashionable suburb of Manchester with a huge mortgage, and Jenny was pregnant with their first child. He saw that it would be all too easy for him to be stuck half-way up the corporate ladder as so many of the managers around him were. The Crown promotion could have led to the kind of stagnation that fills Ashcroft with horror. 'To under-achieve is the worst thing,' he once said.

He had realised he would never make any serious money by sticking with Reed – and he had decided that he wanted to be rich enough not to have to worry about the future of his family. He had watched Jim Slater and John Bentley build up their companies using shares to expand. He had also watched in horrified fascination as the Slater empire collapsed and noted how John Bentley cleverly, or luckily, sold out before the stock market crash of 1973–4.

While he was contemplating the Crown promotion, along came the opportunity that would fulfil his ambitions. The tiny, family-run firm of Coloroll offered him a job. Initially it was to run the export side, which he reluctantly agreed to do for a year. John Wilman, who had known Ashcroft from the Reed days, was already there as head of design. He is still one of Coloroll's greatest assets.

Ashcroft was the right man at the right time. 'It was clear something needed to be done, I just took over and led from the front.' He has been doing so ever since.

It didn't make him too popular initially, particularly with John Bray, the managing director who had taken Coloroll from being a paper bag manufacturer into a wallpaper maker. But, although Bray had probably saved the company from extinction, he was no match for Ashcroft. He joined the company as deputy managing director in 1978, but within months he was managing director and Bray was out.

At that time Coloroll had sales of around £6 million a year and roughly 3 per cent of the wallcoverings market in the UK, and was jogging along quite nicely.

This was the moment Ashcroft had been working towards. All the previous years of obsessionally building up his management theories were about to be put into practice. Even as a private company, Ashcroft's Coloroll received more favourable publicity than many quoted companies. In 1980 it won the *Sunday Telegraph* Best Young Company award, while Ashcroft himself, young and dashing in stark contrast to most chief executives in the manufacturing sector, appeared regularly in the business pages expounding his evangelical theories on management. He became well known for writing three management documents. These were the Blue Book, which lays out the management philosophy, the White Book, which sets financial criteria for every subsidiary, and the Yellow Book, which is an analysis of the market, the customers and the competition.

A vital credo from the Blue Book is 'Death Rae', a humorous term for the concept that managers should be R: responsible for their decisions; A: accountable for their decisions; E: exposed to the effects of their decisions. It includes points on leadership like 'Coloroll is not a "strut and tut" management system. Managers should wander around and discuss.' There are also extracts from Ashcroft's favourite reading such as *In Search of Excellence* and the sayings of an uncompromising Chinese war-lord called Sun Tzu, whose basic premise seems to be that, if officers do not obey the law, they are executed.

By the end of 1984 the company was ready for flotation on the stock market. The date was set for 9 May 1985 and the Coloroll publicity machine swung into action. Starting with an exclusive interview in the *Sunday Times*, a series of glowing articles appeared in the business pages of most of the national press and a series of presentations was undertaken ('road shows' as they are known) to the investing institutions in the City of London and the other financial centres of Edinburgh and Manchester.

Everything appeared to be going to plan. There was huge demand for the shares being offered for sale. The 13.5 million shares offered were 20 times over-subscribed. In other words, investors put up £375 million for the £18.2 million worth of shares available. Ashcroft, still slightly innocent of the vagaries of the City, travelled to London to witness the start of trading on the floor of the Stock Exchange. It was an embarrassing disappointment.

The stock market took an unexpected turn for the worse that week, and when dealings in Coloroll opened most of the 'stags' (people who subscribed to the issue expecting to make a quick profit), and even some of the underwriters, rushed to sell. The shares tumbled from the issue price of 135p to 125p. 'You could almost smell singed flesh in the stock market today as stags burnt their fingers in Coloroll first dealings,' reported the *Evening Standard* City pages that lunchtime.

Ashcroft, who was then just 36 and had only missed his goal of running a public company by the age of 35 by six months, was furious. The day should have been the culmination of what he had been working towards since 1978 when he had joined Coloroll.

Over the next few months the shares continued to fall, touching 101p in the July. Something had gone badly wrong and Ashcroft believed he knew what it was.

Behind the scenes of the slick presentations to the City had been some bitter rows over the structure of the company. The bank that had handled the stock market issue was Charterhouse Japhet. In 1982 Charterhouse had put the consortium together that bought 90 per cent of Coloroll from the family and had provided financial advice since.

The Charterhouse role at that time was vital to Ashcroft; without it he would have been unable to expand the company prior to flotation. But the institutional investors had not been ready to let the 36-year-old Ashcroft be chief executive and chairman. They had insisted that Coloroll go to market with an older and more experienced chairman in the shape of Sam Oxford, the chairman of Magnet & Southern, the building group. The idea was to lend gravitas to Coloroll, as some at Charterhouse feared that the stock market would be wary of a company with such a young chief executive.

Ashcroft objected on the grounds that he had been running Coloroll successfully for over six years, but eventually agreed to Oxford's appointment for the good of the flotation. The fact that the launch went so badly played right into Ashcroft's hands.

By the September, the Coloroll share price was still only 106p and Ashcroft was gearing up to take action. It was not just a question of pride, it was a matter of practicality. One of the major reasons for becoming a public company was to use shares in buying up other companies. Ashcroft needed a healthy share price in order to begin his planned programme of acquisitions. Four months after going public the share price was languishing at 20 per cent below the offer price of 135p. He, and clearly others, felt that the advice from Charterhouse had contributed to the sickly performance of the shares. One of his maxims is to 'locate the problem and take the appropriate action'.

His solution was ruthless and effective. He fired Charterhouse and appointed S.G. Warburg, recognised as one of the top two merchant banks in London at the time. The link was Coloroll's stockbroker, Rowe & Pitman, which was merging with Warburg to form Mercury Securities, a group that proved the most successful of the integrated securities houses after the 'Big Bang' in October 1986.

The effect was almost instantaneous. Within a month, the shares were back to the issue price; within two they were 150p. Ashcroft pushed to become chairman. The market had demonstrated that the Oxford appointment had not had the required effect; if anything, it had confused Coloroll followers who had become used to Ashcroft as the leading figure.

In November he took over the chairman's role and embarked on a hectic programme of acquisition. Since then, Ashcroft has masterminded thirteen takeovers, at a total cost of £400 million in Coloroll shares.

The share price went on to climb steadily to 220p by the end of 1986, then soared to nearly 400p when the market hit its peak in the summer of 1987, providing a strong currency for acquisitions. By the spring of 1989 it was back down to 170p.

Whether they were so-called friendly 'agreed' bids, recommended by the boards of the companies, or hostile swoops, Ashcroft has never allowed sentiment to affect his handling of the integration of the companies into Coloroll. Some months after the supposedly friendly takeover of Fogarty, the duvet company, in 1987, Ashcroft realised that most of the thirteen directors of the group would have to go.

At the time of the deal, Ashcroft had said their contracts would be honoured and he foresaw no massive changes. Nevertheless he realised that their departure was necessary if the company was to perform in the Coloroll mould. Ashcroft told the Fogarty chairman the bad news. He had been a major shareholder and had thus done well financially out of the deal. He was horrified, although he bravely opted to break the tidings to his doomed directors. 'But John, what shall I tell them,' he pleaded. Ashcroft smiled sweetly. 'Tell them you did it for the money,' he said.

Employees or advisers who do not perform are politely dismissed. There is nothing personal. It is just that John Ashcroft's only true loyalty is to success. After the takeover of Fogarty, Coloroll made 200 of the 1,200 workforce redundant. 'Don't you ever worry about what happens to those people, John,' asked a journalist. 'No, never,' he replied instantly, 'I can't afford to. I have to worry about the other 1,000 jobs.'

When Coloroll buys a company, the battle plan to win the hearts and minds of the workforce goes into action immediately following the initial reorganisation. The important thing is to move fast before the workforce and managers become demoralised and start losing money. In the first month after the purchase is finalised, a team of managers goes through the company, examining it for every flaw. But nothing is actually done in that first month, however tempting. Then the action starts. When the management teams sweep in to restructure and rationalise they have a chilling resemblance in style to the Red Devils parachute team. The Red Devils have a reputation for toughness and daring and the same, it is hoped, is true of Coloroll.

Ashcroft reckons to knock a new company into shape in a month. Like so many managers before him, he knows that the easiest way to make money is to cut costs, but knowing where to cut them is what really counts. For instance, Ashcroft will cut back on office staff but values the line managers.

The casualties are generally the top managers. At Staffordshire Potteries five out of seven top managers went, although the remaining two have flourished, and it was much the same story at Crown House.

Often there is a group of ambitious but frustrated middle managers underneath – and sometimes they have been the ones running the company anyway. Denby, the famous pottery company bought along with the Crown House acquisition, was losing £1 million a year and gradually laying off more and more staff. The year after acquisition it made £1 million profit being run by one of the original managers and was recruiting workers again.

The restructuring out of the way, a 'bash' is held at a nearby hall or cinema. 'John believes in getting in front of the workforce as soon as we can,' says Philip Green, the group managing director. 'Basically, it is music, videos and lots of flashing lights and then John does his thing.'

The Ashcroft presentation is slick, punchy, humorous and charismatic. Ashcroft once antagonised a cynical merchant banker by enthusing about 'aura management', but it has not failed him yet. 'He is absolutely wonderful with the girls on the line,' enthused one subsidiary managing director talking of Ashcroft's bi-annual visits.

Coloroll has been the vehicle for Ashcroft to achieve his goals. Although he is quick to give credit to his bright young board of directors, they are all handpicked by him. The team is of his creation. Young, slim and squeaky clean, with a chirpy northern humour, you could take them all home for tea without a qualm. Ask them a question, and out pours the Coloroll philosophy.

Ashcroft has been accused of gimmickry and grandiosity. It is a style that goes with staying in a suite at the Savoy on his frequent trips from Manchester to London (while his co-directors stay at the Meridien in Piccadilly), flying Concorde across the Atlantic and having the Red Devils on hand. But Ashcroft's financial record so far vindicates such behaviour. He also clearly believes it justifies him trebling his salary in 1989.

When Coloroll came to the stock market in 1985 it made profits of £5.3 million. By mid-1989 Coloroll was the largest maker of wallcoverings in Britain and the third-biggest in the United States. It is the largest in household textiles, household pottery and ceramics. The takeover of John Crowther in the spring of 1988 also made Coloroll the second-biggest carpet maker in Britain.

In the financial year to March 1989, sales were £565 million, with profits hitting £55.6 million. But he concedes that the next two years may prove tougher going, as economic growth slows down. Behind his sometimes arrogant manner Ashcroft is also self-critical and takes advice even on minor points. In his early days in the City, Ashcroft smiled almost incessantly. 'Don't smile so much John,' advised a friendly stockbroker one day. 'The City won't take you seriously.' The Ashcroft smile became used with more discretion.

He has not escaped making his share of mistakes, but observers are impressed by his ability to take action quickly to cut his losses or turn the situation to his advantage. However, he occasionally makes long-term enemies.

The mighty Marks & Spencer, for example, dropped Coloroll as a supplier after a series of rows. The main one erupted when Ashcroft decided that Coloroll, as a manufacturer, should open a flagship 'shop' in London's Regent Street. M & S, along with several other retailers, objected strongly to what they saw as a manufacturer and supplier competing with them in retailing. Ashcroft protested that it was merely meant to show Coloroll for what it was, 'one-stop shopping for the multiple retailer'. In other words, a company supplying a large range of products sold by the large store chains. No one was convinced and the shop closed quietly in early 1988.

The high-profile television promotion of the Coloroll brand in its own right also upset M & S, which prefers its suppliers to keep a low profile.

Ashcroft publicly appears not to mind too much, although losing a customer with that kind of high street dominance must rankle.

Socially, Ashcroft's manner is easy-going. He comes across as a relaxed family man who enjoys a good party and the odd game of tennis. But he has few close friends.

'I had lots of mates at LSE and at Reed but I hardly ever see them these days simply because of the time pressure,' he says. It is not unusual for Ashcroft to rise at 6 a.m. and get to bed at 1 a.m. the following morning after a round of hectic meetings. He has built up a sheep farm of 300 Charolais sheep, which win regular prizes at local sheep shows in Lancashire – an activity that has inspired some irreverent press comment. Fellow directors put it down to his need to build something permanent. Running alongside his career plan has been his 'domestic plan' to create a 250 acre self-financing estate. It is both a counterpoint and a fall-back to his business career, although it is difficult to do both – 'Actually I hardly see the sheep these days', he admitted in late 1988.

The farm also involves his wife and three children, a girl and two boys. He is both protective of and ambitious for his family. In business, however, the high achiever shines through.

While admitting, under pressure, to having a split personality (his star sign is Capricorn), he makes no apologies for being confident or arrogant. He believes in himself absolutely and sees mistakes as part of the learning curve.

After the stock market crash in October 1987 Ashcroft became briefly despondent, and the company put out a statement saying that it expected to be less acquisitive in the near future. By early 1988, however, both the market and Ashcroft's morale had revived. He decided it was time to go for a large acquisition that would change the shape of the company.

He and the strategic team at Coloroll identified a number of possible takeover targets. Through their stockbroker, Rowe & Pitman, they built up small shareholdings under the 5 per cent level at which a company must disclose its stake. When the presence of one of those stakes, in a company called Norcros, became public, the news was greeted with considerable hostility both from Norcros and Coloroll's own shareholders who were in no mood for an acrimonious bid battle.

The idea of the Norcros takeover was swiftly dropped and Ashcroft went on to the next target. It was John Crowther, Britain's second-biggest carpet maker.

Although the bid for Crowther began in late April as a friendly 'merger', the entry of another contender – the Thomas Robinson engineering group, run by another young entrepreneur, Graham Rudd – made the bid one of the most bitter in recent takeover history.

It was not of Ashcroft's choosing, but he relished the fight. 'I'm prepared to go to war, isn't everybody', he remarked casually to a friend over dinner in Chelsea in the middle of the £220 million battle. What went unsaid was that he usually wins, as he did then.

His tactics were superb. At the moment Robinson entered the fray, Ashcroft declared that the Coloroll bid for Crowther would not be raised. It was an unorthodox move – normally, contested bids involve a series of offers and counter-offers. But in the nervous City climate of the time it worked wonders. Those investors who were preparing to finance the rival offer from Robinson panicked. If Ashcroft was not prepared to raise his bid, why were they backing a higher hostile offer, they asked, before deserting Robinson in droves. Robinson's merchant bank, Robert Fleming, was forced to fund the bid virtually alone and was left with the prospect of owning a huge number of Robinson shares if its bid succeeded.

On Friday, 3 June 1988, S.G. Warburg's Robert Gillespie rang Ashcroft to tell him that over 60 per cent of shareholders had accepted the Coloroll offer for Crowther in the face of a cash counter-bid worth 10p more from Thomas Robinson. He had won.

By the time the phone call came through, Ashcroft was already in a rare formal board meeting with his co-directors working out the best strategy to assimilate Crowther. Throughout the seven weeks that the bid lasted most of the time Ashcroft had been his usual cool self, although there had been one or two flare-ups.

He was well aware that it was his biggest deal yet. Overnight it doubled the market capitalisation of the company, bringing him his 1990 goal well before time. The prospect of becoming a major industrialist of the 1990s was in sight.

Two days before Coloroll actually made the formal bid for John Crowther, Ashcroft was on a beach in Barbados enjoying a long-promised family holiday. He had long seen Crowther as a suitable acquisition for Coloroll once it got big enough, and had plotted the move carefully initially approaching the directors several months before deciding to go ahead. He had done much of the negotiation with Crowther directors Trevor Barker and Michael Abrahams. Eric Kilby, the finance director, had been left in charge of tying up the deal. But on his return from holiday, Ashcroft jumped into a waiting helicopter and arrived late at night in the Warburg offices. 'He sorted out a couple of points that had been holding us up in a trice,' remarked one banker present. But Ashcroft did not want his holiday mentioned in the press. 'I felt guilty about going at the company year-end anyway, but it had been booked months before,' he said.

Most of the time, though, talking to Ashcroft is more like talking to a computer than to a man. He has proved enviably cool under fire, something he got plenty of during the Crowther episode, and he justifies his ruthless approach as being necessary for the greater good. One of his more chilling maxims is: 'Decide ruthlessly and execute compassionately.'

Leadership comes easily to Ashcroft. People who work with him find his confidence infectious. He sometimes gets uncontrollable fits of laughter and not always at his own jokes. He is a good delegator and a great communicator. On the whole, the view from inside is that it is fun to work for Coloroll; frightening sometimes – but fun.

The record speaks for itself. Most of the directors he recruited in those early days are still with him. Philip Green joined in 1980 as marketing director and was given the job of setting up the textile division. He was group managing director for two years before becoming chief executive in June 1989. (Until then Ashcroft had held both the titles of chairman and chief executive, but he decided that the increasing size of the company required a division of the roles.) Eric Kilby, the finance director, who joined from Arthur Anderson, is the relative newcomer; he has been with Coloroll since 1986, although he has known Ashcroft since 1980.

Even at the beginning, Ashcroft had the vision of the company selling a wide variety of products for the home. His experience at Crown had shown him that the wallcoverings market wasn't big enough to fuel the kind of growth he wanted for the company. Green had read one of the early articles in *Management Today* about Coloroll. 'It sounded exciting and wizzy,' says Green, who then eagerly replied to a Coloroll advertisement for a job. He didn't get it. Then a month later Ashcroft rang him and said, 'You were not right for the job we advertised, but how about this one?' Green, who had spent the three years after graduating from the London Business School working in New York in marketing, was taken aback, and even more so when Ashcroft asked him to go to the company's head office in Nelson the following week. 'Where's Nelson?' asked a bemused Green. 'That's your first initiative test,' replied Ashcroft.

The cultural leap between working in Manhattan and the small textile town of Nelson in Lancashire was vast, but somehow Ashcroft's enthusiasm and sheer force of personality won out. 'It was only a £10 million turnover company then, and it was a terrific gamble,' says Green.

What does he like about Ashcroft? 'I just get on with him; I'm not close to him personally, but then the guys that work for me aren't close to me. I respect him.'

One of Ashcroft's strengths is his ability to delegate yet keep control. 'He actually applies the principles set out in the Blue Book like responsibility, accountability and exposure,' says Green.

Shortly after the flotation, Ashcroft moved the company headquarters from Nelson to modest offices at No. 1, King Street in Manchester, which was just beginning to recover from the recession of the early 1980s. Ashcroft believes in keeping the identity of the group allied with the North West, and he thought it would be a good idea to be near Manchester's important financial community. Only he, Green and Kilby were based there originally. The idea was to separate them from the day-to-day operations of the business so that they could concentrate solely on strategy and development.

Ashcroft believes that if he has the right controls and the right philosophy the separation works. At King Street he can call up the sales and profits of every operating unit on the nationally linked Hewlett-Packard computer system. 'All managers are expected to be fluent in at least two languages. English and Visicalc,' declares Ashcroft. At the Staffordshire Potteries' site at Stoke on Trent the computer can give a picture of the sales and stock position in just 7 seconds.

Once a month there is a team briefing. It starts at the top when Philip Green presents a short report (no more than a couple of pages) on the state of the company, the sales and profits achievements, market position, the problems and the short- and medium-term goals. He presents that report to the divisional directors, who present it to their respective managers, who then present it down the line through middle management to the shop floor. But even at shopfloor level the report is presented to groups of fifteen people or less. The information cascades down through the company so that every single person feels involved.

Ashcroft believes that the twin credos of communication and involvement are especially vital when a company is taken over.

233

On the day the £200 million bid for John Crowther was announced, Ashcroft decreed a special team brief 'so that they heard from us rather than learn about it through the press', and by lunchtime every one of the 6,000 employees had been briefed.

The top team at Coloroll is clean-cut, fighting fit and bright but, above all, it is young. In 1989, Eric Kilby was the oldest at 44; Ashcroft was still only 40, while Philip Green was 36.

Once a company is Colorollised, those that keep their jobs (which to date have been most of the original workforces) are treated generously and working conditions are good. 'The Coloroll employee and management philosophy is based on respect for the individual,' says the Blue Book. The original wallcoverings factory at Nelson now boasts a £250,000 leisure complex complete with a gymnasium and sauna.

Ashcroft believes in the 'entrepreneurial factor' – that is, treating managers as if it was their money they are spending. They are rewarded (or not) according to profits. The board directors' renumeration is directly linked to earnings per share. A bonus worth a third of their basic salaries is triggered on an annual growth of over 20 per cent. The operational directors get paid in line with the profitability of their units, while down the line managers are rewarded according to performance. 'You have to pay them for something they are in control of,' says Green.

Ashcroft insists on instilling the Coloroll culture into every single one of the workforce, and new members have to be worked on particularly hard. The flamboyant presentation is just the start.

Ashcroft and his team have evolved a package to keep employees aware of just who they are working for and why. One part is the team briefing. There is also the ideas scheme, through which any employee can win up to £5,000 plus 20 per cent of the savings resulting from his or her idea. 'How are you doing boards?', placed prominently in factories and offices, tell the workforce of an individual factory or sales unit exactly how they are performing in terms of sales and market share. And there is a children's trust into which the company puts £50,000 a year towards employees' children with severe disabilities.

Directors and senior managers have mixed feelings about the weekend outward bound courses designed to 'bond' them with other managers from different parts of the group. They are driven in groups to a remote part of the Yorkshire moors, given a map and a torch and told to find their way back to base by the following morning without being caught by the enemy (the army). The going was clearly tough. 'It did help us get to know people from other parts of the business, but I wouldn't want to do it again,' said one manager.

Ashcroft also believes in the occasional celebration. In 1987 and 1989 the group held a lavish dinner dance at London's Savoy Hotel, complete with a pipe band and the Red Devils (without parachutes for a change). Naturally the highlight of these evenings was a rousing speech from chairman Ashcroft. 'It was very northern,' said one City editor uncertainly the morning after the first one. In other words, everyone had a jolly good time.

The stock market crash of October 1987 has significantly changed Ashcroft's medium-term plans for the company. Immediately afterwards, when many feared that business activity would come to a grinding halt, Ashcroft contemplated leaving Coloroll and setting up a small family business where he would have a large shareholding, an option he still occasionally considers. By the early spring, however, he was dusting down the acquisitions' file again, coming up with Crowther.

Ashcroft has understood the power and workings of the City more quickly and completely than most young businessmen. When the stock market was bubbling he kept in close contact with major investors and stockbrokers' analysts, usually visiting London at least twice a week. During a takeover those visits were stepped up. To Ashcroft, the lunches and presentations, explaining the rationale behind the company's latest move, are simply part of being a public company chairman.

But after the crash he adapted to the new sombre mood and low turnover in shares. He does not waste time grumbling about the share price, preferring to get on with running the business. 'They're all walking around with their heads under their arms; it's best to stay away,' he says of the City. It has altered his plans for the group too. 'I don't think going for global dominance would be too popular right now,' he joked in the spring of 1982. 'So I think for the moment we have to concentrate on consolidating our business in Britain.'

Ashcroft also got the measure of merchant bankers early on, refusing to be intimidated by their public school and Oxbridge backgrounds. 'They used to have a tendency to treat me like a north country hillbilly,' he said. Now even the pre-eminent Warburg has heard the rough edge of his tongue.

As the company has matured, Ashcroft has become more involved with outside issues. He is keen to promote the North West and, as well as his duties at Manchester University and Business School, is a trustee of the North West Civic Trust and chairman of a recently set up body called North West Business Action. 'It's partly to do with giving something back,' he says, 'and as we push the North West so it pushes us.'

As the British economy slows down, he will have to prove to those inside and outside Coloroll that he is capable of leading the company through more difficult times than it has so far encountered. Occasionally he is tempted to leave, and try something new, but at the last count Ashcroft was firmly committed to Coloroll. 'I can't afford to get diverted. I'm only half-way through what I want to do here,' he says firmly.

XIII

Epilogue

On 19 October 1987, the financial world was turned upside down. After five years of virtually non-stop growth in share prices, stock markets in London and New York fell faster than they had ever done before, further even than the famous Wall Street crash of 1929. Many companies, including some described in this book, saw their share prices halve or more within a few days. Great international heroes of the bull market like Robert Holmes à Court, the Australian raider, found themselves on the brink of collapse, overwhelmed by borrowings. Shrewder or luckier players, like Sir James Goldsmith, who liquidated his investments the preceding August, were treated with new respect.

For a few anxious days, governments around the world pondered the prospect of complete disaster. The chairman of the New York Stock Exchange talked of a financial 'melt-down'. Two months later the world markets had recovered their calm and had started tentatively to move back up again. But, as one stockbroker said, 'Investing in shares will never be the same again.'

The immediate post-crash City was an altogether more un-friendly place for the would-be business builder. The bull market had created heroes whose very share ratings were enough to power them to success. It became a virtuous circle: companies on high multiples were able to buy competitors on lower multiples, giving earnings per share (that all-important measure of corporate health) an inevitable lift. But when the collapse came, it was the heroes of the bull market who often saw their shares fall furthest. Suddenly their currency of growth was devalued and cash became king.

Overnight the fuel that had powered young growing companies – the willingness of City institutions to buy their shares – had dried up. Investors were traumatised – just days before the crash, City fund managers had poured a record-breaking £837 million into the shares of the Blue Arrow recruitment company to fund its takeover of the American Manpower group. Weeks later they had lost half their money. When the markets crashed, many so-called 'experts' and politicians, including President Reagan and Chancellor Nigel Lawson, dismissed the fall as a purely financial phenomenon which had little relevance to real economic activity. But 18 months on it was clear that markets had once again proved their uncanny ability to anticipate the future: the money had spoken.

In America, the twin budget and trade deficits were issues that finally had to be faced, and some unpalatable medicine had to be taken. In Britain, the great Thatcherite economic revival boiled over in a bout of unsustainable over-heating. House prices soared, imports flooded in, wage inflation not seen since the early 1980s returned with a vengeance and the government was forced to push up interest rates to choke off consumer demand and keep the pound artificially high to get the economy back under control.

This was a climate to test the ingenuity and flexibility of many of the companies that had flourished in the Thatcher bull market. Did they have the necessary staying power, the City asked anxiously. Whose company would collapse like a house of cards, like so many of their heroes of the late 1960s and early 1970s? Who would become minus millionaires, like Jim Slater, and who would 'return to go'? Who would survive more bracing conditions and adapt, to emerge as the industrial knights and peers of the 1990s? Which companies had the management structure and resources to cope?

The retailers were in the front line: if government was going to kill over-heating by squeezing consumer spending, it was the high streets that would feel the pinch first. While sales sagged, rents, rates and shop-fitting costs raced upwards and retail square footage escalated wildly, fuelled by the previous boom. It did not take long for the cracks to appear in the weaker companies: those that had piled up borrowings during their expansion were the first to be hit.

George Davies was the first casualty. On 9 December 1988, he was summoned to a Next board meeting at the offices of the City law firm, Slaughter & May. He and his wife were sacked on the spot. It was the end of the City's love affair with the cuddly Liverpudlian, who began his career as a stock controller in the sock department of Littlewoods. Davies was a perfect example of the corporate Peter principle. Next had grown to a size where its creator could no longer control it. Davies, so brilliant in his vision and for a while so stylish in turning his dreams into reality, had fallen into the trap of many before him. He was unable to delegate and work harmoniously with senior executives and fellow directors. The result was a breakdown in communications, which convinced the board that if Next was to survive as an independent company Davies and his wife Liz would have to go.

The demise of Tony Berry a month later was equally dramatic. Having built a nationwide empire of employment agencies from tiny beginnings in 1984, Berry went just one bridge too far in his giant-killer takeover of Manpower. The City had urged him on in the early years, applauding each new deal, but the Manpower takeover, which for a few short months turned Berry into the head of the world's largest employment agency business, broke him. To achieve the takeover he had to promise the City levels of profits that could never be achieved; to fund the takeover his advisers, County NatWest and Phillips & Drew, had to take almost half the new shares issued on their own books in a controversial exercise that prompted a Department of Trade and Industry investigation. In the eyes of the regulators it was the worst City scandal since the Guinness affair, resulting in the resignations of several directors from the parent bank, National Westminster, including the chairman.

Once again, it was the corporate Peter principle in action: while Berry was an astute dealer, he lacked the skills to manage a billion-pound company and showed no inclination to build a strong management team. Indeed, he fired Mitchell Fromstein, the man who had built up Manpower. The board of Blue Arrow, which included Norman Tebbit, the former chairman of the Conservative Party, initially supported him in what looked to outsiders a form of corporate suicide. But eventually a lone rebel director, Dennis Stevenson, succeeded in persuading the directors into an embarrassing volte face. Though it was not disclosed at the time, Berry had committed on appalling error of judgement by investing £25 million of Blue Arrow's scarce resources in a controversial plan by Peter de Savary, the property developer. De Savary's project, put together was to turn some waste land into a giant business, housing and leisure development. Berry had also not kept his colleagues fully informed and when his new chief operating officer, John Sharkey, learned of the project, he joined the Stevenson rebellion. Fromstein was made chief executive, while Berry was emasculated as non-executive chairman and then fired altogether, and finally a second DTI investigation into Blue Arrow was launched. Berry's fall from grace was just as complete as Davies's, and if anything even more humiliating as he was the company's largest individual shareholder.

Richard Branson, whose Virgin Group had come to the stock market at an unsustainable price, showed himself to be a classic example of bull market hype. Written up in the financial press as the great young entrepreneur of the leisure sector, he soon demonstrated his fallibilities. Investors rebelled against his anarchic management style and lack of strategy and, when profits started to falter, Branson – who had appeared to both government and the City as the embodiment of new wave youth capitalism – was suddenly a pariah. Branson reacted by taking his company private, buying out investors at the original issue price of 1986. If they were not interested in his ball he was going to take it off the pitch, and some smaller companies followed in his wake.

Even the Saatchis, whose extraordinary growth had inspired many of the stock market players of the 1980s, demonstrated their feet of clay. In 1989, after eighteen years of unbroken profits growth, the brothers revealed that their earnings were falling. Somehow the Saatchi magic had failed. As the Saatchi share price crumbled, the City speculated about a possible lack of financial control within the sprawling Saatchi empire, which had grown from being a tiny creative hotshop in Goodge Street, London, to be the world's number one ad agency and one of the leading players in management consultancy. The Saatchi brothers, who in 1988 moved themselves to a palatial new headquarters building on the south side of Berkeley Square, had taken their eyes off the ball. By the middle of 1989 it was clear they were in full retreat when they hoisted a 'for sale' sign outside their management consultancy business. The Saatchi dream of a one-stop global supermarket of business services from advertising and public relations through to market research, management consultancy and even banking had crumbled.

The Saatchis had profited through exploiting the economies of scale in the fragmented world of advertising. Berry's great coup, and one that even after the Blue Arrow débâcle had left him a millionaire many times over, was to identify recruitment as a growth market ripe for rationalisation into bigger groupings. Davies had spotted the gap in the clothing market for well-designed coordinated clothes.

But the demise of Berry and Davies showed that what makes a successful entrepreneur is not just the ability to spot a market that no one else can see. It is more, too, than the drive and energy to produce and market the product to fill that nascent demand. Company builders need to keep their feet firmly planted on the ground. They must build a strong management team and, having done that, be prepared to delegate responsibility and power to that team. The classic mistake is to 'believe your own publicity'.

These are lessons that Nigel Rudd and Brian McGowan of Williams Holdings learned very early on: dealers do not often make good managers; if they are to succeed they will have to recruit others to run their creations.

Anita Roddick uses her charismatic enthusiasm just where it is needed – in the market place. The day-to-day management and finances she leaves to her husband, Gordon Roddick, and a team of managers. Michael Green insists he will only expand into those areas where he feels he has the management resources to cope. Entrepreneurs must have a measure of their own limitations and a clear idea of what is and is not possible: they take the best ideas proffered by their eager financial advisers and discard those inspired by over-enthusiasm and a simple desire to earn fees.

Overweening pride, fuelled by City adulation and profile after profile in the financial press, can lead to disaster. 'When you are on the way up, they think you are a genius, when you are on the way down, you're an idiot,' said Sir Phil Harris of City investors after he had sold his carpet empire Harris Queensway.

Davies and Berry might have had some difficulties even if the bull market had roared on, but the collapse in share prices exposed their weaknesses in stark fashion. In the 'flight to quality',

Next, with its huge debts built up during its period of over-expansion, and Blue Arrow, with its weak management, were out in the cold. The share prices of Sock Shop, Ratners and even Body Shop suffered from the Next backlash and the overall concern about high street trading. But, although profits may slow in their growth, or even fall briefly, the underlying structure of the companies looks solid.

Some bull market stocks were made of stronger stuff than Blue Arrow and Next, and emerged from the crash unscathed in business terms albeit with a significantly lower share price. John Ashcroft, the chairman of Coloroll, had his moment of doubt: he initially decided the financial melt-down had put paid to his expansion hopes and went as far as declaring to the outside world that his group would not make any acquisitions. He even contemplated retiring from the company to spend his time minding his Charolais sheep and pursuing some small private business ventures. But three months later he had changed his mind: in April 1988 he mounted a £220 million bid for John Crowther. At a stroke, Coloroll became Britain's second largest carpet maker and virtually doubled its size.

Sorrell did a virtual rerun of his JWT takeover in the spring of 1989 when his WPP group carried off a second American advertising giant in the shape of the Ogilvy Group, while at Carlton, Green was able to seize for Britain a world-famous American brand in the shape of Technicolor and then become a leading player in the international video electronics market through his takeover of UEI. Williams, in taking over Hoechst's Berger paint company, pulled off the kind of dealing coup that earned the company the sobriquet 'The Hanson of the 1990s', while Gerald Ratner, who in the spring of 1987 lost out in the Combined English Stores takeover battle with Next, was able to take his revenge in extracting over 400 CES outlets from Next at distress sale prices. Although many industrial companies found the post-crash City an exceedingly unwelcome place, WPP, Carlton, Williams and Ratners were still able to raise cash from the pension funds and insurance companies with relative ease.

In the half-decade to 1989, people like Green, Ashcroft, and Rudd emerged from obscurity to put themselves firmly on the map of corporate Britain. By the end of the decade a whole raft of even younger City stars were starting to emerge. Howard Hodgson chose the unlikely field of funerals as his territory in which to build a big public company, while the Shah brothers carved out a big slice of the jeans market for their Pepe Group. Still in his twenties, Richard Thompson started to utilise the gargantuan funds of his father, David, co-founder with Harry Solomon of Hillsdown Holdings, one of Britain's biggest food groups. These and others like them may become the giant-killers of the 1990s.

The entrepreneurs in this book may already be familiar faces in the City and most have featured as 'case studies' in management magazines like *Management Today* and *Business*, but it is only recently that their influence has begun to spread further afield into the realms of politics and education.

The taciturn Alan Sugar agreed to talk to the City University Business School, who awarded him an honorary Doctor of Science degree in December 1988. Ashcroft is a Fellow of the Manchester Business School, while Green has become chairman of the Open College. Roddick has become known as much for her radical views on the environment as for her business success. Her desire to put something back into the third world and deprived regions in Britain, like Glasgow where Body Shop has set up a soap-making plant in a deprived area, has made her a hero of the Left as well as of the staunchly Conservative City of London, which is very happy just as long as the profits keep growing.

Even in the notoriously greedy property sector, the Beckwiths have made a point of putting money back into the community with projects like the redevelopment of the Spitalfields vegetable market. They provide sporting facilities for the underprivileged and regularly raise money for charity.

Margaret Thatcher and her government display a keen interest in the careers of these entrepreneurs. As the champion of the Disestablishment, she has much in common with the stars of corporate Britain, and is keen to harness their experience and knowledge. Green, for example, was asked to advise the government on the deregulation of television. They have become the role models of the so-called 'enterprise culture'. A poster campaign on behalf of the Prince of Wales's Youth Trust showing a picture of a young skinhead with the caption 'Help us en-courage him to create wealth, not aggro' demonstrated the revolution in thinking.

From provincial obscurity the new tycoons have been thrown together at CBI meetings, at City seminars, at soirées at 10 Downing Street and at garden parties at Buckingham Palace. They are increasingly aware that they are a recognisable group –

a new force in the land. Ashcroft has hosted a number of dinners and lunches with many of the individuals in this book on the guest list. It is a recognition that they are part of a network, a group of people with common aims, albeit sometimes in competition with each other, who can benefit from exchanging views and experiences.

City cynics say financial genius is a bull market. If a serious recession does hit Britain in the next few years, the durability of these companies will be severely tested. At the time of writing, City investors were sharing disenchantment with the performance of both Amstrad and Sock Shop. Some entrepreneurs may well throw in the towel, content to be taken over by bigger groups. If business ceases to be fun, the temptation for the large shareholders like Mirman and Ross to sell out would be considerable. Those that encounter financial problems will become vulnerable to hostile takeover by older companies or even a newer generation of young entrepreneurs coming up in their slipstream. The prospect of slipping on the banana skin of financial scandal is also an ever-present hazard. But some will prosper and from the characters described in this book will emerge the business giants of the 1990s and the next century. We wish them well.